TABLE OF CONTENTS

SPECIAL MENTION

We would like to specially thank Ashley Tutor for her assistance in the development of this book. Her contributions and thoughts helped us move forward and compile our initial thoughts into a comprehensive formula.

SECTION 0

INTRODUCTION

WHY FEEDBACK IS IMPORTANT

"I need to give you some feedback."

-Every manager at some point their career

What just came to mind as you read that? Did you think "uh-oh, I wonder what they did wrong" or possibly "I hate those words; they're almost as bad as the dreaded 'we need to talk' phrase"? If so, you are not alone. Unfortunately for most of us, the word *feedback* has been paired with the delivery of bad news, usually in the form of how we have screwed up in some way. The problem with this is that feedback is all around us and, if done correctly, is one of the most powerful tools leaders have to impact the performance of their employees.

Before we jump in, let's take a moment to examine just how prevalent feedback is in our lives. From the get-go, we're equipped to provide and respond to feedback. When we were babies and toddlers and somebody did something we didn't like, we cried. When they did something that we did like, we smiled, laughed, and drew them favorably with crayons. These different responses resulted in people doing more of the things we liked and less of those we didn't like. You didn't know you were teaching people from the start, did you?

Unfortunately, most of us   are not taught just how powerful our feedback is and the right ways   to use it—especially when it comes to leaders using it to effect performance. Think about all those bosses you do your best to avoid—the ones that throw tantrums when they don't get their way, the ones who respond to your excellent word by giving you more to do, or the ones you only see after something went wrong.

When we become leaders, most of us make one of our goals to be the opposite of that terrible boss that we had. That's a great aspiration, but then, when it's time to act, we unknowingly find ourselves emulating exactly what we wanted to avoid. We start yelling at our subordinates. We're rude. We're passive aggressive. We're sarcastic. And we give the most work to our best performers. Why? Well, whether we liked it or not, it produced results, and we don't know any better. Not yet anyway.

What If we told you that there WAS a better way? What if there was a way to communicate objective information to your employees? And what if doing this effectively resulted not only in a better workplace but also in employees who value and respect their boss rather than secretly (or not so secretly) loathe and resent them? How do you do this, you ask? The answer is in the science.

Like chemistry, physics, and biology, behavior analysis is a science that tells us how people learn and adapt to a changing environment. In applied behavior analysis (ABA), behavior analysts work with individuals to do two things: (a) establish meaningful goals unique to those individuals and (b) use behavior analysis technologies to ensure each individual reaches those goals. Behavior analysts have worked with all types of settings, including schools, hospitals, factories, government, and businesses. In all these different areas, one thing holds true: to change behavior, we must change the environment.

Leaders Are Always Focused on Performance

One thing that leaders spend a great deal of time thinking about and trying to address is performance problems. Performance problems are a natural part of every organization, and leaders often attempt to minimize or eliminate them as quickly as possible. As a result, the quickest and easiest solutions are usually attempted first. If they don't work, another just as easy or slightly more difficult potential solution is tried. When that doesn't work, the next best solution is tried, and on and on it goes, repeating the process again and again. As if throwing darts at a dartboard, organizational leaders will often simply try every potential solution available to them hoping that one of them sticks. Or as already stated, leaders eventually resort to the initially avoided practices of bad bosses because doing so usually gets immediate results—even if the long-term results are to the contrary.

The cool thing about this is that we, as behavior analysts, know why this happens. And even better, we know how to change it!

Now you may be thinking, "Here we go—these guys are just like the rest. They're going to tell me that everything I'm doing is wrong, and to fix it, I have to spend more time and resources. They don't get it—I don't *have* more time and resources!" If that thought crossed your mind, no worries. What we are going to tell you does not require more time or resources. Instead, it requires a shift in thinking and practice, one which may initially feel more difficult. But with practice, it will become easy and will help you get the best out of your staff.

Why Focus on Feedback?

We can safely assume that you agree feedback is important (otherwise, you likely wouldn't have picked up this book and started reading). However, you may be wondering why we say this is one of the most powerful tools leaders have to impact the performance of their staff. There are several reasons we have dedicated an entire book to feedback.

First, feedback is omnipresent. No matter what, feedback exists. From the quiet you receive when you press snooze on your alarm clock to the laughter you get for telling a joke to your colleagues, feedback is all around us and happening all the time. It also impacts just about everything we do—from showing up to work on time and completing tasks efficiently, to why we send an instant message versus walking down the hall to have a face-to-face conversation. So whether you provide feedback or leave it to someone else, it is almost guaranteed to occur. You might as well figure out how to take the reins and use it to your advantage.

Second, just about everyone gives feedback, but few get the intended results. We can't tell you how many times we hear leaders say things like this: "I just don't get it. I tell them again and again, and they just don't get it right." Or this: "They know what to do—they told me—so why aren't they doing it?" And even this: "As soon as I get them to stop one thing, another problem arises." These statements are made by leaders who have tried providing feedback, but failed to impact behavior the way they wanted to. The reason? ***Feedback f!@#ups.*** They didn't give feedback correctly. Thus, simply providing feedback is not enough; it must be provided correctly to actually have a positive effect on performance.

Third, feedback is a powerful and easy way to improve performance. Once you learn the tips and tricks to make feedback effective, it's the easiest and best way to improve performance. We won't sugar coat things and suggest that learning the different variables that impact feedback effectiveness is easy, but with a little hard work, anyone can master the skills and create high performers anywhere.

That brings us to our fourth point: anyone can use feedback. Feedback is a tool that you can carry with you everywhere you go and that anyone, from entry level employee all the way to owner and/or CEO of the company, can use. In fact, the more people who use feedback effectively in the company, the better off the organization will be.

Our last two points focus specifically on the employee and are the main reasons we decided to write this book. The correct use of feedback increases employee performance, outcomes, and engagement. As Jack Welch famously said, "There are only three measurements that tell you nearly everything you need to know about your organization's overall performance: employee engagement, customer satisfaction, and cash flow." Indeed, employee engagement has become a staple of executive team goals

KNOW OUR JARGON

Reinforcement: Reinforcement is defined by two main characteristics: 1) It is a change in the environment that follows a behavior; 2) it increases the chance that the behavior will occur again in the future when the same or similar circumstances arise.

Reinforcement can both be the addition of something positive (like praise, bonuses, high fives, and high scores on performance evaluations) or the removal of something negative (like avoiding a dock in pay, not getting yelled at by the boss, or avoiding a corrective action write up).

and directives over the past decade and a leading indicator of an organization's overall health.

Over the years, *employee engagement* has been broadly and inconsistently defined without a scientific consensus. However, it has gained popularity in many business circles as an emotional or psychological state of being linked to desirable business outcomes, such as retention and productivity. Unfortunately, a clear and consistent definition of engagement has yet to be produced, leaving employee engagement in the murky waters of professional slang.

To assist in the effort to define this term, we have created an objective definition for employee engagement:

> The rate of behaviors displayed by employees that results in the improvement of the organization.

Thus, the higher the engagement, the more employees are doing to improve the organization. To increase engagement, behavior science lends us another simple strategy: reinforcement. The more a company provides reinforcement for behaviors that improve the organization, the more employees will engage in those behaviors.

Some common reinforcers for engaged behavior are autonomy, meaningful work, and performance feedback (obviously).

How does employee engagement relate to feedback? Well, feedback can be a used as a reinforcer for employee engagement. While many strategies

KNOW OUR JARGON

Response Effort: The amount of effort that a person must put forth to successfully complete a specific behavior or action. This effort has a direct impact on whether the person will actually engage in the behavior. The more response effort, the less likely the behavior will occur.

exist to generate employee engagement, feedback is probably the cheapest and lowest response effort intervention you can use on a company-wide scale.

Why Is Feedback Not Provided More Often?

Knowing that feedback is all around us, it may be confusing as to why it's not used more often. In fact, feedback is one of the most underused tools that leaders have. Let's look at the following example to illustrate this.

Imagine it's the end of the month, and your quarterly reports are due to the executive team in 3 hours. Your reports include your team manager's data and your own analysis on their performance. You, unfortunately, are nowhere near done and about to enter "freak-out" mode. Your hand trembles as it nervously reaches for your third cup of coffee in the last hour in hopes of keeping you awake and alert long enough to get your work in on time. You finally finish fighting with the different layout options, complete the document formatting, and begin analyzing the data from the quarter. Then you realize the report is incomplete, and frankly, it's missing a lot. Your eyes peruse the document with intensity, trying to identify all of the missing components and who is responsible for the absent data and reporting errors.

After about 15 minutes of penetrating report investigation, you identify the following:

Steven, the marketing department manager, did not include an updated profit and loss report, which is an essential part of your report, in his quarterly statement. After quickly generating the report yourself, you realize the numbers are inaccurate and do not account for several budget items or employee salaries. This officially marks the third time Steven has made these same mistakes.

Melissa, the purchasing manager, merged two quarters worth of data into one graph and used a pie chart instead of a bar chart. The bar charts show the progress over time, which allows you to impress the executive team by showing them how much you and your team have completed over the past quarter. That would, in turn, hopefully lead to high praise and maybe even a bonus for your hardworking team members. It takes you over an hour to reformat her graphs; the onboard training she received when she was hired had explicitly explained she should use bar charts in these situations.

You frantically send emails to Steven and Melissa asking why they made these mistakes. After waiting the longest 5 minutes of your adult life, they reply—with enraging similar answers: "I didn't know I was making a mistake," and "I'm not sure how to correct it."

There is no way you will be able to complete *their* work and *yours* before the deadline. You take a slow breath, shake your head, and then lower it in disappointment, asking yourself, "Why is this happening to me?" As you raise your head, a thought screams through your mind, echoing between the walls of your ears, "***Feedback f!@#up!*** If I had given them better feedback in the past, this could have been prevented."

OBM Tidbit

Catch them being good! Sometimes employees engage in behavior that you weren't necessarily targeting, but that you still want to see more of. If you "catch" them doing something that you would like to see more of, even if it is that the behavior you were targeting, provide positive feedback. Quick, in-the-moment, "way to go's" and "thank you's" go a long way!

Yes. Yes, it could have. You get the employees you deserve.

Feedback deficiencies are a major contributor to almost every problem within organizations. Whether it's underperforming departments, projects going over budget, or a high turnover rate, inadequate feedback is almost always involved. At every level of the organizational hierarchy—from employee to manager, to the board of directors—the delivery and receipt of feedback is crucial to success. Employee feedback can significantly impact a variety of different worker behaviors, from employee engagement to employees' own comprehension of their standing within the company, which ultimately has a direct impact on the organization's bottom line.

So if feedback is so important, why don't people use it more? There are several reasons for this, but we will cover the top five:

1. **Old thinking: "If it ain't broke, don't fix it."** As with this old saying, many believe that you should leave well enough alone when things are working well. Thus, many leaders don't provide feedback to employees because they don't want to "mess up a good thing." Behavior science tells us, however, that this is the opposite of what should happen. We know that, for behaviors (or performance) to continue, they must be periodically followed by positive feedback. Even machines need periodic updates, so why would we think people don't?

2. **Thinking that people should just do what's expected and receive nothing for doing their jobs.** This is another error in thinking. We know very few people, if any, who don't want to know they are doing a good job. We look for input about our performance everywhere and often get discouraged when we hear nothing about a job well done. While most are expected to perform the tasks of their position, a "thank you" or "nice work" can be powerful in helping to continue the great work being done.

3. **No time.** Leaders are tasked with the difficult job of juggling several high-priority tasks at all times. Unfortunately, this can be

---

KNOW OUR JARGON

Consequence: an event that immediately follows a behavior and has some effect on the future occurrence of that behavior. Consequences either increase or decrease the likeliness the behavior will happen again in the future when the same or similar circumstances arise.

consuming, leaving little time to focus on employee performance—except when things go horribly wrong. Any time a new behavior is learned, it takes more time, and learning how to provide effective feedback can feel like another thing added to an already way-too-full plate. The problem here is that, when feedback isn't provided or is provided incorrectly, leaders actually spend even more time on performance problems. In other words, learning to provide effective feedback and then doing it consistently can actually decrease the time spent on putting out fires and addressing problems.

4. **Tried it; it didn't work.** Most leaders have tried providing feedback of some sort in the past and have gotten different results. Often times, leaders find that implementing punitive consequences or

MISCONCEPTION

Behavior analysts think of punishment much differently than the rest of the world. It is important to point out that in behavior analysis, punishment is a change in the environment following the occurrence of a behavior that results in a decreased chance the behavior will occur again in the future. This can be the addition of something negative (e.g., your boss yelling at you) or the removal of something positive (e.g., getting your pay docked). The key here is that it follows the behavior and decreases the likeliness the behavior will happen again in the same or similar circumstances.

providing highly negative feedback results in performance changes most effectively. And when they tried to provide more positive feedback, the results were not as good. While this may be true, especially in the short term, the long-term effects of negative and punitive feedback are exponential. Employees learn to do just enough to escape the punishment and learn to get by on the bare minimum. Providing feedback correctly not only establishes strong performance in employees, but it also actually increases discretionary effort, meaning employees work even harder and more productively.

5. **Annual performance reviews.** We have a lot to say about this as these reviews are so commonly practiced yet so completely ineffective. Let's look at the following example for why annual performance reviews are ineffective and what you should do instead.

Cynthia is a mid-level employee who has worked at the company for over 3 years now. Cynthia spent most of her first 2 years at the company being moved from department to department, going wherever the organization needed support. Because Cynthia was never in one specific department for very long, she never received a formal review of her performance. She simply received praise from colleagues for helping them out in their times of need and was then quickly transferred to the next department to help put out the next fire.

FEEDBACK F!@#up!

What went wrong here? Several things. Take note of them now and we will address them as we continue:

1. Cynthia should have received feedback regarding her performance prior to now.

2. Performance reviews should not be used as the tool to providing feedback to underperforming employees. They should be used to evaluate progress and performance as a result of interventions that have already or are currently occurring.

3. Feedback should never be "scathing" or "demoralizing" or include threats.

However, over the past year, Cynthia found a home in the finance department as a comptroller managing the finances of an offsite construction team. Her colleagues appeared to be generally happy with her, and Cynthia felt confident she was doing a good job since none of her managers had ever provided her with a formal performance review or any sort of feedback. The yearly performance review arrived, and Cynthia did not give it a second thought, assuming her performance review would fall into good standing with the company.

After the meeting, Cynthia found her way back to her office, closed the door behind her, and sat quietly at her desk, distraught and staring at her performance review form. A red-checked box at the top of the report and a short phrase next to it stated she had been performing below average. The red-checked box was accompanied by a scathing and demoralizing comment indicating she would need to improve her performance in the finance department or her job would be at risk.

You may be thinking, but Cynthia is the exception to the rule. She should have gotten an annual performance review before her third year. Yes, this is true, but the results of the performance review are not uncommon. Many employees find they have received little feedback regarding their performance and walk into an annual review only to be greeted with lower-than-expected scores.

As a result, annual performance reviews are falling out of favor for more modern, science-based systems of performance appraisal (yep, you guessed it: high-frequency feedback). This phenomenon did not just happen without good reason, and those reasons are listed below:

1. **Often, they don't use data**. Ever been in a manager's meeting and heard about how supervisors are not too fond of doing performance reviews? A big part of the underlying reason is that they're not based on data. Managers are often in a hurry to complete reviews and fill out performance review forms based on memory at the moment they do the review, and the reviews are not based on objective measurements and data that have been monitored and collected.

2. **They are directly connected to an employee's money**. That's right! A poor performance review may cause an employee to lose an annual bonus or lose a raise in their base salary. This can be very

demoralizing for employees.

3. **Contingencies are delayed**. Throughout this book, we will discuss the importance of immediacy with regard to contingencies. Timely implementation of interventions is an absolutely critical component to effective behavior change. Time and again, annual performance reviews fail to effect behavior like we want them to. An employee sitting in a performance review meeting getting chastised for something they did 10 months ago isn't going to connect that event and the verbal lashing they are receiving in the moment. Instead, they will probably develop strong resentment for annual performance reviews and show up defensive for next year's meeting.

4. **360-degree feedback (or lack thereof)**. Performance reviews are just as much about the manager's behavior as they are about the employee's behavior. Remember, the measure of a manager is in the performance of the employee. Performance reviews provide a great opportunity to give AND receive feedback. Unfortunately, however, they're rarely a two-way street and end up focusing on employee inadequacies rather than common goals and the interactions between the two parties.

How could feedback have helped Cynthia?

Cynthia's managers should have provided regular feedback about her job performance, so the results of the meeting would be positive and not a surprise. In addition to answering the question of where an employee stands, which most employees overwhelmingly want to know, performance feedback serves as a consequence that changes behavior. When performance is good, positive feedback acts as a reinforcer, increasing or continuing the behavior. When performance is corrected, feedback acts as a prompt for the correct behavior. Frequent performance feedback can help ensure the following critical-to-success questions are answered.

1. **Why does my job exist?**

Simply put, people want to know that what they're doing matters. They want to know that their position is important to the overall functioning and success of the company. In behavior analysis, we know that this understanding of why a position exists creates motivation and value. Motivation is extremely important as it has two effects on behaviors: (a) it increases the likeliness the behavior will occur, and (b) it makes the reinforcers for that behavior more powerful.

In short, knowing why a position exists is not just for informational purposes. This often overlooked and disregarded point is extremely important—it not only increases motivation to complete the tasks of the position but also actually makes it more likely that these tasks will be completed and that the reinforcers for completing the tasks are more reinforcing. A win all around!

2. **What am I supposed to achieve daily, weekly, monthly, and quarterly?**

Job position descriptions often leave a lot of room for interpretation. It's surprisingly alarming how many people don't actually have a clear idea of the exact tasks and outcomes to expect every day, week, month, and quarter. When expectations are unclear, employees don't always know what to do and often end up doing the wrong things…or waste time trying to figure out what it is they are supposed to do. Understanding what is supposed to happen each day, week, month, and quarter not only helps increase efficiency but also serves as the first step in clarifying expectations that can be tied to performance evaluations. Behaviorally, when you set clear expectations and then measure performance against those expectations, you have not only created a cue or stimulus for the behavior to occur but also now have a consequence that should continue to drive behavior forward.

3. **How can I best utilize my time to achieve my job mission?**

Time management tends to be a bit more difficult to teach than many of us assume. Time utilization increases when expectations are clear; however, we have found that many leaders mismanage their own time by taking on too much, by allowing for interruptions to distract their attention (emails, text messages, social media, etc.), and by underestimating the time it will take to complete a project. Time management is an essential skill for all employees, and feedback can help employees learn and master the skills necessary to be effective time managers.

4. How does my behavior impact others' behavior?

We assume that everyone knows how their behavior impacts others. Unfortunately, most people are not walking around constantly asking themselves, "How is what I am about to do or say going to impact those around me?" Instead, we tend to be focused on how what we are going to do or say is going to impact us. Providing feedback in regard to how a behavior has impacted another person or the larger company often provides insight into behavior that is not initially considered.

5. What behaviors can I change to achieve better outcomes?

In general, people are really good at pointing out when things are wrong. We can spot errors a mile away, and we have no problem telling someone when errors happen. However, pointing out errors is only part of the solution when providing feedback. As you will learn later, the only way to ensure a different error is not made is to provide information regarding the right thing to do. Feedback should include solutions and expectations for behavior that will lead to the right solution.

6. What is the quality of my relationships with my managers, colleagues, and others?

We have heard many managers say, "I don't care if my employees like me. I just want them to respect me." We have found this to really mean that managers care most about the performance of their employees. Managers who say this want a workforce that is high achieving and full of employees who work hard to accomplish the mission of the company. However, those who say this are missing one key thing. We tend to perform highest when led by someone we know, like, and trust. Behaviorally speaking, those who we like and trust are most likely to serve as reinforcers. When our leaders are effectively reinforcing, we do things to get noticed by them, we highly value their feedback, and we will continue behaviors that result in positive feedback because that feedback is a reinforcer. When the opposite is true, managers have a much more difficult time motivating and providing reinforcement for their employees.

In countless companies around the world, employees walk into yearly performance review meetings excited to hear their managers praise their work and discuss raise and/or bonus options. Every year, many of those same employees leave those meetings discouraged and blindsided by the information they receive. This type of discouragement can lead to any number of negative outcomes, and it can ultimately lead to more poor performance or a resignation letter on the manager's desk.

HOW TO USE THIS BOOK

"Life doesn't come with an instruction manual"

~Scott Westerfield

Okay, I Get It. Feedback Is Important, but Where Do I Start?

Now that we have examined the many reasons feedback is so important and why it's not used more often, we are ready to present the feedback formula, which will provide the instructions, guidelines, and considerations necessary to provide effective feedback. Throughout this book, you will learn the many things to consider when providing feedback so that the feedback you deliver results in the behavior change you want. Each chapter within this book will deliver a piece of the formula, so that by the end, you will not only know the best ways to provide feedback but also know when, where, and what impact other environmental considerations may have on the feedback provided. Are you ready?

Wait! One more thing before we get started. You might have noticed a few symbols and pop-outs as you read this chapter. You will see this throughout the book as our way to highlight important terminology, expand upon concepts, and provide additional information. Each symbol will correspond to one of the categories listed below and is meant to aid you in your understanding of the concepts and principles discussed in this book.

KNOW OUR JARGON

Be on the lookout for these as they will provide additional explanations of our behavior analysis jargon. We've learned that it's best when people are not only on the same page but also speaking the same language. We'll introduce key terms that will have you speaking like a behaviorist in no time.

RESEARCH

Sure, we can talk the talk, but we also walk the walk. Behavior analysts have been doing research on all things related to behavior for decades. Now is our chance to show it off.

OBM Tidbit

Organizational behavior management (OBM) is the blending of behavior analysis and business development. There is a wealth of research and concepts in this field that are directly applicable to performance problems. We want to give you just about every bit of information that we possibly can within these pages, so we decided to throw several morsels of tasty info about OBM throughout the book. Enjoy!

MISCONCEPTION

Out with the old, in with the new! No longer do you simply have to go with "what's always been done" or maintaining the status quo. We'll present some old ideas and why they belong buried in the past.

FEEDBACK F!@#up!

Because this book is all about how to provide feedback to increase employee performance, we think it is important that you recognize when things go wrong. Throughout the book you will either see us write "feedback f!@#up" into the text or a pop-out that identifies exactly what went wrong. This way you don't just learn what to do, you also learn what NOT to do.

Okay, now we're ready. We're excited to get started. Let's go!

SECTION I

WHAT AND WHO

1

FEEDBACK BASICS

"You can practice shooting eight hours a day, but if your technique is wrong, then all you become is very good at shooting the wrong way. Get the fundamentals down and the level of everything you do will rise."

~Michael Jordan

If you gathered 100 organizational leaders in a room and asked simply, "What is feedback?," what responses do you think you would get?

You will get some that say, "When I tell them to do something, they do it!" (That's actually just a demand.)

Some might say, "Feedback? I have my HR rep give that to each employee at the end of the year." (An annual performance review? Oh boy. We have a lot to talk about.)

Others will say, "I'll use it whenever I need them to fix something." (That's just a correction. You're getting warmer, though.)

And finally, a select few will say, "Information about their past or current performance to improve, maintain, or change their future performance." (Well damn. Someone read our intro.)

The point here is that the term *feedback* means different things to different people. This is a problem—a rather big one actually. Because this is a common term that all seem to understand, no one stops to clarify the meaning. Instead, most assume they are referring to their definition, when in actuality, each person has a slightly (or not so slightly) different definition of it. What's worse, we have learned that many leaders refer to "feedback" for things that are not even close to it—like that demand we referenced above.

This problem is not limited to leaders; it has been a problem in the field of behavior analysis and, more specifically, organizational behavior management (OBM) as well. In fact, in a 1982 article published in *The Behavior Analyst*, Norman Peterson alleged that feedback, at best, had simply become "professional slang." *Feedback* was just a term that was thrown around as some sort of new behavioral principle. Beyond just the term itself, the mechanisms of how feedback worked were a mystery. Was feedback something that came before employee performance? Or was it delivered after performance? If so, how long after? How exactly did it impact future behavior? Was it something that could be used alone? Was it something that needed to be combined with other potential solutions? These are questions that might not seem too important, but for behavior analysts, our understanding of how these interventions work allows us to find the best solutions for those we serve (and also allows us to be really fun at parties).

Fortunately, the research on feedback, especially in the OBM literature, has continued. We have clarified the definition of feedback and determined the who, what, when, where, and why behind the effectiveness of it.

So what is feedback?

Seems like there should be a simple answer, right? Unfortunately, this is not the case and likely the reason for the many different definitions that have developed. To begin unpacking the definition, let's first look at the impact of feedback.

Survival of the Fittest

Who are you? And why are you the way you are? How did you become that way? And who will you be in the future? These important questions can boggle anyone's mind and keep your head tied up in knots for hours trying to unravel the inner mysteries of that which is you. But what if we told you that we could answer these questions with one simple notion? Guess what? We can. It's called feedback. Feedback is the reason that you are the way you are, the reason you do the things you do, and why you will change (or not change) in the future. Before you rebut, just keep reading. We'll explain.

I'm sure you're thinking there are many other things that created all that is you. And you're right (kind of). Feedback does not account for your genetic makeup, for example. However, it does account for all the things you do, say, think, and even feel. Think of your life as one long series of actions (that we call *behaviors*). When you entered the world, you cried. That crying evolved into pointing and grunting, then to words, and finally to sentences. All of your other behaviors have also evolved in some way—from the time you were born until now. The evolution of these behaviors is due to the feedback you received in response to those behaviors.

Not convinced? Let's look at the following example.

When you were young, how did you talk? Did you use a lot of slang terms? Did you always speak in grammatically correct sentences? Did you curse? Did you curse in front of your parents and teachers? Did you speak differently to your friends than you did to your teachers? Chances are, you didn't speak the same way with everyone. You cursed and used slang with friends. You watched your grammar when talking with your English teacher. And you made sure to not let the f-bomb slip out of your lips when talking with your parents. The reason you were able to speak differently in each of these different situations is because of the feedback you received. Your friends might have given you a high five or encouraged your cursing and made fun of you for not using slang, while your teacher may have given you a bad grade for using slang in class. And chances are, you would have gotten a chancleta (Spanish for flip flop) thrown at your head if you cursed in front of your mom. All of these—grades, encouragement from peers, chancletas flying toward your head—are types of feedback.

Each of these pieces of feedback helped you (whether or not you knew it) determine how to speak in each of the above situations. That same phenomenon happens with everything we do and say each and every day, all the time. The short of it? When you do something that's not well received by others, it is likely that you will not do that thing again in that same situation. However, if it's well received, you'll likely do it again. Think of all those ridiculously cheesy pickup lines that seem ever-present at most bars. People keep using them in the context of being out in a bar for a reason—at some point those one-liners were well received by *someone*.

Now that we know the impact of feedback, let's get back to the definition. Feedback is the information transfer from a mediator to a performer about the performer's behavior or action. The information being

KNOW OUR JARGON

Performance: defined by Daniels & Bailey (2014) – a situation, of one or more behaviors, tasks, and results, which are combined to produce a specific accomplishment.

transferred is meant to impact the performer's behavior in some way. Feedback can be given by anyone, and it can be given about any behavior or action another person has displayed. In this book, we are focused on **performance feedback**. Daniels and Bailey (2014) defined *performance* as a situation where one or more behaviors, tasks, and results are combined to produce a specific accomplishment. Or in other words, performance is the outcome or result of an action or set of actions. A quarterback's performance is determined by how many completions were thrown and how many sacks were avoided (among other things). A surgeon's performance focuses on how many clean cuts are made, the steadiness of their hands, and whether the surgery ultimately fixed the problem.

Putting it all together, as leaders (mediators), we are focused on providing information to our followers (performers) that will affect the outcomes of their work (performance) in some way. This can also work in the opposite direction when our followers (mediators) provide us (performers) information focused on making us better leaders (performance).

Let's look at a few examples.

Martin is a new firefighter just out of the academy. Eager to begin his first shift, he arrives about 10 minutes early. He begins talking with one of the firefighters getting off shift and is so engaged in the conversation that he doesn't hear his new battalion chief, Casey, say it's time to start the daily briefing. All of the sudden he looks around and sees that everyone is gone. He quickly ends his conversation and runs to the conference room, where he slips into a chair in the back, hoping Casey doesn't notice. After the briefing, Casey asks Martin to stay. Casey explains that being on time to briefings is extremely important as they go over all the things that happened during the previous shift and what's expected throughout the current shift. Casey tells Martin to enter the conference room 5 minutes before his shift begins to ensure he is on time.

In this example, Casey is the mediator, and Martin is the performer. Casey provides feedback when he tells Martin the impact of his tardy behavior (performance) and how to correct it. Hopefully this will change Martin's behavior by improving his performance, and he will arrive on time moving forward.

Here's a second example. Carlita is the technology department manager. It is the end of the second month of the quarter, and Carlita reports that her department's net revenue is $2.5 million. The goal for the quarter is $3 million. Upon receiving the report, Carlita's supervisor, Anjun, states, "That's great news. You might even end the quarter surpassing the goal! Keep up the good work."

KNOW OUR JARGON

Feedback is the transfer of information from a mediator to a performer in regards to the performer's performance.

Here, the information transfer, or feedback, comes from Anjun (mediator). Hopefully this feedback will continue Carlita's (performer) end-of-month reports (performance) and the successful management of her department.

So the definition of feedback is the transfer of information from one person to another in regard to the other's performance.

Easy, right? Well, kind of. The good news is that feedback *is* easy. The difficult part is knowing what it is about feedback that makes it so effective. Luckily, years of research have already answered that question for us, and it is our intent to provide all of the details and formulas needed to provide feedback that actually improves performance. Throughout the remainder of this book, we will discuss the important characteristics of feedback, outlined by Balcazar (1985), Alvero et al. (2001), and of course, us. These characteristics include the following:

1. **Source**: The individual or device that presents the information to the performer. We call this the mediator.

2. **Participants:** The people whose performance is the topic of feedback. We refer to them as performers.

3. **Performance**: The actual behaviors, actions, tasks, and so on that are the focus of feedback.

4. **Type:** The intended direction performance will move once feedback is given. Performance can increase, decrease, or remain stable. The types of feedback we will discuss are positive, corrective, and negative.

5. **Temporal Dimensions:** How soon after the performance or before the next performance that feedback is delivered. We discuss these as consequences and antecedents.

6. **Medium**: How feedback is communicated to the performer. This can be done in person or by phone, email, instant message, graph, and so on.

7. **Privacy**: Who is present when feedback is delivered and who has access to the feedback.

8. **Formality:** How rigid the feedback is. Sometimes feedback needs to be documented or follow a formal process; other times it does not.

9. **Physical Environment:** The objects and other stimuli in the actual space where feedback is provided. Physical environment can largely affect how well people receive and respond to feedback, so the environment should be considered when preparing to provide feedback.

10. **Frequency:** How often feedback is provided to the performers.

11. **Content and Delivery**: The actual information provided as feedback and the way in which it is provided.

Now that we're all on the same page and share the same definition of feedback, it's time to jump in and start working through the different characteristics of feedback and how to use them to make feedback more effective.

2

SELECTING THE WHAT AND THE WHO

"Learners need endless feedback more than they need endless teaching."
—Grant Wiggins

We mentioned that feedback includes a mediator (the person providing feedback) and a performer (the person receiving feedback). We also clarified that performance feedback focuses on any action, task, or behavior that produces a specific accomplishment. While on the surface, this is pretty straightforward, there are some considerations that must be considered. Thus, we will now focus on identifying the right things to provide feedback for, who should provide the feedback, and who should receive it.

Feedback Is Everywhere.

Feedback is a reaction to almost everything we do, and the more feedback we get, the more we can appropriately adjust our behavior to meet a goal. The same holds true for our employees.

Meet Johanna. She's on a weight loss journey and recently bought an activity tracker to support daily exercise and calorie tracking. She has a daily step goal, and at any point of the day, she can see how close (or not so close) she is to reaching her goal, prompting her to step it up if she's too far behind. In this example, the activity tracker is the source of Johanna's feedback on her health goals.

Now consider Luis. Luis loves video games. He spends his free time trying to earn new inventory, collect money in his pretend bank, and beat progressively challenging levels on all three of his gaming consoles. He does look on forums for cheat codes every once in a while, but for the most part, he has learned how to play each game based on the feedback delivered instantaneously through the push of a button, joystick, or trigger. All the complex button combinations required for a badass fight to victory and the ever-so-slight turn of a racing wheel on a bendy virtual road have been a result of learning through a response and consequence—or put more simply, engaging in a behavior and contacting immediate feedback. Such frequent and immediate feedback gives Luis the opportunity to excel quickly and is another reason he enjoys video games so much. For Luis, the video game is the source of feedback for his playing behavior.

Martha is our last pseudo-individual. She works for a large corporation in one of those cubicle offices with 100 people who don't know each other's names. She was just hired because she has years of experience in her position, yet she doesn't know the ins and outs of this new corporation's policies, mission, or culture. She's been working for Corporation X for 6 weeks and she's still not quite sure what the higher-ups would see as an exemplar finished product or what she's doing well or where she needs to improve. However, most of her calls end well, with the consumer happy, and she gets all of her assigned tasks done on time. Martha assumes she's doing a good enough job because no one has complained about her work, but she is becoming quickly disgruntled by management's total disregard for recognition, training, and leadership. In Martha's case, the source of feedback comes from two places: first, the consumers with which she has spoken and, second, upon task completion within a deadline (by her own monitoring). However, her managers have implemented another *feedback f!@#up*, *as feedback should* have come from a supervisor or manager (or a colleague at the very least). Unfortunately, there's been zip, nada, zero feedback. Dissatisfied with her current work situation, Martha is re-evaluating whether this company even deserves her experience and dedication.

Performance feedback with clear expectations drives motivation, engagement, and productivity in a work setting. However, Martha's scenario is an overly common example of what organizations have to offer their workforce. The remedy to this is threefold. First, you have to know which behaviors or actions should result in feedback. Second, you have to determine the appropriate person or persons to receive the feedback. And finally, you have to know if it is you, someone else, or some other thing that should be providing the feedback.

What Deserves Feedback?

We have discussed that feedback happens all the time, whether or not you plan for it or mean for it to happen. And if left to the rest of the world, there's a chance that your employees will receive the wrong feedback and will begin doing things that don't your organization toward its goals. But we also know that supervisors cannot be everywhere all the time, providing feedback to employees on every single thing they do (or don't do).

Joy has her master's in business administration with a focus on entrepreneurship. She has been hired to head up your new entrepreneur division, which focuses on creating tools and providing services to those launching businesses of their own. Joy is a rock star. She graduated at the top of her class, and her answers were near perfect during her interview. Additionally, she seemed eager, excited, and like someone who would not only fit in well with the team but also effectively lead them.

Joy has now been with the company for about 6 months, and it's time for her bi-annual review. You, as Joy's leader, are a bit disappointed with what you have seen as Joy has not thus far accomplished what you thought she could. As you are reviewing the past 6 months, preparing for her review, you reflect upon what happened, trying to figure out how to pull Joy out of this 2-month slump she seems to be in. You're not sure when her eagerness started fading and her performance started slipping, but you do know these past 2 months have not had the results you needed. Moreover, there has been a drastic change in Joy's accomplishments.

Even though you're still not sure where to begin, Joy walks in. You decide to begin with a question to get her perspective. You ask, "How do you think things have been going thus far? Are you reaching your goals? Do you feel that you're being productive?"

Joy smiles and says eagerly, "I absolutely love working here, and I am so thankful that you invested in me. I also feel that I have been incredibly productive as we not only met our 6-month goals in just 4 months, but we also started a new project that will be launched in the next few weeks."

FEEDBACK F!@#up!

Here you waited 6 months to provide Joy any feedback. Feedback should be provided consistently and often to ensure performance continues. Here, you have learned that Joy's performance slipped because she met her goal. Had you provided feedback, chances are her rock star performance would have continued. Finally, had you provided regular feedback to Joy, you might know something about this "new project" that is about to be launched.

You, knowing nothing of this "new" project look at her puzzled. "What new project?"

Joy frowns and pauses. "The project that Bill told us to begin. He came to me the week you were out, but I assumed that, since you two are partners, you knew?"

Let's stop there. As you can see, there will be several questions for both Joy and Bill to get to the bottom of what happened. However, there is one thing that you could have done to not only avoid being blind-sided by this new project, but also to ensure Joy remained on track. You could have given her consistent feedback regarding her performance.

Joy knew what the 6-month goals were and when she accomplished them within 4 months, and the only person who provided feedback was Bill, who told her to focus on something else. The only feedback she actually received on her performance was meeting the goal before the deadline.

Thus, she didn't know what to do next and assumed this new project was the way to go. After all, you never told her it wasn't.

This leads us to our four rules regarding *what* should result in feedback.

Rule 1: Provide feedback on accomplishments and goals.

Feedback should always be focused on the accomplishments and goals of the individual, team, department, and/or company. Employees are hired to help the company reach its goals, so all feedback should be focused on anything that moves the company closer to or away from a goal. In the example above, feedback should have been provided on Joy's accomplishment of meeting the goal early as well as her work toward that accomplishment in the first 4 months.

Had you provided Joy feedback regarding her work in the first 4 months, chances are, she would have continued that work rather than looking to switch gears. This brings us to our second rule, which goes hand in hand with Rule 1.

Rule 2: Provide feedback on the behavior or the results of the behavior.

In today's world, we often look to the internal characteristics of a person to explain why something did not occur how we wanted. We don't recommend doing this ever, but especially when providing feedback. Telling someone they are lazy or stupid or highlighting even the positive characteristics of brilliance or creativity doesn't actually give them any information about what to do next. Remember, feedback is information transfer from the mediator to the performer regarding the performer's performance. The purpose is to impact the next performance in some way. The best way to do this is to focus on the actual things that person did (the behavior and actions).

If you observed someone interacting with a customer in a way that would likely increase sales, then tell that person exactly what they did correctly: "You kept a smile on your face, really seemed to listen to what they were saying, and ensured you got it right by rephrasing in your own words. Keep it up!"

If you aren't able to observe the actual interaction or work, focus on the results, or accomplishments. If your number-one sales agent makes four sales in one day, focus on the sales that were made. You could say, "Wow! Four sales in one day—nice work there. You are really going above and beyond."

Both of these situations provide the performer information about what they did to receive the feedback, allowing them to continue reaching their targets.

Rule 3: Provide feedback on things the person can control.

Nothing is worse than to receive feedback on something that you have absolutely no control over. Take our earlier example with Joy. Had you decided to provide feedback to Joy on Bill's decision to direct the team in a new direction, Joy would likely be frustrated and discouraged. Joy has no control over Bill's decisions and has no way of determining which partner to follow. In this example, the better resolution would be to focus on the behaviors that Joy did have under her control—that of hers and her teams. Thus, even though she met her goal before schedule, if you wanted her to continue with the same momentum, feedback should focus on that.

Here's what you might say: "That's awesome that you met the goal 2 months prior to schedule. I would have liked to see that momentum continue through the fifth and sixth months to determine if we could have gone further. In the future, even if goals are met ahead of schedule, please continue to work on them to see how far we can go."

This feedback provides Joy with the information necessary for her to make a change in what she does in the future. Next time, whether or not Bill attempts to change her direction, she hopefully knows that she should continue working toward and beyond goals until you say something different.

Rule 4: Provide feedback on things that are measurable.

Companies set goals and then measure progress toward them so that changes can be made when necessary. The same holds true for performance. The way to know if someone's performance is moving the company toward a goal or away from it is to measure the progress, or results, and their impact on the company. Thus, when you're providing feedback, always make sure that the feedback provided is about actions that can be measured.

You're likely thinking, "Wait, I have to measure everything now, too??!?!!?"

Not exactly. We will dive into measurement and tracking the effectiveness of your feedback later. For now, just remember that, when deciding what to give feedback about, choose something that *can* be measured, even if it isn't being measured right now.

In short, when deciding the *what* of feedback, remember that you should always focus on the *measurable* behaviors or actions (or outcomes of those actions) that the person can control. Do this, and you have figured out the first step in the formula: What should result in feedback? Still not sure? No worries! We have provided the decision tree below to help guide you through the questions to ask and what to do depending on how you answer the questions.

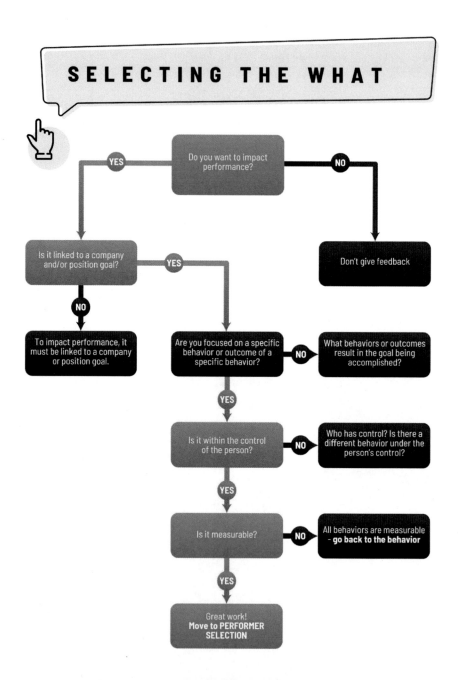

SELECTING THE WHAT

Do you want to impact performance?

YES

NO

Is it linked to a company and/or position goal?

YES

Don't give feedback

NO

To impact performance, it must be linked to a company or position goal.

Are you focused on a specific behavior or outcome of a specific behavior?

NO

What behaviors or outcomes result in the goal being accomplished?

YES

Is it within the control of the person?

NO

Who has control? Is there a different behavior under the person's control?

YES

Is it measurable?

NO

All behaviors are measurable – go back to the behavior

YES

Great work!
Move to PERFORMER SELECTION

Once you have gotten all the variables correct, you have completed the first step in the feedback formula. Nice work! To celebrate, let's start writing our formula:

EFFECTIVE PERFORMANCE FEEDBACK =
(The Behavior/Action/Outcome) + (x)
**x = everything we have not yet discussed. Be patient—it's coming!

There's one final point to remember when selecting the what: while we can provide feedback on **any** behavior, only feedback that focuses on the behaviors and outcomes under the **control** of the individual will make a difference. Feedback provided on the behaviors of others or outcomes outside the control of the individual will simply lead to frustration and resentment.

Who Deserves Feedback?

Now that we have a general idea of what should result in feedback, it's time to move on to the who...meaning *who* should be the recipient of the feedback. We're sure you're thinking "the performer, of course." You are correct, but before you get too settled into thinking that we are simply pointing out the obvious, take a moment to think of ALL the performers you have encountered today alone (we are secretly hoping that it's not first thing in the morning and you are home alone). If today is a work day, you've likely already encountered several performers, each of which is doing something to move the company toward its vision and mission (at least hopefully that's what they're doing; if not, they need some feedback!).

For most of us, there are five distinct categories of individuals we encounter at work: supervisees (both our own and other people's), our supervisors, our peers, ourselves, and our clients. Most of these individuals should be recipients of *your* feedback. The exception is other people's supervisees, who should receive feedback from *someone else*—likely one of your peers. Let's go through each of these in detail.

Supervisees – This one's obvious, right? We're sure you've learned by now that some of this stuff may seem obvious and logical, but under the surface, it's not always quite as easy as it initially appeared. The performance of our supervisees is the best measure of our leadership skills. When they fail, we won't say that the leader failed, but rather, the leader must learn and adapt and help supervisees succeed. An inexperienced supervisee will require much more feedback and support than a more seasoned employee, but *both* will still need feedback. A supervisee who is performing below standards will need a lot more feedback when compared to an elite performer, but again, *both* need feedback. The difference in all of these examples is a matter of how much feedback is needed in terms of quantity and specificity (we'll get there soon).

Supervisees come at all levels. For those who are in their first leadership positions, a supervisee may be a frontline staff or even a peer (if you're shift manager or floor leader). However, as you move higher in the organization, you will be accountable for increasingly more people. However, we expect that higher-level leaders rely on their direct reports to the next direct reports and so on in a hierarchical fashion, as deemed by the organizational structure. Leaders can (and should) provide feedback to all levels of employees under them. The more removed a leader is from a position, the less likely it is that feedback will be provided; however, do not discount the power of the CEO's feedback to a frontline worker as the CEO walks through the assembly line. This can sometimes be the most powerful feedback provided in an organization.

FEEDBACK F!@#up!

Providing feedback to leaders is one of the least common practices in business. It seems that we have adopted a "since they got here, they should know and have mastered everything" type of attitude. Unfortunately, there is not much further from the truth. As a leader, it will be important to not just learn how to provide feedback to your supervisors, but also teach your supervisees how to provide feedback to you.

Supervisors – We divide this category into two groups (one of which is accounted for in the group above): (a) the leaders you supervise and (b) the leaders who supervise you.

All leaders need feedback, too. When providing feedback, coaching, direction, and so on, supervisors need feedback about their performance and its effects on their supervisees. If a leader is providing ineffective feedback, that person needs to know. Additionally, your supervisors need to know when they are doing things right and when they need to change. Often times, we assume that the highest leaders in the company don't need any feedback. They're the ultimate leaders, so they know everything, right? Wrong. Even the highest-level leader at the largest company in the world needs feedback. And because this is so often overlooked, chances are this person needs more feedback than the rest of us. Don't shy away from telling your supervisor when they are helpful, what they did that worked well, and when things could be improved. Finally, as a leader yourself, seek out feedback from your supervisees.

Peers – We all need feedback. Team members and peers are no exception. We need to tell those we work most closely with when they do things right, when they impress us, and when things go wrong. We personally love team members who can help us correct mistakes before our boss finds out! We are certain you feel the same way. Peer feedback builds stronger teams and creates a more positive culture. Additionally, there may be times that you observe someone else's supervisee, and it is not appropriate for you to provide them with feedback. Instead, provide the feedback to your peer, who can in turn either pass on the great news that someone caught them doing things well or solve the issue.

Ourselves – We've all heard the old saying that "crazy people talk to themselves." However, every one of us talks to ourselves, whether it's out loud or a little voice in our heads. And believe it or not, we can actually provide feedback to ourselves—and you probably have before! Providing yourself feedback is part of self-monitoring. If you have ever congratulated yourself for reaching a goal or crossed out a completed task on your task list, you have provided yourself some feedback! This feedback is important for a number of reasons. First, it is always good to gage how you think you did on something. If working toward a goal, you want to cheer for yourself for reaching it. If you aren't reaching it, chances are you need to "have a talk with yourself" to figure out what to change. If you're not in the habit of giving yourself feedback, start thinking about how you can start. Also, keep in mind that, if you are to receive feedback from yourself, you want your staff to provide feedback to themselves as well. This may be an important skill to teach!

Consumers – Most companies think about getting feedback from their consumers (which we will discuss very soon!); however, a lot don't consider providing their consumers with feedback. This is a significant oversight; just as we want feedback from them, consumers sometimes need feedback from us. This may come as second nature to those in customer service or sales; however, it should be second nature to all of us. However, because our consumers are not purposely taking actions to move our company toward its goals, this type of feedback is not performance feedback, so we will not focus on it other than to say that it might be something to think about.

Now that we know all the different groups of individuals who should receive feedback, the important thing to determine is who *exactly* should receive the feedback *for what you have decided to give feedback on.* You have just ensured that you're giving feedback about the right thing, so now it is time to determine which individual or group of individuals should receive the feedback.

The easy question to answer here is "who did it?" Sometimes it's obvious who needs feedback. There are times that you observe a supervisee do something and then immediately provide feedback regarding it. However, there are other times that the answer to "who did it?" is not so clear. Sometimes there is more than one person responsible for the outcome. Other times there is no clear "owner" of the outcome. And still other times there is someone who had nothing to do with the final outcome, but played a role in getting there. All of these individuals should receive feedback.

Juneice is a customer representative for a cellphone company. She works in the call center that handles customer complaints about contracts and service. Juneice receives a phone call from a very disgruntled consumer explaining that she recently switched the phone service (we'll call it Cells4You) and got an upgraded phone. The phone that she wanted was not going to be released for a couple weeks, so she was going to wait until its release and then switch. However, when talking with the sales agent, the agent stated that she could set up a new phone line for free with a free phone so that the switch could occur that day. The consumer stated that she was told there were no penalties, contracts, or hidden commitments. However, now 4 months later, the consumer is calling because she wants to get the extra phone line disconnected. She was told there would be a cancellation fee of hundreds of dollars and that she would owe for the purchase of the phone. Juneice's supervisor overhears this call and begins thinking about who should receive feedback.

To help Juneice's supervisor, let's go through the questions we may ask, which are outlined in the simple decision tree below, to determine who should receive feedback (in other words, to identify the performer).

You can see we are only adding one simple question to our formula... who performed the action or is responsible for the outcome? Label this individual by name and by position to determine if they are a supervisor, supervisee, peer, or yourself.

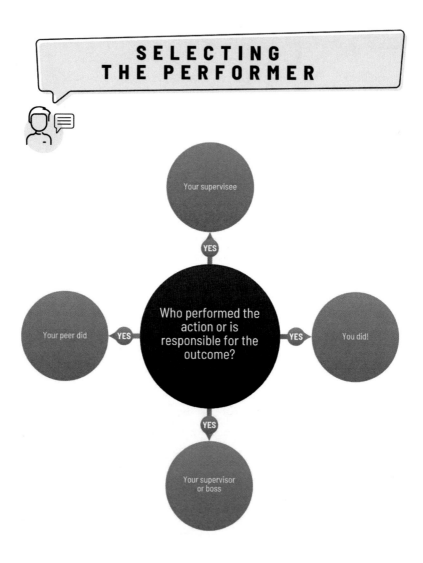

SELECTING THE PERFORMER

Your supervisee

YES

Who performed the action or is responsible for the outcome?

Your peer did   YES   YES   You did!

YES

Your supervisor or boss

Here's how our feedback formula works with this information added:

EFFECTIVE PERFORMANCE FEEDBACK =
(The Behavior/Action/Outcome) + ***(The Person)*** + *(x)*.

Who did it?

The easiest way to identify the performer is to determine who actually did the performance. Sometimes this is easy. You want to give feedback on that spectacular touchdown caught despite triple coverage? That's easy—provide it to the person who caught the ball. You want to provide feedback for the new fire captain who clearly and flawlessly directed everyone on the scene? Again, pretty easy—provide it to the captain. Additionally, it's generally better to provide individualized feedback whenever possible. One Harvard business writer said, "A great individual is better than a good team" (Stibel, 2011), which is a statement with so much value.

Think of it this way: The decision-makers within an organization want to retain their top performers, right? Hopefully, attempts to minimize turnover rates involve showering quality employees with professional development opportunities and ways to grow within the company. How else do entry-level employees eventually get to an all-star level or maintain top-performer status? One reason is receiving clear and consistent feedback about their performance as it relates to their individual job responsibilities within an organization. But why is feedback on individual performance important, and why is it usually better than group performance feedback? Get your pen and paper ready; more lists are coming your way…

Feedback provided on an individual level is the way to go for the following reasons:

1. It positively influences the likelihood that feedback will be *specific* and makes it much easier for the performer to begin tracking their own performance.

2. Individual feedback allows a leader to identify goals that are appropriate to the staff member's current skills and mastery level. To deliver individualized feedback, a manager or leader must take a look at specific, individual performance—which, in turn, provides the mediator with more frequent opportunities to identify areas that

MISCONCEPTION

Positive Reinforcement vs Reward vs Bribe: Contrary to popular belief, positive reinforcement is not synonymous with a reward or a bribe. Positive reinforcement is the process of presenting something preferred following the behavior that results in that behavior occurring again in the future. Reinforcement is not presented because negative or problematic behavior occurred; it is solely based on the occurrence of positive behavior.

Rewards are items and activities that are perceived by the deliverer to be preferred. Rewards are delivered after a behavior; however, are vaguely linked to the behavior or do not have any effect on the future occurrence on the behavior. While reinforcement is directly linked to the behavior and increases the likeliness the behavior will occur again, rewards may increase morale, but will not effect the behavior. Examples of rewards include pizza parties at the end of the month or giving candy to someone for a correct response (when the person does not like candy).

Bribes are promises of rewards that are presented prior to the wanted behavior occurring. They are presented only because an unwanted behavior has occurred and the promise of this reward is meant to end the problematic or unwanted behavior and replace it with the wanted behavior. It is often confused with a way to "motivate" the individual to perform; however, the problem is that the individual learns that they first have to demonstrate an unwanted behavior before the offer is made. This creates a chain of behavior that is not optimal. The difference between a bribe and reinforcement is that reinforcement is presented only because of the wanted behavior while bribes become available only because of the unwanted behavior.

Example: There are 3 additional reports that need to be complete prior to the end of the day. Your goal is to get your supervisee to stay late and complete the reports.

MISCONCEPTION

Reinforcement: Prior to the end of the day, you enter your supervisee's office and say "We have these 3 reports that must be done before the day ends. If you do them, you will likely have to stay late. If this happens, I would like to give you a ½-day tomorrow. Can you please stay late and complete the reports?"

Reward: The supervisee stays late to complete the reports. The next day you present him with a $10 gift card to Starbucks not knowing that he hates Starbucks.

Bribe: Your supervisee comes into your office and says "see you tomorrow!" You ask if the last 3 reports are complete and your supervisee replies "no – I was going to do them tomorrow." You remind your supervisee that they are due today and ask if they can stay late to get it done. Your supervisee replies that they have plans tonight. You then offer to give a ½-day off tomorrow if they stay and get the reports done.

need improvement and to set goals for the performer.

3. It generates faster learning. Since the effectiveness of feedback relies on specific and timely information, individualized feedback generates a more rapid acquisition of novel skills and continues to improve already-developed skills.

4. It enables quick detection of both strong and weak performers. Think back to your high school days when group projects were administered; you were either deemed the over-achiever (leader of the group) who did most of the work, the mid-worker who met the minimum standard of whatever they were assigned, or the leech who most team members affectionately describe as the student who did little to nothing except wait for everyone else to finish the project. Oh, don't you love it when a teacher allows all the group members to conduct a "performance evaluation" at the end of the project to help determine an appropriate

grade for each student? Those moments usually result in sweet, sweet revenge. The moral of this example is that there may be only one or a handful of individuals keeping the "great results" boat afloat, while others piggyback on the top performer's glory.

5. Feedback primarily based on team performance can lead to detrimental effects for both the top performers and the weaker ones.

- **The top performers:** Without individualized feedback, work morale and stellar performance may dwindle (slowly or suddenly) because the performer's efforts are not being recognized frequently enough. Ask yourself if you know what each of your team members contributed to a project's end results. If it's not clear to you, then it's impossible for you to provide valid and accurate feedback—positive or not—to each performer within a group.

- **The slackers:** Okay, a *slacker* label is a little harsh (although some have rightfully earned this badge). It is true that low-performing staff may not meet performance standards because of a lack of motivation or insufficient contact with positive reinforcement. However, it's also possible that a staff member may not be performing at optimal levels because they aren't equipped with the skill set to do so, or perhaps the staff member does not have a clear idea about the expectations of their job role or the responsibilities within it. Not only does individual feedback reduce uncertainty in job roles (Goltz et al., 1990), but failure to examine team member performance at the individual level greatly increases the chance of missing gaps in performance deficits.

6. Individualized feedback develops and strengthens rapport between the performer and mediator. This fact holds true only under the assumption that positive feedback is given at a higher ratio than corrective and negative feedback. Delivering an abundance of positive feedback brings added benefits to the leader by generating discretionary effort from their employees in a variety of work tasks.

7. Individualized feedback helps create value in the work that staff is doing and should clearly show *how* their efforts are positively

impacting the business.

8. An employee who understands precisely what they are doing well and where they should improve supports the development of intrinsic reinforcers. A response that produces a (reinforcing) consequence natural to the task is an intrinsic reinforcer. In a work context, pride in a job well done and confidence in the ability to do a job well are examples of intrinsic reinforcers that will help maintain a team member's performance even when other consequences, including feedback, have been reduced. Bill Parcels, a two-time Super Bowl-winning coach astutely said, "Even small successes can be extremely powerful in helping people believe in themselves. When you set small, visible goals, and people achieve them, they start to get into their heads that they can succeed" (Heath & Heath, 2010, p. 143) Parcels hit on an important point—mastery in addition to positive feedback for personal achievements helps develop meaning, pride, and ownership in the work performed. Performance assessment can increase intrinsic motivation (intrinsic reinforcers) by providing information about the individual's demonstrated and attained level of competence (Archer-Kath et al., 1994).

9. Individual performance feedback enables a leader to evaluate changes in a performer's behavior after feedback delivery. That is, providing individualized feedback can help you answer questions regarding whether any implemented changes based on that feedback have increased desirable performance or whether a different or added intervention is necessary.

As you can see, there are many reasons a leader should heavily consider an emphasis on delivering performance feedback at the individual level. It may seem like we think all feedback should be given individually, but we know this approach has its place. There are other times where group feedback is more appropriate.

Remember those three players who were supposed to cover the receiver? What about their coach? Who should the coach provide feedback to? All three of the players? Or each of them individually? What about a sales team that did not meet the monthly goal? Who gets the feedback then? Clearly, based on these questions, there are times that group feedback has benefits. For this, we move to our next question.

Are two or more individuals working toward, and all responsible for, the same performance goal?

If the answer is "yes," then group feedback is more appropriate, keeping in mind that you're targeting the behavior of each individual in the group. Groups don't behave; people in groups behave. Let's look at the benefits of group feedback.

1. If feedback is being provided for a group performance, it implies that all team members are collectively working toward the same performance goal. This means the group members will push each other to be successful and will probably gently nudge (or totally harass) a teammate who slacks off. Why is this important, and what does it mean for the leader? This extra source of feedback potential increases the opportunity for reinforcement because peers serve as mediators of feedback among each other. In addition to an increased frequency of reinforcement as co-workers give each other positive and corrective feedback, the immediacy of contact with feedback following performance also changes. More specifically, the time between performance and feedback reduces. Recall from the first few chapters that both the frequency and immediacy of reinforcement are important controlling variables in consequences administered to change behavior.

2. A focus on group performance feedback can be efficient, particularly for a priceless commodity called *time*. It takes a supervisor a lot of time and effort to deliver effective feedback to every team member, so a group approach can minimize the time and frequency of providing individual feedback. If a group feedback approach sounds attractive to you because of time management, keep in that while you may free up more time in your day by giving group feedback, it could come at the expense of lower individual performance gains.

3. Group feedback is critical when the results of individuals working together matters most. Department feedback and feedback for people who work in crews, assembly lines, or sports teams are prime examples of when group feedback, in combination with individual performance feedback, is ideal.

A leader or manager determines whether to provide individualized or group performance feedback, or even a nice mix of the two (yes, pick this option when appropriate). To determine who the performer or performers are, always trace back to who is responsible for the outcome or goal. If it's a group, it's okay to provide group feedback. In all other situations, it's best to err on the side of caution and provide feedback individually.

Worried about forgetting? Remember to refer to the "who receives feedback" decision tree below to help guide you.

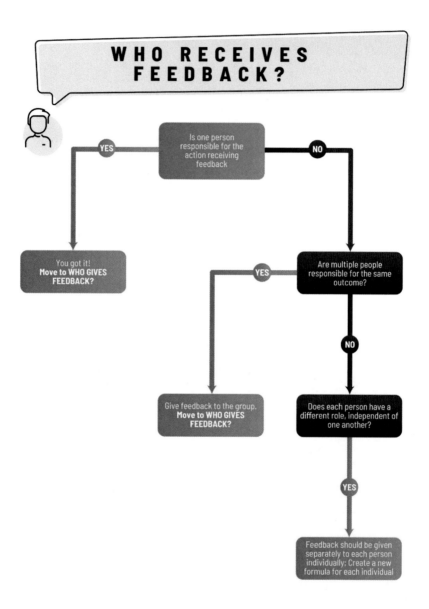

WHO RECEIVES FEEDBACK?

Is one person responsible for the action receiving feedback

YES

NO

You got it!
Move to WHO GIVES FEEDBACK?

Are multiple people responsible for the same outcome?

YES

NO

Give feedback to the group.
Move to WHO GIVES FEEDBACK?

Does each person have a different role, independent of one another?

YES

Feedback should be given separately to each person individually; Create a new formula for each individual

And now, we are ready to add to our feedback formula:

EFFECTIVE PERFORMANCE FEEDBACK =
(The Behavior/Action/Outcome) + *(The Person)* + **(The Number of People)** + *(x)*

Let's see what else is included in *x*. Up next, the mediator—the person giving feedback.

Who gives feedback?

Hopefully you're jumping up and down right now, hand up shouting "I do! I do!" If you are, great work so far. You understand that you're one of the most important people in this equation. However, you're not the *only* person, and as a leader, you're responsible for helping others provide feedback as well (if they're not already).

The key here is not determining who should provide feedback (because everyone should), but instead determining who is the right person in the right moment. To determine this, we have to first understand why different people provide feedback. As you may have guessed, those who receive feedback are also those who should *give* feedback: supervisors, peers, supervisees, consumers, and ourselves. Let's dive into each category to determine when each person should provide feedback.

Supervisors – This category might seem like the most obvious one. If you are in a leadership position—that is, a position where you're overseeing the work of others—then you absolutely need to provide feedback. While it may seem obvious, employees all over the world fail because their supervisors and managers will not provide them with *objective* feedback based on *observable performance*. However, there are also leaders out there who give such feedback and do it well. We're hoping that, with the guidance in this book, you find yourself in the latter category.

Peers – Throughout our careers, we are bound to make certain decisions that we're not 100% sure of. It is therefore important to build a network of trusted colleagues who can offer advice and, of course, provide us with feedback. Additionally, as mentioned earlier, it is often better to find out you're doing something incorrectly from a peer than from a supervisor. Those teammates who look out for one another have stronger teams and are the members who are more likely to get promoted. Be the team member that looks out for your peers and helps them by both encouraging and complimenting their hard work and helping to correct when errors occur. Also included here is anyone you may also consider a mentor. Mentorship is a special type of relationship where one person is guided by another, more experienced person who isn't necessarily their supervisor. Seeking a mentor, especially when you're engaging in behaviors outside your comfort zone, is crucial to ensure you're going in the right direction.

Supervisees – Supervisees are an excellent source of feedback and should ideally be regularly providing it. There are a few reasons that this does not happen more often. First, we all were children once. And being a child is somewhat similar to being a supervisee in that there is someone who sets the expectations and then tells us if we are achieving them. As children, many of us were not encouraged to tell our parents, teachers, or other authority figures what we were doing wrong (chancletas might have come flying our way, after all). This hierarchical learning—the idea that we are not to tell those above us what they are doing incorrectly—carries into adulthood and continues throughout our lives. And even though most of us were never explicitly told to not tell our parents and teachers when they were doing something right, child feedback has typically been disregarded as invalid. The difference in the workforce is that we are not children, we do have perspective that the supervisor might not have, and we have plenty of valuable feedback to offer. And that is true of your supervisees as well. So how do you get your supervisees to provide more feedback? You teach it, elicit it, and then reinforce it! Don't be that manager who assumes you're doing a remarkable job because no one said anything. Be the leader who knows there is likely something terribly wrong if no one is saying anything. Here are some things to keep in mind when asking supervisees for feedback (Lees, 2017):

- Ask for feedback that is both positive and corrective. The first time you do this, you will likely see that not much will be offered. However, simply asking for feedback introduces that this is appropriate and wanted—and it shows your supervisees that you value them.

- Ask about specific topics and behaviors that you recently engaged in. If you're not getting much feedback, even when you specifically ask for it, try asking more specific questions. For example, if you gave a presentation, you could ask, "What did you think about the presentation? How was the delivery? What did you like most? How can I make it more effective next time?" Assuming there's room for improvement, using "how can I" rather than "can I" also sends the message that you expect correction or constructive criticism.

- Don't underestimate how easy it is to become defensive. Even when asking for corrective feedback, it is remarkably easy to find yourself feeling defensive about what you're hearing, especially if you don't agree with it. Remember, though, by becoming defensive or immediately providing a counter argument, you risk punishing the feedback, making it less likely the supervisee will share in the future. Instead, reinforce the very fact that they came to you and were honest. Additionally, one strategy that works well when feeling defensive is to ask for specific examples and/or ways that you could improve. This takes the focus off your personal work and puts the focus on solutions instead. It also teaches supervisees to come to you with solutions to criticism and issues rather than simply dumping them on your plate.

- Don't ask for feedback just for the sake of asking for it. In other words, don't put this book down, call a supervisee into your office, and ask for feedback simply because we said to. One of two things will happen if you do this: (a) you will come across as insincere, discouraging your supervisees to provide you with feedback, or (b) you will get defensive because you will receive critical feedback you weren't expecting. The reason to ask for feedback is to gain input on how you can improve your own performance. If you're not looking to do this, don't ask for the feedback. However, if you genuinely value the input of your staff and use it to improve your leadership skills, ask for it often!

Consumers – Consumer feedback allows us to know how we're doing as a company. While providing consumers with feedback does not result in improved performance for the company, receiving feedback from them can. Focus on evoking consumer feedback about the things that you and your staff can control. This can take the form of a quick survey that consumers fill out in person or complete online at a separate time. Here are a few things you want to consider:

- You want surveys to be completed as soon as possible after the customer interaction. As time passes, customers are likely to forget about the interaction and are far more likely to complete a survey right after the interaction ends. This is why many companies will ask consumers to agree to a satisfaction survey prior to being transferred to an agent.

- Keep the surveys short. The longer the survey, the less likely it is that a customer will complete it. Think about it: When is the last time you had the time to complete a 30-minute survey that asked question after question? When you ask customers to complete a survey, they're doing so on their own time and have almost nothing to gain for doing so. The shorter the survey, the better.

- Keep questions as objective as possible. Likert scales (e.g., the classic 1–5 scale) can be tricky to make sense of. The second that we receive anything but a perfect score, the panic alarms sound. Tie questions to measurable behavior that (a) you can act on and (b) is tied to significant results.

- The single most important question to ask is whether the consumer will be a repeat customer and/or recommend your company to a friend. While this does not tell you exactly how to improve performance, it does give you immediate feedback regarding whether *something* needs to change.

Ourselves – We highlighted the importance of receiving feedback, as a leader, as a supervisee, and as a peer. Feedback from others helps us improve our skills. Unfortunately, you will not always be surrounded by people who are consistently providing feedback. To remedy this, we recommend two things. First, elicit feedback from others. We discussed how to elicit feedback from your supervisees, but do the same with your supervisors and peers. If there is something you want to know about specifically—maybe you're preparing for a presentation or a peer observed you provide feedback to an employee, for instance—ask someone who observed you or who can observe you doing a role play (if you are preparing) to provide feedback. Additionally, ask your supervisors for their input on your work. The second solution is to provide feedback to yourself (yes, you are both the mediator and the performer here).

Believe it or not, it is possible to provide ourselves with feedback. This is called self-monitoring (you can probably guess why it's called this). Self-monitoring is what we do when we taste the new recipe we cooked and say "this is yummy!" or when we step on the scale and say "I shouldn't have had that second piece of cake yesterday." We self-monitor and give ourselves feedback all the time without necessarily thinking about it. When it comes to our own performance, there are some things to consider. Let's look at the pros and cons of self-monitoring first.

The Pros and Cons of Self-Monitoring

The advantages of a self-monitoring approach to feedback delivery and performance improvement far outweigh any disadvantages or process development headaches. Ready to hear why? Self-monitoring does the following:

1. **Generates immediate feedback**. When we discuss *when* to provide feedback, we will review just how important the immediacy of feedback (and any consequence, really) is in producing performance changes. Can't wait? Here's a quick sneak peak of what's most important to know: The closer in time the feedback follows a behavior, the more likely that it will impact that behavior, thus making it more or less likely to occur in the future under similar conditions. Delayed feedback is not nearly as effective and accounts for one of the main reasons that performance reviews are useless and ineffective in generating desirable performance outcomes.

2. **Reduces dependence on others**. Since self-monitoring systems provide immediate and frequent feedback, they decrease the need for additional feedback from supervisors, bosses, and peers. Notice we says *reduces*, not *eliminates*. Self-monitoring of our own behaviors provides us immediate feedback about what is going well and what might need to change. Additionally, if we can teach those around us (especially our supervisees) to provide themselves with their own feedback, or help create a self-monitoring system that provides them with immediate feedback, we decrease the amount of feedback we need to personally provide. Self-monitoring systems can also help us, as leaders, collect information on the actions our staff are performing that we cannot easily observe. For example, say you are a lead trainer, and you have

five trainers who each work with individual clients working toward weight loss. You can't both observe the work of the trainers and work with your own clients at the same time, but you can still monitor the trainers' performance and provide them with feedback by creating a self-monitoring system. An easy way to do this is to create a chart that reports how quickly each client is reaching their goal. The trainer is responsible for client progress, so having the trainers monitor their clients and provide themselves feedback regarding how effective they are as trainers allows them to make adjustments as needed. Asking them to then report their self-monitoring results to you allows you to provide feedback without having to do the extra work of monitoring the trainers yourself.

3. **May produce quicker acquisition**. Achieving a predetermined goal may occur more quickly because feedback is delivered often. Think about your own goals. When you monitor your own progress toward these goals, you don't have to wait for someone else to tell you how you are doing—you already know! This more immediate feedback allows you to give yourself a pat on the back when you're doing well or make immediate changes when you're not moving in the right direction.

4. **Clarifies expectations**. Self-monitoring relies on tracking measurable behaviors and/or outcomes. This process has positive outcomes for both you and any supervisees you may create a self-monitoring system for. For you, creating a self-monitoring program forces you to think about specific goals and what actions will move you toward accomplishing those goals. This helps ensure clarity on the behaviors, actions, and tasks that are most important to goal achievement. Similarly, your supervisees get the same benefits when you create a self-monitoring system for them. When doing this, you not only clarify for yourself what your supervisees should be doing but also help communicate the same clear expectations to your supervisees.

Of course, when something sounds too good to be true, it usually is. We need to be honest in telling you that self-monitoring has some potential disadvantages, too.

1. Self-monitoring as a source of feedback does not mean you or your boss are completely free of the responsibility to monitor staff performance or deliver feedback. You still need feedback from your

leaders, especially when you're asked to do something new or different. Similarly, your supervisees need feedback, too. We will discuss this in more depth later, but for now, note that self-monitoring is better to use for behaviors that are already established. They are less effective when you are trying to learn something new—after all, how do you know if it's right if you haven't done it before?

2. A tendency to fabricate data can develop. When given too much freedom or when the wrong consequences are in place, employees may be very tempted to fabricate data, for two reasons in particular.

> **FEEDBACK F!@#up!**
>
> Any time someone's performance is directly related to a strong reinforcer (such as a bonus, raise, or promotion), that person should not solely be responsible for monitoring their own progress. The problem here is that the reinforcer is so strong it creates motivation to achieve it, no matter what. Even the most honest people will be motivated to "fudge" a little if it makes the difference between that promotion or raise they've been working so hard for or remaining exactly where they were – with all of their hard work going relatively unnoticed.

Let's say Lucia's performance bonuses or other privileges are tied to performance gains evaluated via self-monitoring. Here, Lucia is likely motivated to get a bonus and the other rewards offered for her performance. Even if Lucia is an extremely honest person, not having anyone else check in on her progress is likely to result in a bit of fudging—especially if her scores are close.

The situation could be different in other scenarios. Instead of allowing employees to earn desirable outcomes for performance gains, the boss at Ronald's office penalizes failure to meet outlined goals with reprimands, suspension, and eventual termination. The employee at this office might fabricate data, not to gain access to bonuses, but to escape the reprimands and other negative consequences.

In the first example, data fabrication continues to occur because it gets the employee something they want; in the second example, misrepresentation of data occurs because it helps the staff member avoid a very unpleasant situation. In reality, it's possible for data fabrication to be maintained by a little bit of both of these contingencies.

You might be thinking, "That makes sense, but it will never happen to me. I am of sound moral character and always tell the truth." And we believe you. We really do. But we also know behavior, and we know that given the right circumstances, everyone is more likely to fudge, no matter your moral standing or values. That's the problem with relying on those internal characteristics rather than sticking with what is observable. Someone may be completely against lying and falsification of data; however, if fudging just the slightest bit will help you keep your job (and you have a new baby and spouse at home counting on you to provide), chances are you will fudge the data.

So how do you combat this for yourself (making fudging the data less likely) and for your staff? We offer two ways to remedy data fabrication issues:

a. Conduct intermittent integrity checks. Every so often and without warning, a manager or supervisor must monitor the performance reflected in the self-monitoring results. This is done not only to check for deliberate skewing of data but also to ensure that observer drift has not occurred. In relation to self-monitoring, *observer drift* refers to any unintended change in the way a performer uses the self-monitoring measurement system that results in measurement error. Sometimes this drift occurs because the individual's interpretation of what they're measuring changes, or perhaps the intended behavior to measure is too difficult to measure. The frequency of integrity checks will depend on the employee's current performance, history of accurate data collection, and the complexity of both the system being used and the performance outcomes being tracked.

b. Ensure that reinforcement and feedback sources regarding performance are not solely found in data collected from self-monitoring. Yes, recognition from the boss and other potentially positive consequences associated with performance improvement and accurate data collection should be administered through self-monitoring. However, an employee depending on only one way to get those "extras" is a recipe for fabrication disaster. More specifically, focusing on only one reinforcement source creates contingencies that support unethical behavior.

FEEDBACK F!@#up!

Two things went wrong here. First, as we discuss in the paragraph, the difficulty of the response was so high that it was unattainable. Behavior science tells us that there is a point at which the cost of the response (whether it be the effort to complete it, the length of time it takes, or the perceived likeliness one will get it correct) becomes too high and the reinforcer loses its effectiveness. You see this here with Natalie. The effort involved in finding a notebook, carrying it around, and putting data in two places outweighed the reinforcement she would receive.

Second, instead of reinforcing Natalie's efforts of recording her food intake, her trainer actually punished her efforts. Behavior analytically, punishment is something that occurs after a behavior that results in the decrease of that behavior in the future. Here, Natalie's behavior of recording her food intake was met by her trainer telling her she didn't do it correctly and more work for Natalie. To encourage Natalie to continue her efforts, her trainer should have provided Natalie some positive feedback regarding her efforts and asked if there was a way for her to add in a notation of times she ate. Lucky for him, Natalie is a behavior analyst and she provided him with feedback regarding this!

3. Asking staff to monitor their own performance increases the amount of work they have to do. You may be thinking, "So what? It benefits everyone in the long run." While that's true, people don't always place high value in delayed positive consequences. Before people have the chance to determine any benefits of changes made in a work or even personal situation, the primary perception is that the change will equal more work. Behavioral scientists have repeatedly shown that increasing the amount or the difficulty of a task greatly *decreases* the likelihood of an individual initiating or completing an effortful task.

Every day, people avoid behavior that is really the best thing for them in the long run: starting a new workout program or beginning to increase physical activity, quitting their strongest addiction (e.g., smoking, coffee, junk food), and adopting certain child-rearing techniques that require a lot of time and energy are just a few examples. Monitoring your own work performance is another example; it takes more time and is "one more thing to do." Given that, don't be surprised if you're met with rolling eyes, sighs, or a total lack of participation when it's introduced to your supervisees.

Here is the perfect example of how self-monitoring goes wrong. Natalie, one of our authors, has been working with a private trainer to accomplish both workout and weight loss goals. One of her largest challenges is eating right. She tends to eat sporadically or go without eating all day, leaving her starving and making poor nutrition choices late at night. To remedy this, her trainer asked her to begin keeping a food journal. He also gave her an app to download to her phone that automatically calculates calories and tells her how much more of each nutrient she needs to eat each day. A behavior analyst who loves data to the core, Natalie began excitedly. She recorded every single thing she ate, down to the seasonings she used to season her food. After the first week, she observed that her eating habits were changing. The feedback of seeing "zero calories" at 2 p.m. changed her behavior of not eating prior to 2 p.m. However, as she excitedly showed her trainer her tracking and progress toward goals, she was told that she was not doing it correctly. The app did not record the times that Natalie ate each day, and given that was one of her largest issues, her trainer told her she needed to write a separate journal with the times that she ate each item. Natalie, faced with having to figure out how to carry a notebook around with her at all times and remember to enter her food logs in two places, failed at both tasks. She was no longer encouraged by the app because it didn't have all the right information, and she was overwhelmed by the extra work. Now, instead of self-monitoring, food logging became just another task—one that she had no time to do. Thus, she stopped tracking everything.

So how do you tackle this issue? We've got answers for that, too!

a. Make self-monitoring easier with sufficient training. Ensure that staff demonstrate both mastery and fluency for *all* the steps of self-monitoring before allowing them to use it independently (steps for training are detailed in the next section). Also, keep in mind that self-monitoring should *not* be used to teach a new skill or improve a skill the staff member cannot do consistently or independently.

   If you are developing a self-monitoring system for yourself, choose a system that will not be too much extra work and one that actually provides you value. Self-monitoring systems should quickly tell us whether we are on track. If you don't get that information, then you're not doing the right self-monitoring.

b. Reinforce self-monitoring use and accurate data collection. As stated above, do not provide reinforcement exclusively for self-monitored data collection or performance improvements, but definitely include self-monitoring as one way to achieve reinforcers. Remember, one advantage of self-monitoring is that the procedure itself generates feedback and produces intrinsic reinforcers for the individual using it. However, this happens over time, so additional sources of reinforcement are needed to get your team self-monitoring efficiently and consistently when it's first rolled out.

   For yourself, finding feedback for progress is a bit more difficult; however, you can seek out feedback from your peers and supervisors from time to time. Share your successes with those who will provide objective feedback regarding your progress. But be careful: We tend to share our successes, but not our failures. Seeking out feedback when you are not reaching your goal can actually result in useful feedback that will move you forward. Get in the habit of frequently sharing your progress, no matter how good or bad.

Now that we have jumped all the way down the self-monitoring rabbit hole, we are going to bounce back out and return to our original question—who should provide the feedback? We have discussed the different groups of people who can provide feedback and specific situations for which each person is most appropriate. Unfortunately, there are some other things that must be considered as part of the formula before you can decide the exact person to provide feedback. This includes identifying the impact on performance you want the feedback to have, when the person is available to provide feedback, how feedback will be delivered, and how formal or private the feedback should be. Accordingly, we're going to leave you hanging for just a bit. Don't worry, though—we promise to fill this in. For now, just remember that anyone **can** give and everyone **should** give feedback, but not everyone **should** provide feedback about **everything** to **everyone.** There's a time and place for everything.

3

TYPES OF FEEDBACK

"For every minute spent in organizing, an hour is earned."

–Benjamin Franklin

Meet Clide. Clide was just hired at a Fortune 500 company and has been charged with turning the business around. Turnover is high, profits are down, and the business is on the verge of bankruptcy. Clide is the company's last hope. During his first month, he spends a lot of time observing the managers of the company and how they interact with the frontline staff. He pays special attention to when they interact with staff and what their topics of discussion are when they do interact. To his disappointment, he notices that most of the managers only interact with the frontline staff when something is wrong. What's worse is that they don't provide any solutions. They only point out what is incorrect and set the expectation for it to be fixed immediately.

The problem here?

There are several problems, actually. We will use them to walk through our next topic—what type of feedback should be provided?

When considering what type of feedback should be provided, you have to first determine what you want to happen. We boil it down to one of two things:

1. **You want something to happen.** Here, the employee is not doing something that they should be doing. It could be making sure the check boxes are all checked on a daily report, responding to emails, or arriving on time to meetings.
2. **You want something to stop.** Here, the employee is doing something that needs to stop. This could be using work time to order birthday presents or plan that next vacation, engaging an unsafe behavior on the assembly line, or yelling at customers. Whatever it is, there is a clear focus that it needs to stop.

The most common problem here is that, when things start going wrong, we tend to only focus on what needs to stop. Stop turning things in late. Stop not responding to emails. Stop yelling at the customers. Just stop.

Why is this problematic?

Well, there is a law of behavior that is very similar to a law of physics: You can't stop one behavior without another one surfacing. Just like with matter, you cannot completely get rid of it. It can change shape, form, consistency, and so on, but it will never completely go away. Behavior is the same. You can get rid of one behavior, but it will change shape, form, and consistency to morph into a new behavior. We tend to assume that the right behavior is what will occur in its place, but we overlook the complexity of this. Things are often not simply either or—just like there is usually more than one way to complete a task, there is definitely more than one way to screw it up.

Have you ever had this happen?

You're called into your boss's office for an error. Your boss proceeds to tell you, in detail, how you screwed up. You are then told "go fix it" and sent on your way. Be aware, this is definitely a *feedback f!@#up!*

Knowing what we did wrong is half of the equation. However, knowing what was incorrect does not automatically lead you to the correct answer. A good example of this is when you tell a child to "stop running," and the child stops and then immediately begins skipping. Technically the child did exactly what they were told. They stopped running. However, the correct behavior (walking) did not emerge because you did not give any indication that what you actually wanted was for the child to walk, not that you simply wanted the child to stop running.

All too often, we assume that the correct answer is obvious to our followers and, as a result, provide little to no information about it. We assume that people are well trained, that they have been told before, or that they should somehow just know. It's our experience that this is not the case. More often, people don't know what to do to fix the errors, or they know in theory what to do but haven't yet mastered the skills necessary to solve the problem.

Feedback is information transfer from the mediator to the performer. Performance feedback is information regarding a skill, task, or action related to the organization reaching its vision. *Effective* performance feedback is information that leads to the improvement of performance. There are three types of feedback: two are effective, and one is ineffective. Let's look at effective feedback first.

Positive Feedback

Positive feedback is information about the correct behavior or action. It focuses on what was done correctly and what you would like to see more of. Here's an example:

Werner is a manager at a department store. He is walking around assisting some of his employees stock the shelves when he observes one of his newer supervisees, Jocelyn, interacting with a customer. Jocelyn is fully engaged with the customer, answering questions and making the customer feel very welcomed. Werner makes eye contact with Jocelyn, gives her a thumbs up, and mouths "great job!"

Here, Werner witnessed something that his supervisee did that he wants to make sure she continues. He let her know by providing positive feedback as soon as he saw it happen. Hopefully, she will do the same things for the next customer as well.

Corrective Feedback

Corrective feedback is information about the incorrect behavior and how to fix it. It allows you to identify the problem and provide a solution to how to correct the problem. Let's see how it works.

Adrian is leading a meeting with her managers. In this meeting, each manager is supposed to submit their report, as a PowerPoint, at least 24 hours prior to the meeting. Adrian then combines the PowerPoint files so that each person can report without changing things over. She is rather disappointed because one of her managers, Hayden, did not submit his report prior to the meeting. Before the meeting began, Adrian took Hayden aside and asked him if he was prepared to present. He stated that he was. Adrian, pleased that he was prepared, provided this feedback: "I'm glad you are prepared for the report and look forward to seeing it. Please remember to send me all of the reports at least 24 hours prior to the meeting so that I can combine them. This cuts down on our transitions between reports and makes the meetings run quickly and smoothly. Next week, please submit your report no later than Tuesday afternoon."

In this simple example, Adrian did not simply tell Hayden what he did incorrectly; rather, she also told him exactly how to correct it. While it may sometimes seem obvious what to do and what the expectation is, it has been our experience that employees often state "they didn't know" when provided feedback regarding sub-par performance.

This leads us to our third type of feedback.

Negative Feedback

Negative feedback, like corrective feedback, is focused on what was done incorrectly. The information provided from the mediator tells the performer what was wrong. The purpose of negative feedback is to stop something. The examples below are all examples of negative feedback:

- "Stop doing that!"
- "No, that's not how it's done!"
- "You should know better!"

Most of us have received negative feedback of some sort at least once from a manager. In fact, it is almost alarming how often negative feedback is used. Why is it used so often? Primarily because it's not completely ineffective. Negative feedback usually does stop something. However, while those shows featuring loud and abrasive bosses screaming and insulting employees makes for entertaining television, it is the last thing you should be emulating.

Let's look at Holly. Holly is a bartender. In the food service industry, employees are commonly taught to deliver services to customers in a friendly and courteous manner. However, Holly has been observed regularly delivering services to customers with a very abrasive and sometimes rude tone that some may find particularly offensive. Noticing this, Jeremy, the bar manager, signals to Holly and sternly says, "Holly, stop speaking to customers so impolitely. You're going to scare them away and get us poor reviews." Holly returns to making drinks, adjusting the volume and tone of her voice.

Negative feedback is different from corrective feedback in that negative feedback only tells you what not to do. We hear negative feedback a lot. Think of the parent who yells ahead to their child to "stop running." We already know what happens here, right? The child stops running, but begins to skip. The parent, becoming frustrated, then begins to yell at the child again. The problem? The child actually responded to the feedback. The child stopped running. However, the parent did not specify what the child **should do instead** of the unwanted behavior. Not specifying what to do instead leaves it up to the individual to decide, and the child in this example does not fall in the minority by coming up with an alternative that is still wrong. Corrective feedback provide the solution in that it identifies what is incorrect and **solves the problem** by clearly communicating the correct response. Additionally, by communicating the correct behavior, you create an opportunity for the response to occur and to provide positive feedback, making it more likely the behavior will occur again in the future.

Remember Clide? Now we know why Clide was disappointed and a likely next step he will take to help start turning things around. Our guess is that he will train his staff to provide *positive* and *corrective* feedback, rather than the *negative* feedback he observed.

For this part of our formula, we are focused on whether we want the action to continue. If we want the action to happen again, we provide positive feedback. If we want it to stop or change in some way, we provide corrective feedback. Use the decision tree below to guide you in making this choice.

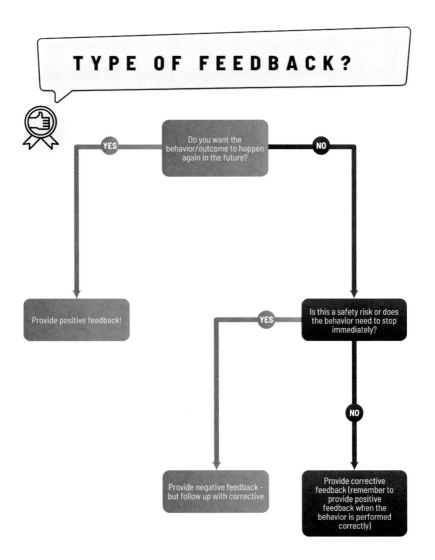

Let's add this to our formula:

EFFECTIVE PERFORMANCE FEEDBACK =
(The Behavior/Action/Outcome) + (The Person) + (The Number of People) + **(The Type of Feedback)** *+ (x)*

SECTION II

WHEN AND WHERE

4

THE TEMPORAL LOCATION OF FEEDBACK

Time is abstract, timing is a science.

~Adam Ventura

Left Waiting

It's late on a Tuesday morning, and you are sitting uncomfortably in your old leathery office chair, imprisoned in your undersized cubicle, just waiting. No matter how you try to readjust yourself on the seat—front to back, side to side, or even a quick spin around—for some reason it just seems to make you more uneasy. The waiting is unbearable. Every time you look at the digital clock affixed to the wall, time, without any prior notification or care for your wellbeing, appears to be speeding up. You can't stop it, and to make matters worse, you start thinking that the end of the day is going to arrive with you still waiting.

Different versions of "what's taking so long?"—versions with and without colorful curse words—bounce back and forth in your head like an irritating, never-ending game of pinball. You try to distract yourself with answering emails and chatting online, but every time you click send, that infernal computer keeps informing you of the current time, which, like an avalanche of unfortunate events, prompts you to take a deep breath, sigh, and begin tapping nervously on the manufactured wood on the top of your desk.

Periodically, your office-neighbor leans over the shaky and worn-down cubicle wall and asks how you're holding up. You look up with frustration, stress beaming out of your eyes, and say "not good" in a tired and sarcastic tone, as if you want them to just go away so that you can go back to worrying in peace.

Not getting the message, your officemate brazenly asks, "How many hours has it been?"

You don't even turn around this time to look them in the eye. Instead, you simply just extend your right arm and blast four fingers out of the palm of your hand like a firecracker exploding from your grasp. "And with no answer?" They reply in mild shock.

It's at that moment, that your boss walks casually over to the entrance to your area and in a cavalier tone delivers his next *feedback f!@#up*, "Hey, great work on that presentation this morning, I thought your content was well sourced, the graphics were creatively placed, and your productivity trends look promising. Can't wait to see next month's numbers. Hope your day is going well!" You sat there while they were talking, almost paralyzed by your disbelief.

The entire interaction took 15 seconds. *15 seconds!* You spent 3 days working on that presentation and then waited for 4 hours and 13 minutes to get 15 seconds of feedback. Unsatisfied with the feeble attempt at communication, you spin your chair around, turn off your monitor, pick up your bags, and tell your nosey-nearby-resident that you're leaving for the day. While storming out of your cubicle, you mutter under your breathe, "This company doesn't deserve my time."

Timing Is Everything

In a recent TED Talk©, Bill Gross, the CEO of Idealab®, described five key elements to business success: ideas, team, business model, funding, and timing. He concluded that one key element impacted the success of any new venture more than the others. That's right, you guessed it—timing.

Consider two examples:

1. Do you remember a company called "Ask Jeeves"? Started in the late 90s, Ask Jeeves was originally an Internet business and search engine focused on answering questions. It was fantastic. It answered our questions, solved our problems, and showcased some of the most advanced search algorithms ever developed. While this search engine was genius and way ahead of its time, the key problem is that it was way ahead of its time. Ask Jeeves never really reached its full potential despite being re-branded as Ask.com. Eventually, most consumers replaced it with another startup you may have heard of—Google, Inc. Google wasn't so much better that people should have switched over; it just started at the right time.

2. What about Friendster? Do you remember that company? Yeah, we don't either. Friendster was one of the first social media networking sites ever developed, way back in 2002, and it was later re-imagined as a social gaming network site that also failed. According to research, people in 2002 were not ready to share the intimate details of their lives on a social networking platform. Apparently, someone forgot to tell Facebook that when it got started in 2004.

The lesson: Timing is everything.

Dictionary.com defines *timing* as "the selecting of the best time or speed for doing something in order to achieve the desired maximum result." This fundamental (and somewhat abstract) concept is critical not only in high-level business dealings but also in interpersonal interactions, as evidenced in the delivery of effective performance feedback. Knowing the best time to give feedback and the effects of scheduling can greatly impact the successful delivery of feedback. Don't worry, this chapter will take the *time* to make sure you know exactly *when* to deliver feedback.

So when *is* the preferred timing for performance feedback?

The best time is immediately following after the behavior is performed. (With a couple exceptions, of course. There is never a rule that applies *ALL* the time.)

There's a lot to say about delivering feedback immediately after a performance has occurred. However, first we want to explore exactly what it means to provide feedback immediately after the performance.

Survival of the Fittest

Have you ever taken time to think about who you really are, how you got to be this way, and whether you will change or stay the same in the future? Chances are, at one point in time you either reflected on how you came this far or thought about who you wanted to be one day. What if we told you that we knew the answer to all of this? Do you have any idea what we might say it is?

We'll give you a hint: It's only one word.

Good guess!

But it's not "feedback."

KNOW OUR JARGON

In behavior analysis the word "consequences" refers to something that happened after a behavior that had an affect on the future likeliness of that behavior. Consequences can either make it more likely or less likely the behavior will occur. Knowing a consequence occurred only tells us the behavior will change, but it does not tell us how that behavior will change.

The answer is "consequences." When you think of the word *consequences*, you're probably thinking of bad things (e.g., "accepting the consequences of your actions," "time to face the consequences," "sir, you cannot name your twins 'Truth' and 'Consequences'). However, a consequence doesn't only refer to unpleasant events; the term is much broader than that.

Before we jump into this, we want to warn you that we might geek out just a bit. We will do our best not to go too far.

You remember that we like to ensure we have the same shared understanding when it comes to terms and definitions, right? Consequences is another one of those words that can easily become "slang." It's used often in our everyday language, and most people mean slightly different things when they talk about the consequences of something. For us behavior analysts, we are usually on high alert when this word is mentioned because consequences are some of our favorite things. But we also know that most everyone else in the world does not view them as we do. Let's see if we can bring you to our side.

Consequences are simply events that occur after a behavior or action that have some sort of effect on the future occurrence of that action or behavior. There are several things that are important about consequences, and we will highlight some of them. Of course, if you want to know more and geek out with us, pick up a book about applied behavior analysis. It will certainly tell you everything you ever wanted to know about consequences (and likely even more). For our purposes, we need to know the following:

1. Consequences happen *after* something has occurred.
2. Consequences can either make it *more* or *less* likely that same thing will occur again.
3. Consequences are unique to the context in which they occur.
4. Consequences are the reason you are who you are and you do what you do.

FEEDBACK F!@#up!

This could have easily been avoided had the individual who offered her the position clarified the appropriate work attire.

Do you remember your first job? In case you don't (and, really, even if you do), we'll provide you with the following example. Adrianne is a 16-year-old girl who just got her first job working in a grocery store. She wore a suit to her interview and had not yet received the uniform that others wore, so she decided to wear a suit on her first day as well. Impressive, right? Not really. Her job was to stock the shelves and gather the carts outside and bring them inside. Not only did others keep misidentifying her as someone shopping, but also her feet were incredibly sore after her first day. She learned from the consequences of mistaken identity and hurting feet, and on her second day of work, she wore slacks, a polo shirt, and tennis shoes. At the end of the day, no one mistook her as a shopper, and her feet felt great. Thus, she wore the same outfit again the next day. Additionally, on her first day, while gathering carts, she removed them one by one from the cart holder. She found that the carts kept rolling away, and she was chasing them down across the parking lot. However, she also found that, once she had two or three carts together, they were less likely to roll.

OBM Tidbit

Training is one of the most important aspects of a new position. Many companies fall short in ensuring the skills required by the job are actually mastered. Organizational Behavior Management (OBM) research tells us the best way to ensure someone has actually been trained is to provide performance or competency assessments prior to the end of training. Interestingly, OBM research has also identified that the most important aspect of training is the feedback received on performance of the new skills. How many trainings have you been in where you have gotten a chance to practice your new skills let alone received feedback on your performance of the new skill? Our guess is not many.

Thus, learning from the consequences that followed her cart gathering on the first day, she did not let go of the first cart until several were linked together. Again, Adrianne learned from the consequences she contacted. Eventually, Adrianne became a pro at gathering carts, learning the tricks of the trade as she practiced each day.

We're sure you have similar stories of learning new skills and entering new companies and positions. Your behaviors, and the things that you now do, have all been shaped by the consequences you contacted! You talk the way you talk, dress the way you dress, and even complete your job responsibilities the way you do because you have contacted different contingencies that made it less likely the other things would continue to happen and more likely the things you do now would repeat themselves.

RESEARCH

The concept of selection by consequence was originally coined by B.F. Skinner in the early part of the 20th century as a framework for his approach to the study of the behavior of organisms. Skinner modeled his "behavior of organisms" framework on Charles Darwin's notion of natural selection.

Darwin discovered that organisms, and the environment they existed in, were working together through the use of an extremely elaborate and sometimes cruel system of consequences that advanced the natural selection of genetic structures in the evolution of species that resulted in all of the living beings that exist (and no longer exist) on our planet today. Simply put, if an organism could not exist comfortably in their environment, they would adapt to the changes or go extinct, which is where we get the concept of "survival of the fittest".

Behavior analysts refer to this as *selection by consequences*, meaning that it is the consequences that shape, change, or maintain what we do. It is this concept that explains why we are more likely to do some things, while other people are more likely to do other things. It even explains why you may do one thing with your significant other when the two of you are alone that you would never do in front of your friends. Consequences are essentially the main reason we do, think, say, and feel what we do. They are so powerful that you can predict what someone might do the next time something similar happens if you know the consequence that followed the action the first time that they did it.

Feedback is similar. And like consequences, feedback can have one of four effects on behavior. It can increase it. It can continue it. It can decrease or stop it. Or it can change it. As we noted in the previous chapter, positive feedback is information that conveys the performance was good and should continue. Positive feedback is used to increase or continue behavior. Negative feedback is meant to do the opposite. It is meant to stop behavior. But remember, we already discussed that negative feedback simply leaves you open for something different (but still not correct) to happen. Thus, corrective feedback *not only stops the unwanted action but also provides the performer with the necessary information to do the right thing.*

Consider another example. Emily heard a funny joke when eating with her parents and their friends last night. She wants to share the joke with her colleagues, so she tells the joke while they are in the breakroom eating lunch. Emily delivers the punch line and starts laughing. But when she looks around the room, everyone looks a bit confused. After what seems like a lifetime of awkward silence, one of her colleagues says, "I don't get it." Chances are, Emily will not tell that joke when she works overtime this evening with the late shift. Why? Because the feedback she received from colleagues during lunch indicates that the joke was not well received.

Feedback is not necessarily a consequence, but it can be used as a consequence. Remember that feedback is information transferred from a mediator to a performer. Thus, in order for feedback to be **effective**, it has to follow the same rules that consequences follow to be effective. In other words, just because a consequence happened just after a certain action does not mean that the consequence will actually influence whether the specific action occurs again. Certain rules must be followed for that consequence to have the effect you want. We'll list them and then dive into them specifically.

1. Timing is Everything.
2. Specificity Brings Clarity.
3. Value Determines Strength.

Now let's dive in.

Components of Effective Performance Feedback as a Consequence

Emilio is the manager of a mid-sized family restaurant that can get quite busy at times. The restaurant has a variety of experienced employees along with some newly hired staff members, primarily working as servers. When it gets busy, staff members go a thousand miles a minute, engaging in a variety of behaviors at any given moment—placing the ticket with the cooks, writing an order down at a table, bringing the food to the tables, filling water, and so on.

Emilio recently picked up a copy of this book and has been reading the first few chapters. He has learned that positive feedback increases and maintains behaviors and decides he is going to try it out on his four new servers, Johan, Shannon, Azumi, and Walter.

Component 1: Timing Is Everything

Johan is a bit newer to the restaurant business. In fact, he's a bit new to working in general as this is his first job. He's trying hard, but would benefit from additional training and, of course, feedback. He values feedback that he receives from Emilio and the rest of his coworkers, but has learned that this feedback can be sparse due to the lively nature of the restaurant. Therefore, when he receives feedback, it greatly affects his performance.

As this is Johan's first job, it is expected that he would make several mistakes as he learns not just the restaurant business but also general expectations of employees. Emilio finds this to be true as Johan occasionally forgets portions of orders, delivers plates to the wrong tables, drops silverware, and forgets to mention the weekly specials. Emilio is concerned about and wants to fix these things, but only remembers that positive feedback is the best way to increase and continue behavior. He focuses on what Johan is doing right, and there are several things Johan is doing well. He greets customers warmly and with a smile, he recommends his favorite dishes when asked, he regularly checks on his tables to make sure they have everything they need, and he offers the dessert menu at the end of the meal.

At the end of the night, Emilio decides to take a stab at this feedback thing. However, just before he calls Johan over, the restaurant is slammed with a late-night rush. By the end of the night, Emilio is so tired, he engaged in his first *feedback f!@#up* and decides he will provide the feedback to Johan the next day. Unfortunately, the next day is even busier and once again, Emilio does not get a chance to provide feedback. This continues for a few weeks until Emilio finds an opportunity to provide feedback. He tells Johan that he really likes how he interacts with the customers. Johan, worried that his performance has been sub-par due to all of his errors, is elated with this feedback. He smiles and makes a mental note to himself that he is a great server. The next day, Emilio watches Johan to see if the feedback helped fix Johan's errors. He sees that it didn't. In fact, he observes that there are a few things—like offering dessert at the end of the meal— that Johan isn't doing anymore. Emilio hasn't paid much attention for the past few weeks, so he's not sure when these changes started. Discouraged, Emilio wonders if this book was a good investment. Maybe he should have continued to read in the time he was waiting to give feedback.

The scenario with Emilio actually highlights one of the biggest mistakes that leaders make when providing feedback: they wait too long. The longer you want to provide feedback, the more likely it is that the feedback will not be effective. *Why?* In order for a consequence to be effective, there must be a direct link between the behavior and the consequence. In other words, it must be clear that Action A resulted in Consequence A. The longer you wait to provide the consequence, the more likely it is that other actions will occur. The more actions that occur, the more you have to sort through to determine which of those actions actually resulted in the consequence.

Let's look at an example to illustrate. You just got home from a long day at work. You're a pharmaceutical salesperson, so you spend most of your day traveling to and from different doctors' offices. This day you went to seven different locations. You park your car in the garage, take a long hot bath, and go to bed. The next morning, as you're warming up your car, you see the "low tire air" signal in your car. You get out and see that your tire is flat. *How did this happen?* You think back to all of the things you did the prior day and try to remember if there was a construction site, a pothole, or something else that could have punctured your tire. You also look around the garage and your driveway to see if there is something there. You can't figure out what caused the flat and quickly give up and begin changing the tire.

If the tire had gone flat immediately, you would have known exactly what happened. However, because your tire did not go flat until the next morning, you have to sort through the many different locations you drove to try and determine exactly what happened. Chances are, you will never know. Consequences and feedback work the same way. The more time that passes, the more events you have to sort through to determine just what exactly resulted in the feedback.

The other problem with waiting is that other consequences or feedback may be introduced, changing the behavior in a way you did not want. Johan's offering of dessert following the meal is a good example of this. Initially, when Emilio first observed Johan, Johan was offering dessert to each table at the end of each meal. However, when Emilio observed again several weeks later, he noticed that Johan was no longer offering dessert. *What happened?* Most likely, Johan offered dessert consistently when he first began. However, time and time again his customers said they were full and declined ordering anything. Johan was receiving *immediate* feedback from his customers that they did not want dessert. This feedback resulted in him offering it less and less often until he finally stopped offering it altogether. The problem is that, because Emilio was not providing immediate feedback, Johan received it from other places.

A Timely Fix

Luckily, Emilio does not give up that easily and decides to read a bit more about feedback. He reads this chapter and realized his errors (surprised that his very problem was actually the discussion of the book!). He decides to try again to see if he can get Johan back on track. As luck has it, the next day the restaurant is offering a new dessert that Johan is especially excited about. In his excitement, he offers it to his first table of the day as they finish their meal. They decline. Remembering that the timeliness of feedback is important, Emilio approaches Johan as he takes the dishes to the kitchen and says, "Great job offering that new dessert. Even though that table didn't order it, I bet you will get a few that will as long as you keep offering it. Thanks for making sure to follow through on the desserts." Emilio watches as Johan walks to his next table as they finish their meal. Sure enough, Johan offers the dessert menu and discusses the new dessert of the day. They order! Excited to see this feedback thing working, Emilio approaches Johan again as he takes the plates to the kitchen and says, "Way to go! You continued offering and got an order. Keep it up." As the day continues, Johan continues to offer dessert to each and every table. Some accept, more do not. Emilio quickly gets distracted with the other requirements of his job, but makes it a point to periodically check in to make sure Johan is still offering desserts, providing a quick "thumbs up" when Johan does. To Emilio's surprise, Johan continues offering desserts even the next day. It seems things had gotten back on track!

Conclusion: The more immediate the feedback, the more effective it will be!

Component 2: Specificity Brings Clarity

Feeling really good about what he was able to do with Johan, Emilio decides to move on to his next new employee, Shannon. While Shannon is not new to the workforce, she is new to the restaurant industry. Emilio enters the restaurant and sees Shannon and the rest of the employees hard at work. He issues the good old-fashioned "Excellent work everyone!" as he walks by. As he walks to the back into his office, he hears Shannon offer dessert to a table. Thinking how ironic since this was the very thing he just worked on with Johan, Emilio decides he should provide feedback to Shannon about this as well. After all, dessert sales make a huge impact on the budget. Unfortunately Emilio performs his next *feedback f!@#up* and walks by as Shannon is leaving the table and says, "Hey, Shannon, great job today! Keep it up!" Shannon smiles, thanks him for the encouragement, and continues her day.

Emilio finishes up some things in his office and decides he will spend a bit of time observing Shannon during the lunch rush. He wants to see what she is doing well and what to improve, so he can try out his new skill.

After a few minutes, Emilio frowns. Shannon just cleared a table, but did not offer any dessert. He gave her immediate feedback this morning about this very thing. *Why didn't it work?*

Whatcha Talkin' 'bout, ~~Willis~~ Emilio?

Emilio provided Shannon feedback immediately following her offering of desserts. However, this did not impact whether she offered desserts to the next table. The reason for this is the second component of effective consequences; it must be behaviorally specific. When feedback is vague, it leaves room for guessing or assumptions. And we all know what happens when you assume. Shannon, who was issued a "great job today!" from Emilio, did not make the connection between the "great job" and her offering of desserts. Instead, she made a different connection.

Emilio did not observe the initial part of the meal and was not aware that the customers initially came in disgruntled. Evidently, they had walked in just before two other parties, but the hostess did not see them, resulting in the other two parties being seated first and Shannon's customers having to wait a bit for a table. Shannon opened with her usual smile and "how's it going today?" only to receive an ear full about how poor the service is and that the family would have left, except they were starving and leaving would have further delayed their meal. After listening to their concerns, Shannon assured them that she would talk with the hostess and management to make sure the restaurant developed a better way to monitor who comes in first. She also reassured them that she would do everything she could to turn things around for them. By the time the family ordered their food, they were smiling and joking. When Emilio told her "great job," Shannon assumed that he was noting how she turned things around and made a repeat customer from what was going to be a bad review. She didn't even connect that it was about offering dessert.

While Emilio was spot on for the timing, he wasn't specific. When things are vague, it is usually the thing that stands out most that people assume. In this example, the thing that stood out most was Shannon's role in creating satisfied customers when they started out being disgruntled. Offering desserts was something she did regularly, so it did not stand out to her. Had Emilio been specific, Shannon would have been clear, likely resulting in her continuing to offer dessert to her other tables.

This time Emilio was not as discouraged as he remembered that he stopped after the first component. Reading the second component, he realized where he went wrong. He provided generic praise, which places a blanket on everything. Specific praise ensures the employee knows exactly what resulted in the feedback. Having more clarity now, Emilio goes back out to the floor to observe Shannon once again. This time he notices that Shannon is friendly and personable with customers, ensures their drinks are always filled, and brings their food as soon as it is ready. He also notices that Shannon is making several errors. She sometimes forgets to bring the silverware, she is inconsistent about offering dessert, and she takes several orders at a time when things get busy, entering all the orders together instead of one at a time.

Since Emilio is not yet sure how to correct things, he decides to focus on what Shannon is doing well to ensure she continues doing these things well. As she leaves a table with drink orders in hand, Emilio says, "I really like how you welcomed the customers before taking their drink orders. Way to make them feel that you care." Shannon, pleased with herself, thanks Emilio for the feedback and makes a note to herself to always welcome customers before taking drink orders. And the note worked as she does this again with her next table!

Emilio, thrilled that he figured it out, gives himself a high five and a pat on the back. He is really getting this feedback thing down!

Getting into the spirit of things, Emilio decides to provide a bit of extra feedback to Shannon after he sees her greet a table with a friendly interaction, but keeping it efficient. Emilio quickly approaches Shannon and provides specific feedback on her efficient and friendly interaction and throws in extra praise for encouraging the customers to look at the specials. "Way to be efficient, Shannon!" Emilio boasts. "You engaged positively with the customer and made it quick. That's *exactly* what I want to see— especially when we're busy. Great job listing the specials as well. Upper management really wants all staff to be doing this, so it's great that you did. You're on fire today!"

Conclusion: Being specific makes feedback more effective!

Component 3: Value Determines Strength

With Shannon and Johan on the right track, Emilio turns his attention to his third new employee, Azumi. Azumi is the most experienced of the three new employees as she has worked as a server in a different restaurant. She is used to doing things a certain way and knows that they are not done exactly the same here. However, she keeps forgetting the new way of doing things and resorts back to old habits. They are small things, and the job still gets done. Thus, Azumi doesn't think it's a big deal. Emilio, however, doesn't agree. He observes Azumi and sees that she often brings bread to the table *after* drinks are ordered rather than before. He also notices that she offers to fill up drinks for tables that are not her own. While this is great teamwork, it also undermines the staff waiting on those tables and makes them appear to be incompetent. Since Azumi is the most experienced of the three new employees, Emilio expects her to be the best. He is disappointed to see that she isn't.

As a result, everything that Emilio learned thus far about feedback got tossed to the side and the *feedack f!@#ups* started flowing. Emilio began correcting Azumi, pointing out every little thing that she did wrong. Azumi, who was often praised by her colleagues for helping them out, gets very annoyed with Emilio. She doesn't understand why he is picking on her. Azumi quickly develops a distaste for Emilio, and since she has never seen him wait on a table, she also assumes that he truly knows nothing about her position. Let's see what happens as a result.

Emilio enters the restaurant feeling quite encouraged by his work with Shannon and Johan. He is so excited that he immediately provides Azumi with more *feedback f!@#ups*: "Great job greeting the customers— friendly and efficient! I love how you offered the dessert menu before bringing the check, too. And the way that you incorporated the daily specials with your recommendations was genius." Azumi, having never received positive feedback from Emilio and being well versed in these things, shrugs her shoulders and says a quiet "thanks." Emilio is a bit taken aback from this reaction and decides that maybe he needs to provide more positive feedback. After all, Azumi has been working there for about 4 months with little to no feedback. Stepping it up, Emilio spends the next hour providing positive feedback about every single thing that Azumi does correctly—from greeting the customers to putting enough ice in the drinks, to offering dessert. Azumi politely accepts his feedback each time and continues working. After the hour ends, Emilio is a bit confused. Shannon and Johan were so appreciative of the feedback, and Emilio could see the results of the feedback almost immediately. Why is Azumi not so appreciative? And why does it seem that she just continues as if she never received any feedback?

There are two things at play here.

First, Azumi does not value Emilio's feedback. In order for feedback to be effective, it either has to be of high value to the person receiving it or it has to be paired with something valuable. In this example, Emilio was both paired with a log of negative and critical feedback early on and was not seen as a credible boss, given that Azumi thought Emilio didn't know how to be a server. These two things resulted in Azumi not valuing Emilio's feedback. As a result, the feedback provided had little effect on Azumi's behavior.

And Now, the Exception: When Things Go Wrong.

Feeling that he had mastered this feedback thing, Emilio turns his attention to Walter, the fourth and final new employee. Emilio—feeling especially energized due to his success with Johan, Shannon, and Azumi— decides he will try to decrease the time it takes Walter to take the food from the kitchen to the table. Emilio notices that Walter carries items one by one and walks fairly slowly through the restaurant. He wants Walter to put all food items for one table on a tray and carry them to the table at the same time, ensuring everyone receives their food at the same time.

Preparing for a quick observation and the feedback session with Walter, Emilio reviews the three components he just learned:

1. **Provide feedback immediately:** Emilio is ready to jump in immediately the next time he saw Walter take food to the table.
2. **Be specific:** Emilio chose one behavior—the number of items Walter carries to the table at a time—and is prepared to state exactly what he wants to happen.
3. **Ensure feedback is valuable:** Emilio has spent the past few days focusing on ensuring he has good rapport with Walter. He also provided positive feedback to Walter regarding how full to fill drinks and offering desert at the end of a meal. Walter responded, so Emilio thinks he is ready.

Emilio exits his office to begin his observation when he sees Waltcr carrying several empty dishes to the kitchen. On his way, he passes Johan, who is carrying a sizzling-hot plate. Walter, who obviously cannot see over the top of this large stack of dishes, is about to run right into Johan.

"STOP WALKING WALTER!! FREEZE!!" Emilio yells. Emilio is so scared Walter will run into Johan, causing Johan to drop the plate and causing injury to either Johan or a customer, that everything he just reviewed about feedback goes out the window. But is Emilio wrong?

Earlier, we stated that the best time to provide feedback is immediately *after* the behavior occurs. However, in this scenario, had Emilio waited for the behavior to finish, the result would have been dangerous and likely resulted in injury of one or more persons. Scenarios like this, where there is risk of injury to another, are the exception to the rule above. In this situation, feedback should not wait until after the behavior occurs. Instead, it should be provided **immediately in the moment** to prevent the potentially disastrous outcome.

You might have also noticed that Emilio did not provide corrective feedback. He provided negative feedback in that he simply told Walter what not to do. Safety issues provide us with another exception to our rules in that it is okay to provide negative feedback in the moment to get the dangerous behavior to stop **as long as** the correction is provided during follow up **before** the next occurrence of the behavior.

In summary, when safety issues arise, one should never wait for the behavior to occur or finish occurring, resulting in continuation of the unsafe behavior. Unsafe behaviors should always be stopped **the moment you realize they are unsafe** to prevent any potential injury from occurring. Additionally, it is okay to provide negative feedback in the moment to stop the unsafe behavior as long as you follow up with corrective feedback before the behavior happens again.

Building value brings effectiveness.

There are a few things you can do to build the value of your feedback.

1. Establish value in both yourself and your feedback.

2. Pair feedback with something valuable.

Have you ever had someone in your life who was always critical of everyone and everything around them?

Bart is an example of this. Bart is the type of person who always finds something to complain about. The food wasn't seasoned well. The waiter didn't refill his soda fast enough. That movie wasn't really all that funny. The special effects sucked. The concert was too loud. No matter what happened, Bart always finds something to complain about. You are thinking of trying a new restaurant. You know Bart tried it the other day. Are you going to ask for his opinion? If so, he'll probably say something like, "It was okay, but the food could have been better. It was only lukewarm when I got it." Are you going to let that deter you from trying the restaurant? Chances are, Bart's statements about the restaurant will do little to influence whether you go to the restaurant because Bart *always* finds something wrong.

The same holds true when providing performance feedback. In order for the feedback to have an effect on the behavior, the feedback and the person delivering the feedback (the mediator) have to be valued by the performer. There are many different ways one can build value in themselves. Here are some general guidelines.

1. **Be genuine.** *Genuine* is a common term in the English language, but it is not always well defined. Behaviorally, being genuine involves two things:

    a. **Say-do correspondence:** Say-do correspondence means that you do what you say you will do. Your words and your actions match. If you commit to something, you follow through with it. It also means that you demonstrate behaviors that are in unison with the things you are saying. If you ask about someone's day, you don't then turn away or walk off. Instead, you wait and listen to their answer. The more your words and actions match one another, the more genuine you are.

    b. **Specificity:** You provide details regarding what you are saying. If you say someone is awesome, you state what behaviors they demonstrated that made them awesome. If you say you are excited for them, you tell them why you are excited. Those who are genuine speak in behavior-specific terms rather than make broad statements regarding others.

c. Let's look at a few examples:

    i. You say, "You're so awesome, I'm going to try and come to your speech tomorrow." You then don't show up. Not genuine.

        1. This is not behaviorally specific—why am I so awesome?

        2. There is no say-do correspondence. You say you will come to my speech tomorrow, but you don't.

    ii. You say, "I really appreciate how you listened to me vent the other day. I want to return the favor. What's going on?" And then you sit down next to the person, leaning in. Genuine.

        1. Your statement is behaviorally specific. You described exactly what you appreciated.

        2. There is high say-do correspondence. When you stated you wanted to return the favor, you engaged in behaviors that showed interest (sitting down, leaning in).

2. **Be objective.** We live in a world of subjectivity, where evaluations, opinions, and yes, feedback often rely on what we think or how we feel. Unfortunately for subjectivity, it is just as easy to discount an opinion you don't agree with as it is to value one you agree with. It leaves too much room for interpretation. However, objectivity does the opposite. It brings clarity to the issue and removes any judgment. Think about the family that Shannon encountered, the one who had been seated only after two other families arrived and were seated. Subjectively, they could have said, "Your hostess sucks. She doesn't care about her job. She should be fired." Shannon would not have known what upset them or how to fix it. In fact, given that Shannon is good friends with the hostess, she might have become defensive, arguing that the hostess does care about her job and is usually quite excellent. Fortunately, the family was objective in

their description of what happened. They told Shannon that they were not addressed until after the two other later-arriving families were seated. When we are objective with others, we build value. Why? Because people know we are not simply judging them or stating an opinion. Objectivity keeps the judgment and labels out of it, increasing the value of what is being said.

3. **Be consistent.** *If you're not consistent, you're non-existent.* People value consistency above most other things. We want to know what to expect, even if it is expecting something mediocre. Take McDonald's, for example. There is not a McDonald's in just about every country and town across the world because they make the world's best hamburgers (sorry McDonald's, no offense). McDonald's thrives because no matter where you go—whether it's in Warrenton, MO, New York City, or Beijing, China—you know what to expect. The hamburgers look the same, taste the same, and smell the same. It is their consistency that keeps them ahead. Thus, when it comes to you, a great way to build value is to be consistent. Don't show up as Person A on Monday, Person B on Tuesday, and a toss-up between the two on Wednesday. People will avoid you if they don't know what to expect. Similarly, if your feedback is not consistent, it will not be valued.

4. **Focus on how you can help.** There is no better way to build value than to offer help, especially when it might be inconvenient for you. We value those who can help us and who are willing to pull up their sleeves and put in the hard work when things get tough. Think about a supervisor you had that always stood on the sidelines to point and direct, making sure to never get their hands too dirty. Now think of the one who jumps on the assembly line when you're short-staffed and offers to help with the late-night reports so you can make it home at a decent hour, too. The latter supervisor is the one who will be more highly valued. When you're willing to help, people know you care. And when they know you care about them, your value increases.

Let's go back to Emilio for a minute. For Emilio's feedback to be effective with Azumi, he first needs to focus on building his value with her. Reading this, he decides to focus on these four guidelines to increase his value. However, Emilio realizes this may take some time as he knows building and repairing value can be a lengthy process. He doesn't want to wait until he has fixed this problem to provide feedback. Lucky for him, there is another way to increase the value of the feedback: deliver it with something of value.

There are many times that our feedback alone is not valued highly enough to impact behavior the way we need. This happens to everyone, even those of us who have established ourselves as highly valuable. In these situations, and as a general rule, deliver feedback along with something that is of high value. This ensures that your feedback will result in the change you anticipate.

How does one do this, you ask?

Let's see what Emilio does. Emilio takes a bit of time to learn what is of high value to Azumi. He learns that money and time off are highly valuable to her. Emilio also learns that Azumi loves chocolate candies. Knowing that he can't just give her a raise or extra time off, he decides that he will bring in a box of chocolate candies and deliver them along with his positive feedback. The next day, Emilio enters the restaurant and greets everyone warmly. He then spends about 30 minutes observing the staff, focusing on what Azumi does correctly. He sees that she consistently offers the daily specials, suggestions based on what the customer wants, and dessert. He then asks Johan to cover Azumi's tables for the next 10 minutes and asks that Azumi meet him in his office.

Azumi, nervous that she has been called to the boss's office, enters hesitantly. Emilio smiles warmly and invites her to sit down, placing the box of chocolates on his desk. He offers Azumi a piece of chocolate and says that he just wanted to check in with her on how things are going. He tells her that he noticed that she is very consistent in her discussion of the daily specials, of her recommendations catered to what the customer is wanting, and of the available desserts. He offers that he is really pleased and impressed with this and thanks her for having such consistency and attention to detail. Azumi smiles and says, "Thank you. I've been really trying to focus on these things as I know it helps the business—and my tips." Emilio agrees and affirms that she's using a great strategy. Azumi pauses, waiting for Emilio to criticize her, but Emilio says, "That's all. I just wanted to check in with you and let you know that I've seen your hard work." He offers her another chocolate as she heads out of his office.

While Emilio did not specify that he brought in the chocolates because he wanted to reward Azumi's hard work, he delivered them along with the positive feedback. This pairing can be done a number of different ways, but the main point is that sometimes you have to do a bit extra to increase the value of your feedback. The most effective way to do this is to provide access to something of value to the employee based on positive feedback. In other words, when you tell the employee they are doing an excellent job, you offer them something of value. The added benefit of this is that it also pairs you with positives as opposed to negatives.

We will give Emilio a gold star for his work with Johan, Shannon, and Azumi. It seems that he is really getting the hang of this.

But What About When Things Need to Change?

You probably noticed that we just spent a lot of time discussing positive feedback; however, we have not yet touched on how to use corrective feedback as a consequence. One reason for this is that positive feedback should be the main focus. We go with the research on this one—which says positive to corrective feedback should be delivered on an average of a 4:1 ratio. However, we know that employees make mistakes and that leaders need a way to correct these mistakes. Corrective feedback is used when a behavior needs to be changed—or when we need to stop one thing and replace it with another.

A Quick Note About Negative Feedback

We have already stated that we do not recommend the use of negative feedback. It only focuses on what to stop doing and does not provide any help or guidance about what should be done instead. However, there are times that we need something to stop immediately. These are usually related to safety issues when continuing the action will likely result in someone being severely injured. In these situations, saying a quick "stop that!" or "watch out!" is warranted—as long as some guidance about what to do instead is provided at some point in the near future.

A good example of this is the example above where Emilio needed to stop Walter's walking immediately so that he did not run into Johan and cause him to drop the hot plate. In this situation, it is not only okay to use negative feedback but also to provide it in the moment as the behavior is occurring.

Outside of these instances, we recommend using corrective feedback instead. Corrective feedback not only stops the unwanted behavior but also ensures the replacement is of the right thing.

The Better Way—Corrective Feedback

One thing that all behavior analysts know and try to teach the world is that *all* behaviors fill a function. In other words, every single behavior ultimately results in a consequence that keeps the behavior going. Or as we like to say, everyone does what they do when they do it because it works for them in that moment. Corrective feedback provides an alternative. It replaces the things that are incorrect, but working for that person, with the correct thing that should work even better.

Let's look at Gus, who works at a bar, to illustrate. The bar is incredibly busy today, and one customer becomes quite chatty with Gus, asking him all sorts of questions about different drinks and shots. This conversation leads to other off-topic comments and questions about the geographic area and other things to do. While Gus typically does not mind this sort of small talk, it is incredibly busy this day, so the questions and comments are preventing him from getting to his other customers. To end the interaction so that he can move on, Gus interrupts the customer and says, "Do you know what you want to drink, or should I give you more time?" The customer retorts, "Geez. I didn't know it was wrong to ask about the neighborhood. On second thought, maybe I'll go to the bar down the street where I won't be so unwelcomed." Lucas, Gus's supervisor, observes this interaction.

When things die down a bit and there is a lull in customers, Lucas takes Gus aside. He expresses that he understands why Gus found really annoying to have a customer ask irrelevant questions and not order a drink when there were other people waiting; however, there is a better way to redirect that would prevent the customer from leaving. Lucas provides some suggestions for how to do this. Gus agrees, thanks Lucas for the support, and returns to the bar.

When using corrective feedback, follow the same components as you follow when providing positive feedback, plus one more. Let's first briefly look at the first three components in the context of providing corrective feedback.

Component 1: Timing Is Everything

As with positive feedback, when using corrective feedback as a consequence, it is best to provide it as close to the event as possible. This increases its effectiveness by ensuring the connection is made between the performance and the feedback.

Component 2: Specificity Brings Clarity

Remember to be specific. This is especially true when you're correcting a behavior. Make sure that you state exactly what happened that was incorrect and exactly what to do to correct it. In the example above, Lucas could have said, "Don't be rude to customers; instead, be nice and welcoming to them." This is not very specific. Lucas and Gus may have different definitions of rude, and Gus may have initially welcomed the customer warmly. Instead, Lucas should say something like this:

> It seemed to upset the customer when you interrupted him and asked if he was ready to order. Instead of doing that, wait for him to finish and point out that there are a lot of people waiting. Maybe say something like, "I would love to keep talking, but can we pause this for a minute while I take everyone else's orders? Do you know what you want in the meantime, so I can get to work on that?" This might have gone over better, and we would have kept the customer.

Here, Lucas is specific and provides Gus with an exact alternative to what he said. This takes the guesswork and assumptions out of it and provides Gus with an exact model to follow.

Component 3: Value Determines Strength

The more we value something, the more we incorporate it. The feedback you provide must be valued by the performer. If not, it will be discounted and tossed aside. We discussed some ways to increase the value of positive feedback above. You can do the same with corrective feedback. You can first focus on increasing the value of your interactions with staff.

You can also pair your feedback with an effective consequence. With corrective feedback, the consequence may not be preferred. It could be something the person wants to avoid, such as a writeup or docked pay. But remember, even if there is a punishing consequence as a result of the poor behavior, once the behavior is corrected, then positive feedback and consequences should follow.

The Additional Component: Sandwiches Are for Eating and Eating Only

A lot of people love a good sandwich! I'm sure you can think of your favorite sandwich right now. Maybe it's warm with cheese melted over your favorite meat with all the right sauces and dressings. Or maybe you prefer them cold with the vegetables piled high. Whatever sandwich is your favorite, I'm sure the Feedback Sandwich did not come to mind. No one wants to consume a feedback sandwich, so don't try and feed it to anyone! Not sure why we are so against them? Let's focus on what we do like first – and we promise we won't leave this out. For now, please just refrain from using them in any interaction that you have.

If you do need to give constructive feedback, don't be afraid, and follow the Nike™ slogan: Just Do It™. In the end, the employee will respect you more for your direct approach and transparency than if you tried to conceal the original intention of your meeting between to loaves of contrived positivity. So remember, meat without the sandwich can be just as appetizing.

We just covered a lot of information regarding providing feedback as a consequence (immediately after the behavior or outcome). Before we move on to other times that feedback can be provided (yes, we do know that it is impossible to *always* provide it just after the behavior), we will look at one more example.

Gary is a salesperson at an electronic store. This electronic store can get particularly busy, as most do from time to time. As such, it's not uncommon for the sales team to face a mob of customers on any given day. Gary's supervisor, Yolanda, frequently roams around, observing her supervisees from afar as they interact with customers. On one particularly busy day, Gary is pounced upon by a particularly unruly customer. The customer curtly demands (not asks for) assistance.

"Hey, you!" The customer shouts toward Gary. "What deals to do you have on printers today? Your printers are normally overpriced, so I'm surprised to see that there is a sale."

Gary, remembering his training, sheds any signs of annoyance and greets the customer with the warmest smile he can muster. "Good afternoon, sir. I'd be happy to help you find a printer that best fits your needs and your budget. You are correct. We have a great sale today on some of our newer models. Are there any particular features you are looking for?"

Way to go, Gary! If you were Gary's supervisor, I'm sure this would warrant some positive feedback as soon as he was done interacting with the customer. He took a potentially unpleasant interaction and turned it into a potential sale. Good thing customers are always reasonable and equally pleasant, right?

Unfortunately for Gary, this customer wasn't. The customer snaps back at Gary, "Listen here, buddy. I'm not some kind of sucker that you can trick into buying something he doesn't need. All I want is a printer that prints in color and is easy to use. I don't need anything fancy, so keep it under $100."

Gary's heart is pounding, and he wants to tell the customer off. He holds firm and smiles through the pain, but the berating continues. Gary can't hold it anymore and in a very quiet voice mutters to himself, "Well then maybe you should actually let me help you." *Oh, oh. Did the customer hear that?!* Gary frantically thinks to himself. Unfortunately for Gary, the customer heard him and begins fuming, demanding the manager at once.

Seeing this interaction going downhill fast, Yolanda, who was nearby, quickly steps in to diffuse the situation. "Excuse me, sir. I'm the manager," she says in firm and authoritative tone. As the customer is about to begin his tirade on Gary, Yolanda quickly interrupts with a series of questions about what exactly the customer is looking for. Yolanda expertly navigates the conversation, quickly and fluidly interrupting the customer the moment he seems to be going on a tangent. Yolanda successfully guides the customer to what he is looking for and points him toward the register.

Gary, standing there the whole time, is stunned. Bewildered, he asks, "How…did you do that?"

"You're going to get customers like that, unfortunately," Yolanda explains. "I know it's very difficult to not give them attitude back, but that won't do you any favors. It's easy to get distracted when customers go on tangents, so what I do to keep them on track and away from the useless side-comments is start asking them questions about what they're looking for. I've found this keeps them on track and allows me to make the sale without getting into the back and forth."

Yolanda then begins to give Gary a few examples of questions he could ask. "You can ask them about anything that they might've had in the past, what they liked about it, what they didn't like. Remember, you know the products, so you can start narrowing down based on what they tell you. The purpose of the exchange is to make the sale and make the customer feel heard. What I'd like to see now is a few more interactions with customers. Over there, we have few customers at the customer service stand. Go assist them, and I'll be standing nearby within earshot."

Gary walks over to the customers and begins to replicate Yolanda's approach. As soon as Gary has successfully finished the interaction, Yolanda walks over to him and immediately provides positive feedback. "Great job, Gary! That's exactly what I want to see. You asked questions and narrowed down their options. I liked that you made a few suggestions as well. I'd like to see you keep doing that throughout the day." Gary nods, feeling more confident.

In this example, Yolanda used corrective feedback to teach Gary a more effective way to interact with customers and potentially get a sale. And when he tried it out, she gave him positive feedback for his progress. This is how you put the two together to get steady progress from employees. Correct what's wrong, and praise what's right.

Before we move on, here are a few final notes about the positive impacts of providing feedback immediately following the performance.

1. **It helps create a dialogue, making feedback less stuffy and more conversational.** It's far easier to remember the important details when the event discussed just occurred. Nothing is worse than fumbling for examples of when the behavior may or may not have occurred. Feedback delivered in the moment leaves little room for objection.

2. **Delivering feedback helps acceptance of feedback.** Behavior analytic research from the past half-century emphasizes the importance of immediacy when delivering consequences, indicating that the consequence (feedback in this case) is more likely to impact the future occurrence of behavior the more immediately it is provided after the behavior. Or in other words, the longer you wait, the more likely it is that your feedback won't have the effect you want. Additionally, the longer you wait, the more likely it is the feedback is provided after a *different* behavior than the one being discussed, impacting *that* behavior instead of the one intended. Thus, remember, provide performance feedback as soon as possible or else you might change the wrong behavior.

RESEARCH

More than 60% of employees report their employer has not given useful feedback in the past six months, and as a result, they experience surprises during performance reviews (Cornerstone OnDemand 2013 U.S. Employee Report).

3. **Immediate feedback also allows the individual to alter performance before it's too late.** And by "too late" we mean before performance strays beyond what can be fixed in a reasonable amount time or with a practical amount of resources. Imagine being told you were greeting customers incorrectly the *entire* year...

4. **Immediate feedback is especially important when teaching new skills.** People who have been doing a job for a long time have a good grasp of acceptable levels of performance. New hires or trainees, on the other hand, do not. Immediate feedback provides them with information about their performance right away, making the learning curve much smaller.

Becoming good at something—anything—takes a lot of practice.

However, just because you practice something over and over again doesn't actually mean you will get better. You get good at something based on the feedback of your practice. Thus, if you only receive feedback on one attempt out of 1,000, your performance probably won't improve much, if at all. The reason? Behavior is fluid, meaning it regularly changes shape, form, frequency, duration, and intensity. If feedback is provided during each occurrence, the behavior begins to take a different shape and happens more or less often.

When You Can't Follow....Try Leading

We know that providing immediate feedback regarding performance all the time is impossible. Sometimes providing feedback is inappropriate, and sometimes the supervisor isn't available. The good news, however, is that you can provide feedback at other times and still get positive results.

By leading, we mean before

If you cannot provide feedback just after the event, that leaves you with two options: (a) wait until the next time a similar event will occur and provide the feedback just before that, or (b) provide the feedback sometime between the event that just ended and the next event. We'll start with the second most effective time, just before the next event.

KNOW OUR JARGON

Antecedent: an event that immediately precedes behavior and has some effect on whether or not the behavior will occur.

RESEARCH

The role of the antecedent is one that can be traced back to the very origins of behaviorism, decades before B.F. Skinner began his work. Turning the clock more than a century to the 1900s, the primary focus of psychology was on mental processes and the study of consciousness; things that could not be seen, but only spoken of in theory. It was around this time that a graduate of the University of Chicago named John B. Watson began to pioneer what would become to be known as behaviorism.

In his famous article, "Psychology as the Behaviorist Views It", Watson made a very bold claim. He said "[Psychology] is a purely objective experimental branch of natural science. Its theoretical goal is the prediction and control of behavior. Introspection forms no essential part of its methods, nor is the scientific value of its data dependent upon the readiness with which they lend themselves to interpretation in terms of consciousness" (1913).

Watson described psychology not in terms of mental processes, but rather, in terms of observable behavior, specifically, the effect that environmental events, stimuli, have on subsequent behavior. Thus, his views became known as stimulus-response psychology, or S-R psychology. Watson believed that human behavior could be predicted, controlled, and improved. He famously, or infamously (depending on who you ask), boasted: "Give me a dozen healthy infants, well-formed, and my own specified world to bring them up in and I'll guarantee to take any one at random and train him to become any type of specialist. I might select – doctor, lawyer, artist, merchant-chief and yes, even beggar-man and thief, regardless of his talents, penchants, tendencies, abilities, vocations, and race of his ancestors.

RESEARCH

I am going beyond my facts and I admit it, but so have the advocates of the contrary and they have been doing it for many thousands of years" (1924). These claims were perhaps a bit too bold as they are still used to discredit his ideas and behaviorism in general. Watson, however, was merely planting the seeds for future behaviorists. His ideas would continue to be cultivated, especially by the founder of the experimental analysis of behavior, B.F. Skinner. However, a major takeaway from Watson's work was the importance of the events preceding behavior, the antecedents. In one of the most well-known psychological experiments and highly controversial (by today's standards), Watson conducted "The Little Albert Experiment." In this experiment, Watson aimed to provide empirical proof that preceding stimuli could be conditioned to evoke a fear response (crying). He presented his participant, baby Albert, with several stimuli, which initially had no effect. This included a rat, a rabbit, and a Santa Claus mask. However, one stimulus that evoked an immediate response was the sound of two metal pipes clanging together. In subsequent trials, Watson began presenting these neutral stimuli together with the sound of the metal pipes. Eventually, after repeated trials, Watson found that the previously neutral stimuli now evoked the fear response through a history of learning. Unfortunately, he was unable to reverse this due to Albert being pulled from the experiment. While the method Watson used to prove his point was highly questionable and unethical by today's standards, the lesson is clear: a history of learning can result in preceding stimuli evoking a response. As a bit of trivia, Watson left the field of psychology not too long after the Little Albert Experiment and wound up in advertising, where he employed the idea of pairing stimuli together. This practice can still be found in use today.

When you provide feedback just before the next occurrence of the behavior, it is called an *antecedent*. In behavior science, antecedents are different from consequences: antecedents set the stage for behavior, while consequences summarize the performance (forgive our poor attempt at a theater reference). There are different types of antecedents, and again, if you want to jump into the behavior science hole with us, please do so by reading books on behavior analysis. When thinking about feedback, or the information transfer from a mediator to a performer, the difference is that the antecedent provides the information as a reminder or cue for the correct behavior to occur.

Let's look at an example to see the difference.

Angela is a new teacher at a local high school. Her principal, Herbert, is observing her teaching class. During this time, he made the following notes:

1. She is prepared for class. Her lesson plans are written; she writes an agenda on the board and follows it.

2. It seems she follows a schedule as students came in and immediately began working from the prompt on the board.

3. She called on students evenly—every student was given a chance to respond.

4. She corrected mistakes.

5. She did not provide any positive feedback other than "okay."

Here is what Herbert's feedback may be if he provided it immediately following the observation.

> Angela, I enjoyed observing you today. It seems that you are well prepared for class and that the students know where to look for the day's activities. I also liked that you called on the students evenly. One thing that we have focused on this year is providing four positives for every corrective. I noticed that you did not provide many positives. I would like you to focus on this and provide students with positives as much as possible. You can praise their effort or willingness to participate, even if their offered answer is wrong.

Herbert's feedback here is both positive and corrective. He was specific, stated exactly what was good, and then offered a correction for what needed attention. Since the feedback was provided just after the lesson, he did not need to reference or provide exact examples as the lesson was still fresh in both Angela's and Herbert's minds. But what if Herbert had to leave halfway through the class and could not provide feedback until just before the next class. How would his feedback be different? Let's see.

It turns out that Angela has a planning period next, and then the day is finished. Herbert, called into other meetings, decides to check in with Angela the next morning, before her first class. This is what he says:

> *Angela, I enjoyed observing your class yesterday. It seems that you were well prepared for class and that the students knew where to look for the day's activities. I am glad to know that you write the agenda on the board along with the initial prompt for students to begin when they enter your class. I also liked that you called on all of the students evenly, giving them all a chance to respond. It seemed that you kept track of this using some sort of popsicle stick system. I love this! One thing that we have focused on this year is providing four positives for every corrective. Yesterday, the most positive feedback I heard was "okay." I know that the students were almost always wrong, but there are other things that you can provide positive feedback about. You can thank them for offering an answer. You can applaud their effort. Or you can even comment on how they all entered the classroom and immediately got to work. Today, I would like you to focus on providing as much positive feedback as possible.*

The main difference in Herbert's alternative feedback is that it contains a few more specific details and an instruction of what to do next. The purpose of feedback when it is given as an antecedent is to effect the performance that is about to occur. Feedback as an antecedent, however, serves as a reminder or instruction for what to do next. While the distinction may seem minimal, there are some differences in the effect it will have on the performer's behavior. Most importantly, feedback provided just before the next occurrence of the task operates as a signal that, if the task is done correctly, it is likely that you (or possibly someone else) will provide a positive consequence.

It might be helpful to look at the difference between positive and corrective feedback to see how providing it just before the person does the next task can function as an instruction or cue of some sort. Let's consider another example that highlights this difference.

Melinda is a sales manager and sits in on sales calls with the different sales agents in her department. Today she sits in on Scott's final call of the day and notes some key things about his behavior with the potential customer. Since it's his final call, Melinda decides she will provide the feedback the next morning before Scott makes his first call of the day. The next morning, Melinda approaches Scott and says the following:

> *Scott, I want to check in with you on a few things that I observed during your last sales call yesterday. Today, I want to make sure that you focus on a couple things that I think will help bring about more sales. First, I want you to try and listen more so that you can get a better idea of what the person might find interesting to purchase. You can do this by asking more open-ended questions and following up with questions prior to making an offer. For example, you can say, "What are you using right now?" Then ask, "How is it working out for you?" You might also ask things like, "If there was one thing you could improve, what would it be?" The answers to these questions will tell you exactly what the customer is looking for and help you decide the best product to offer. Please try that on your first call.*

Here, Melinda gave corrective feedback along with specific instructions of what to do next. Given that it was provided just before Scott's first call, it is serving as an instruction. Hopefully, he does this well and receives a "nice work" and a sale for his efforts!

Now let's look at how positive feedback can also serve as an instruction.

Randolph is a unit director at a large hospital. The hospital recently instituted a new policy to reduce the number of sharps injuries (those that result from improper use of sharp tools like scalpels and needles) within the operating room. Immediately following the training on this, Randolph observed Byron in the operating room, noting that Byron handled each sharp with great care and followed the new policy exactly as instructed in the training. The next day, Randolph caught Byron just before his first surgery of the day and said, "Byron, I noticed that you followed the new policy on handling sharps yesterday with perfection. I'm excited to see you continue that today!"

In this example, Byron was likely focused on the new policy since he just finished a training on it. However, the next morning, he might have been thinking of other things (such as the coffee stain on his shirt that resulted from him rushing due to being late for surgery). The feedback serves as a reminder and gets him focused back on the new policy, making it more likely he will continue following the policy.

As with providing feedback as a consequence, there are some guidelines to follow when providing feedback as an antecedent. Let's dive into them.

Guideline 1: Try to provide feedback before the very next opportunity.

Waiting is bad. In general, most of us hate to wait. We hate to wait for the doctor. We hate to wait in line. We hate to wait in traffic. Why?

FEEDBACK F!@#up!

Providing feedback both when the behavior is correct AND when the behavior is incorrect is important. As you can see here, there was no feedback provided to keep Byron's behavior going when he was doing things right. When things started going wrong, the feedback Byron received was exactly the same as when he performed things correctly – there was no feedback. When the consequences are the same for both correct and incorrect behavior, there is no way to know which is which. While it is best to provide feedback in both instances, it would have been better to provide it in at least one of the instances (either when Byron performed correctly or when he performed incorrectly).

Waiting wastes time. With feedback, waiting not only wastes time but also makes the feedback less effective. When you're providing feedback as an antecedent, you likely couldn't provide it as a consequence. Whether the feedback is positive or corrective will have differing effects on the performance.

Waiting for positive feedback may decrease the behavior.

We know that positive feedback is used to increase or maintain a behavior. This is true. But the lack of any kind of feedback can actually result in the eventual decrease or even stoppage of the behavior. Let's look at the example above with Byron and Randolph. Byron initially received positive feedback and then again followed policy regarding sharps in the operating room. However, this time, assume no one provided feedback. The next day, the same thing occurred; Byron followed policy, and, unfortunately there was a **feedback f!@#up**; no feedback was provided. This continued for a month. Byron continued to follow the new policy, yet received no feedback from anyone. Then, one day, Bryon made a small error in how he handled a sharp. No one was injured, and the operation was still completed with success. Byron still received no feedback. The next day, Byron made another mistake, reverting back to the previous way that he used to handle sharps. Again, no one took notice. However, three weeks later, when Randolph returned to observe Byron, he noticed that Byron was no longer following policy. *Why?* Well, when Byron did follow policy, no one took notice, AND when Byron didn't follow policy, no one took notice. In other words, Byron received no feedback either way, leaving it up to him to figure out what to do.

The moral? If you want to keep a behavior going, you must provide consistent feedback—especially for new behaviors.

Waiting for corrective feedback ensures the performer continues incorrectly.

When you observe an employee performing incorrectly, but wait to correct it, you are ensuring that the performer continues incorrectly. Our guess is that no one really wants an employee to continue doing the *wrong* thing. The only way to correct the performance is to provide feedback. In addition, it is quite frustrating to receive feedback that you have been doing something wrong for 6 months, yet no one said anything.

Meet Mira. Mira is a warehouse employee and is coming up on her first biannual review. She is excited as she knows this evaluation is tied to a raise and the potential to enter the training program for the supervisor position. Mira believes she will receive excellent ratings as she has always arrived on time, often works through her breaks, and ensures all tasks are complete prior to leaving, even if it takes her a bit longer. She has never asked for overtime, so she is hoping her supervisor has taken notice of the times she has stayed late to help out. What Mira doesn't know is that it is against company policy and actually a liability and legal issue that Mira has not taken breaks at times and stays after without pay, given that she is an hourly employee. Her supervisor noticed this and must give her feedback regarding it so that it will stop. Additionally, her supervisor is concerned that Mira cannot finish all of her tasks within her regular work day. Warning! Mira's supervisor is about to perform a ***feedback f!@#up***. Do you know what it is? Read on to see if you're right.

When given the review, Mira is not only shocked, but incredibly frustrated. For the past 6 months, she believed she was going above and beyond, often staying late because she was helping her colleagues, not because she could not finish her own tasks. When provided the feedback from her supervisor, she not only complained, asking why she was not told this earlier, but actually submitted her resignation. She indicated that she was really excited to have the opportunity to advance her career, but now that she knows her supervisor waited for months to correct her, causing her to miss the opportunity for advancement, she no longer felt supported or felt that this was a company that valued its employees.

Did you get it right? The ***feedback f!@#up*** here is multilayered. Feedback was not provided immediately, allowing the mistakes to continue. Mira thought her behavior demonstrated her dedication and strong work ethic and had no way of knowing that it was against policy and introduced a liability for the company. Also, Mira's supervisor assumed that her working through breaks and staying after was a reflection of her inability to complete the job in the allotted time. They did not determine if this was actually the case and provided corrective feedback based on the assumption. Finally, Mira's opportunity for advancement became contingent upon this one instance of feedback, which seems unfair given she wasn't told these things before or allowed any time to correct her behavior.

Unfortunately, things similar to this happen all the time. Employees begin doing things that they think are helping the company when in actuality they are not. However, supervisors don't get around to telling the employees about it until it is time for a performance review. To avoid the negative outcomes of this, provide feedback as soon as you see something needs to be corrected.

Waiting to provide feedback is one of the largest mistakes that supervisors make. While providing feedback immediately following the behavior or outcome isn't always an option, try to provide the feedback before the next instance. This approach will increase the chances that the feedback is effective and that the performer does not continue the inadequate performance.

Guideline 2: Provide specific detail about the performance.

When observing staff or reviewing outcomes, take specific notes regarding performance. Everyone forgets details as time passes (which is why eye witnesses are usually so unreliable), so recording the details will ensure nothing is lost. Provide these details to not only ensure the performer remembers the instance but also ensure the performer knows exactly what to keep doing and what to change. Let's see how specific details can make a difference with Denise.

Denise works at a debt collection office. Her primary task is to call people from the list of names that she is given on a monthly basis and come to an agreement regarding their outstanding debt. Each collector is also given a monthly goal. If they reach that goal, they are eligible to receive a bonus. Hector is Denise's supervisor. He regularly observes his employees work and provides immediate feedback after observing a call (feedback as a consequence). He also provides individual feedback at the beginning of each day. One morning, Hector asks Denise to visit his office. He provides feedback regarding her current numbers. He tells her that she is "getting close" to her goal, and with "a little extra effort," she will likely reach her goal before the end of the week. Feeling encouraged, Denise leaves Hector's office to start her day. She decides that she will try to make double the calls today to ensure she reaches her goal.

Denise begins making her calls for the day, rushing each person to a decision. She interrupts people a few times as they provide her with long explanations about why they didn't pay last month and focuses on getting a final number. Hector observes this as he is doing his daily observations and frowns. He is surprised to see this change in Denise as she usually builds excellent rapport with the people she is calling. Hector believes this is one of the reasons Denise is able to get to her target; people like talking with her and then figure out how to pay at least something.

What happened? **Feedback f!@#up!** Hector provided feedback as an antecedent, which created an instruction for Denise. *Put in extra effort to reach your goal.* The problem is that "put in extra effort" was not clearly defined. Hector did not provide the details about what he meant by "extra effort," and Denise was left to conclude that the solution was to get through more calls. Unfortunately, this was not the right solution, and even though Denise made 50% more calls that day, she actually got fewer dollars agreed to for payback.

Had Hector taken the time to provide specific details about what he observed Denise do during her calls that made her successful and provide her with specific instructions about what "a little extra effort" meant, it is likely she would have had a different outcome.

Guideline 3: Provide feedback as a consequence as well, especially when correcting.

Remember that, while antecedents make it more likely the action will occur in that moment, the best way to ensure a behavior happens (or doesn't happen) again in the future is to provide a consequence. This is especially important when corrective feedback is provided to ensure the corrected behavior continues. Let's look at an example to put this into perspective.

Kabir just finished the police academy. As a new police officer, he is assigned to partner with Alicia, who is now on her 10th year with the force. While patrolling the neighborhood, they see someone run a stop sign. Kabir, anxious to do his first traffic stop, asks if he can take the lead. Alicia agrees, thinking the traffic stop is routine and a great way for Kabir to gain some experience. Kabir walks to the car and taps on the window. He engages in small talk for a few exchanges and asks the driver for their license and registration. The driver, friendly and compliant, asks why they were pulled over. Kabir responds by saying he will tell them after running their license. He heads back to the car, runs the license and registration, and proceeds back to the pulled over car. Kabir, not exactly sure if he is ready to write his first ticket, tells the driver that they rolled through the stop sign without stopping. The driver apologizes and thanks Kabir for allowing them to leave with a warning. Alicia and Kabir walk back to the car, and as soon as Alicia is about to provide feedback, a car speeds by going about 20 miles over the speed limit. Alicia turns on the siren and lights and proceeds after the speeding car. The car pulls over, and as Alicia and Kabir walk toward the car, Alicia says, "This time tell the driver why you pulled them over as soon as you begin talking with them. Don't wait to run their information. It's better to always let people know why they're being pulled over."

Kabir walks to the car and taps on the window. The driver rolls down the window and greets Kabir. Kabir responds by saying, "Hello. I pulled you over today because you were going 19 miles over the speed limit. Is there an emergency?"

The driver responds, "No. I honestly was thinking about this feedback my boss gave me today. I thought I was doing really well at work, but then, after 4 months of my supervisor saying nothing to me, I get called in his office and told I'm doing horrible work. I'm sorry officer; I'm just really upset about it." Kabir smiles and says that he's sorry to hear that (and thinks how thankful he is that his partner provided him feedback just before he walked to the car). He asks for the driver's license and registration and walks back to the car. Alicia, who observed the interaction, praised Kabir for telling the driver why he pulled them over, asking a question about why and maintaining a conversational tone of voice. Kabir smiled, knowing he was quickly improving, and it was only his first day of work!

In this example, Kabir was provided feedback first as an antecedent and then as a consequence. The consequence was provided to ensure Kabir knew that he did exactly what Alicia instructed. This approach will increase the chances that Kabir continues to tell drivers why they are being pulled over as soon as he approaches their cars.

The middle isn't always bad.

In a perfect world, supervisors would be able to provide feedback either as a consequence or as an antecedent. However, we know the world is not perfect, and there are times that neither just after or just before an employee is going to perform a responsibility will work. In these cases, there is a third option; however, it should be used as a last resort and only when necessary. *The reason?* Because it's not as effective. Yet even less effective feedback is better than no feedback, so when you are not able to provide feedback just after or just before, choose a time that is between to two.

For example, Nadine is a traffic lawyer. Her clerk Rebecca is currently in law school and finishing her last semester. In fact, she is in process of taking her last set of finals. Nadine has been providing Rebecca as many experiences as possible so that she is ready to practice independently once she passes the bar. The other day Nadine noticed that one of the filings for appearance was completed incorrectly. It had already been submitted, and by the time Nadine noticed, Rebecca was heading out the door. Rebecca did not come in the next day as she had a big exam, and on the following day, Nadine threw a celebration party to congratulate Rebecca for completing law school. Not wanting to provide corrective feedback in the middle of the celebration, and because there was not anything that could be done about the incorrect paperwork at the moment, Nadine decided to wait another day to provide feedback. The next day, Nadine called Rebecca to her office. Nadine showed Rebecca the file for appearance, with the incorrect portions circled and written-in notes about how to correct it. Nadine then instructed Rebecca to follow up with the court to determine if the file for appearance had been accepted anyway or if they needed to resubmit.

In this example, it was not optimal to provide feedback to Rebecca as soon as Nadine realized the error. Additionally, it is not known when Rebecca will file another appearance, so Nadine provided the feedback at the next best moment. To ensure that everything is corrected, Nadine provided specific details about what was incorrect and how to correct it. She then provided Rebecca guidance and instructions on how to correct the current mistake.

More often than not, you'll likely find that you're providing feedback between instances of performance. As stated before, it is better to provide feedback than not at all, and we recommend that feedback is provided at the next best chance and provided frequently, even if not at the most effective times. Later, we will discuss how often feedback should be provided; however, for now, provide it no more than a few days after the performance occurred. This timing will ensure the event is still present in the performer's memory and that the performer has not had too many chances to continue repeating any mistakes.

Let's take a look at the decision tree to walk through the questions and answers for how to decide the best timing for your feedback. Here, the question is regarding the temporal location of feedback regarding the current performance and the next performance.

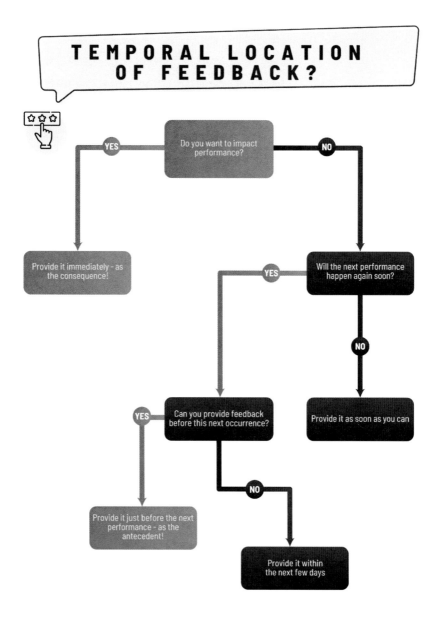

Now we're ready to add this to our formula:

EFFECTIVE PERFORMANCE FEEDBACK =
(The Behavior/Action/Outcome) + *(The Person)* + *(The Number of People)* + *(The Type of Feedback)* + **(The Temporal Location)** + *(x)*

5

THE MEDIUM OF FEEDBACK DELIVERY

"Images act like shortcuts to our brains, and that is why visuals are so powerful."

~Ekaterina Walter

One of the largest stressors in today's workplace is miscommunication. While advances in technology have made it easier to work with others in different geographical locations, it has also increased the rate of miscommunication for those who are not careful. In addition to increased stress, miscommunication can lead to incorrect performance and, worse, poor quality in services.

Clear communication in which the performer receives the same message the mediator sends is pertinent for feedback to be effective. However, more often than not, we hear the stories about communication exchanges that leave one person feeling good and leave the other person walking away confused. In our experience, we have heard people at every level and in every position say the same thing at one time or another: "I don't understand why this keeps happening. I know I told them what to do." Of course, the individual not following through on the request could be not doing so for a number of different reasons. However, it is our experience that one of the most common reasons is that the performer received a message other than what the mediator sent.

Effectively delivering a message can be affected by a huge variety of things—from the actual words used to the emotions, the cultural practices, the medium used to communicate, and even the location in which the communication occurred. Because feedback is so pertinent to the success of others, in the next few chapters, we discuss the different components of communication and how to maximize them.

When determining the best medium for delivering feedback, you must first consider the different parts of communication that are present. Most linguists include language, paralanguage, and nonverbal communication as the three main components of communication. Communication is most effective when all three components are present. As you remove different components of communication, the message is less likely to be received the way it was intended.

The chart below illustrates the effectiveness of communication based on modality and which components are present. Keep in mind that, even though a communication modality may not be as effective, there are things you can do to increase its effectiveness.

MOST EFFECTIVE

Medium	Conveys
In Person Face to Face	Language, paralanguage, nonverbal
Video Conference	
Telephone	Language, paralanguage
Instant Messenger on computer	Language
Handwritten Notes / Cards	**Emojis can introduce an amount of paralanguage/ nonverbal; however, should be considered in a business setting and with different cultures
Emails	
Text via phone	
Unopened / unread documents	Missed communication

LEAST EFFECTIVE

It's Always Better When I See You

As the chart displays, the more varied types of communication present, the more effective the communication will be. Let's look at the following example.

It's Monday, and Betty is having "one of those days." She woke up late, causing her to not have time to grab her morning coffee. Worse, on her way to work, she got into a huge fight with her sister about whether to place their dad in a nursing home. As Betty pulls into a parking space at work, she takes a deep breath. Trying to put her argument and her worries about her father to the side, she gives herself a quick pep talk just before getting out of her car. She walks by two of her colleagues on her way to her office and starts feeling that the day might not be so bad. Just as she turns on her computer and begins checking her email, her phone goes off. It's a text message from her supervisor saying, "Jim called. His order is wrong. Fix it before you do anything else!" Betty sat silent looking at her phone for a minute. She took another deep breath, knowing this day was not going to get any better.

Yes, we know. Betty is a victim of a ***feedback f!@#up.*** The feedback Betty received did not follow many of the rules we've already discussed. That's one of the problems with text messages. We tend to shorten them and send them quickly, leaving out key details. Additionally, it is impossible to tell whether the supervisor is upset with Betty. The only thing that's clear is that Betty needs to address the situation immediately.

Now let's consider that Betty's supervisor picked up a copy of this book and thought through what might happen if he sends a quick text to Betty. He needs to communicate with her as quickly as possible and didn't see her when he went by her office this morning. Thus, he decides an email will allow him to easily provide more details.

Take two. Betty has just entered her office and sits down to her computer. She still had the same morning, but now her phone does not ding with a message. Instead, she opens her emails and sees the following subject line from her supervisor "OPEN IMMEDIATELY – JIM ORDER WRONG." Now she's thinking, "What could be wrong with Jim's order. We went over it three times." Betty clicks open the message. It reads as follows:

Betty,

    I didn't see you in your office this morning, and this needs to be addressed immediately. Jim called. He said that his order is wrong. He said that he only received half of the items he ordered and wants to know where the rest of his order is. He is really mad as he stated that he stressed the importance of everything being there today. Make this your first priority to fix this morning.

Fortunate for Betty, her supervisor never actually sent this email. She didn't have to stare at the computer wondering if she would lose her job or get ripped apart later that day when she met with her supervisor. Because her supervisor read this book, he knew that the best way to deliver feedback is in person. Even though Betty was not in her office when he first walked by, he decided to grab a cup of coffee and head back to her office. Maybe she was just running a few minutes behind this morning. When he returned, Betty was in her office, turning on her computer. She looked a bit frazzled, which was unusual. He gently knocked on her open door and peeked his head around the corner. "Got a minute?"

Betty forced a smile and said, "Sure. Come on in."

Betty's supervisor entered the office and sat down in the chair across from her desk. "Are you okay this morning? You look…you look like something is on your mind."

Betty normally always kept her home life separate from work and didn't want to introduce any drama. She smiled halfway and said "Thanks for asking. I'm okay. There are just a few things going on in my personal life with my family. And on top of that, I was late this morning, and I really hate arriving late to work. I will be fine, though. I am ready to start the week and focus on something productive!" Betty tried her best to put some excitement in her voice. This was not lost on her supervisor.

He responded, "I'm glad that you are okay, and I hope your family stuff gets worked out. I know that can be stressful." He paused a minute to make sure his message was genuine. He really cared about his staff and hated to see them go through difficult times. After a moment, he leaned back in his chair a bit and placed his hands on his knees. He leaned in a bit, placing his weight on his elbows, and only then said the following:

I received a call from Jim this morning. He's the manager over at ABC Corporations. He said that the shipment of letters was not correct, something about only receiving half of the letters. I'm not sure if he meant that he only received letters A–M, or if he received all letters but only half as many sets as he wanted. You know how he can go on and on and not always be too clear. Can you call him this morning, find out exactly what happened, and try to resolve it? I would have someone else do it, but you are always so good at figuring out the exact problem, and he seems to respond more positively to you than anyone else.

Gold star for Betty's supervisor! When he delivered the feedback in person, Betty was able to receive the entire message. She knows that her supervisor is not upset with her, nor will she be in trouble. She also has some information about the problem and why she was asked to call Jim. She feels good knowing that she has more success with this client than anyone else.

As the example clearly shows, delivering feedback in person is always best. We recommend it any time it's possible. Delivering feedback in person allowed Betty's supervisor to learn a few key things that he would not have known without the face-to-face interaction. First, he learned that something was bothering Betty. He picked up on her body language and nonverbal communication. Using this information, he was able to adjust his feedback to increase the likeliness Betty received the correct message. Second, he provided more details than he could have through text or email. In person, we tend to explain things in more detail than we do when writing or typing a message. In our example, those added details were not only important for Betty in finding the solution for Jim, but also in her knowing that she was not in trouble. Finally, Betty was able to better interpret the message by watching and hearing her supervisor's body language and paralanguage. The supervisor's relaxed posture and calm tone of voice sent the message that he was not upset. Additionally, the pause after asking if she was okay sent Betty the message that her supervisor cared. These small details can make all the difference in the message!

That being said, we know that feedback cannot always be delivered in person. There are times that waiting for the optimal moment to deliver feedback face-to-face would eliminate any effectiveness of providing feedback. In these moments, consider the following when deciding what modality to use.

A Picture Is Worth a Thousand Words

When you can't be face to face with someone, the next best thing is a video chat. While nothing beats the real thing, videoconferencing is a close second. With videoconferencing, you can still observe the person's facial expressions and some of their body language, in addition to hearing the tone of voice and rate and inflection of speech. In today's world where so many of us are working remotely and working with those across the country and world, videoconferencing is a great way to bridge the geographic gap that makes in-person meetings few and far between. When you're providing feedback through videoconference, here are a few things to keep in mind.

1. **If you're in the building, do it in person.** Videoconferencing is an excellent solution when you are unable to physically meet with the person. However, it should not be used as a shortcut or because you already got your steps in for the day (and don't need the extra 200 to get to your supervisee's office and back). While this might seem obvious, we have run into these situations. Don't be a lazy boss—instead, walk the distance to deliver feedback in person.

2. **Be free from distractions.** Picture this: You are talking with someone through video, and while they're looking toward the camera, their eyes are moving from left to right, back to left, and again to right while you're talking. You ask a question to confirm they are actually listening and not caught in some cyber bliss, and their response is, "Can you repeat that?" Sitting in front of a computer introduces a world of temptation—from emails to instant messenger, to that project that is due 2 hours after the meeting. We suggest being free from these distractions any time you are videoconferencing, but it is especially important when providing feedback. You want to ensure the performer understands the importance of your feedback, and the best way to do this is to give it your undivided attention.

3. **Watch your words.** While it's easier to interpret someone's message when you can hear their tone of voice and see their facial expressions, videoconferencing does provide some limitations to how much body language can be observed. As a result, there is more reliance upon the actual words being used. Be thoughtful about the words you use, and be sure to use the most objective language possible.

This will minimize any confusion or miscommunication.

4. **Be aware of body language.** Looking into a camera may seem weird, especially because we are used to looking at the person when talking with them. However, when you look at the computer screen, at the person, instead of into the camera, it usually looks as though you are looking down. Try your best to look into the camera when talking, but don't make it weird by staring directly into it. Additionally, keep in mind that your body language should match your message. Whether discussing positive or corrective feedback, make sure your posture is open by placing your hands on either side of the chair (resting on the arms of the chair) or on the desk in front of you. Lean forward to show interest and engagement.

Hearing Is Better than Reading

There are times when meeting in person or through video are virtually impossible. In these times, use the telephone. While the person receiving feedback cannot see your facial expressions or body language, they can hear the tone and pitch of your voice. It is much easier to interpret the meaning behind the words when you can hear the inflection of a person's voice. If possible, use this only when providing positive feedback as it's always best to provide corrective feedback in person or through videoconference. However, if the choice is between a phone call and a text or email, pick up the phone.

Like when videoconferencing, be sure you are free from distractions and completely focused on the task at hand. There's nothing worse than to have a phone call with a supervisor who seems like they are focused on everything other than what you're saying. Don't be that supervisor.

Finally, keep in mind that the person cannot see you. Thus, you need to articulate and verbalize your head nods, agreeances, puzzled looks, or disagreements. Phone conversations have removed a large portion of communication, so words are also more important. Be sure you have prepared for the call and have chosen your words carefully to reduce the chance of miscommunication.

Some Communication Is Better Than None

Unless providing positive feedback, we do not recommend using email, texts, or handwritten notes. However, there are times that using these modalities to provide positive feedback can be useful. Here are a few pointers when considering which modality is best.

Email

Remember that most of us receive numerous emails per day. We tend to skim the subject line and quickly open the most important emails while flagging the others for later. To ensure your feedback is not marked "for later review" or, even worse, not flagged at all (yes, we all have emails we have never read), use a subject line that calls the receiver's attention to it. Subject lines like "Great job today," "Heard some good news," "Taking a minute to thank you" send the message that something positive is written in the email, making it more likely it will be opened.

Emails are the most formal of all written communication, so be sure to use business language. Do not use slang terms or abbreviations. Also, depending on the climate and culture of your organization, emojis may not be appropriate.

Instant Messenger & Texts

Instant messenger apps have made communication throughout organizations easier and more efficient. These apps are an excellent way to get questions answered quickly, avoid unnecessary meetings, and collaborate with team members across the world. We are huge fans of instant messengers—except when it comes to feedback. If you're anything like us, you probably have your instant messenger app on your phone and computer so that you can respond quickly whether you're sitting at your computer, working out at the gym, picking your kids up from school, or meandering somewhere between those tasks. This widespread accessibility is excellent for increasing the ease of communication as you can answer questions and respond even while you're doing other things. However, because we're often typing on our phones and at least sometimes doing other things as well, it's easy to type a quick response. When providing feedback, however, you want the message to be anything but a quickly and carelessly typed response. Thus, when you're using instant messenger to provide feedback, we suggest following these guidelines:

1. **Only state the positive.** When typing and sending texts, keep the messages positive. Save corrective feedback for face-to-face meetings.

2. **Be sure to check for typos.** It's easy to type a message and click send quickly. However, if you're anything like us, you tend to have about a million typos per day. There's nothing worse than accidently sending a curse word or some other typo or incorrect autocorrect. Feedback is important, and the importance of the message is undermined when the message is filled with typos or incorrect words.

3. **Use emojis when appropriate.** The one cool thing about text messages and instant messenger is that we can send emojis and gifs. These allow us to share emotions through written word that we are not able to share with just words. When providing positive feedback through instant messenger or text, it's okay to use emojis. The only thing to note is that you still need to be conscious of your audience and keep the emojis and gifs business-appropriate—especially when sending texts or messages to a subordinate or supervisor.

Handwritten Notes

Handwritten notes are not talked about like they were in the past. It seems that we have made communication so convenient that we have lost sight of handwritten notes. However, receiving a card or quick handwritten note with positive feedback sends the message not only that the person did something great but also that you thought enough of them to take the time to write the feedback out. Handwritten notes are an excellent way to provide positive feedback to your employees. Try writing a few each week as a way to show your staff that you truly appreciate them.

It's awesome that we have so many different ways to communicate with one another. The advances in technology have helped increase business and communication across the world. It has allowed us to work virtually, to work with offices in other countries, and to collaborate in ways that were much more difficult 10 or 20 years ago. It's easy to get caught using these technology advances for ease and to decrease time, and we recommend using them when other modalities are not available. However, if you are in the same office (or will be within the next few days) or can meet with the person face to face, the good old-fashioned in-person meeting is the best way to provide corrective feedback. When that's not possible, make your best attempt to schedule a videoconference. Also, be sure to use the other advances in technology to increase the ease and rate of positive feedback you provide. We'll discuss how often it should be provided soon, but for now, keep in mind that using different modalities can help increase how much positive feedback you can provide given the limits on your time and other responsibilities.

Now that we have highlighted the pros and cons of different mediums—and stressed the importance of providing feedback in person whenever possible—we are now ready to talk about where to provide feedback. More specifically, we will discuss the privacy and formality of feedback. Before we move on, though, let's update our formula:

EFFECTIVE PERFORMANCE FEEDBACK =
(The Behavior/Action/Outcome) + *(The Person)* + *(The Number of People)* + *(The Type of Feedback)* + *(The Temporal Location)* + **(The Medium)** + *(x)*

To assist in the decision about what medium to use when providing feedback, use the decision tree below.

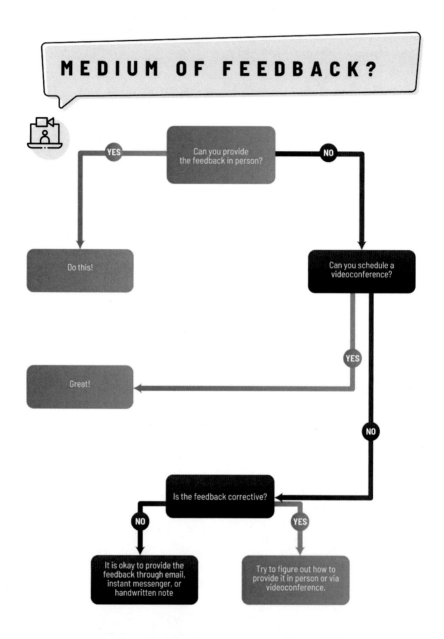

MEDIUM OF FEEDBACK?

Can you provide the feedback in person?

YES — Do this!

NO — Can you schedule a videoconference?

YES — Great!

NO — Is the feedback corrective?

NO — It is okay to provide the feedback through email, instant messenger, or handwritten note

YES — Try to figure out how to provide it in person or via videoconference.

6

WHERE TO PROVIDE FEEDBACK

"Location, location, location." – Anonymous Real Estate Agent

A Haunted House of Feedback

You're walking down a long, dark, lonely hallway with your briefcase in one hand and a ball of sweat in the other. The only noise you hear is your own heart beating in lockstep with the sound of your feet as you nervously walk past your colleagues' offices and toward your boss's ~~dungeon~~ office. As you approach the office, you grab the steel door handle. The cold temperature on the handle sends shivers up your arm as you pry it open.

Once inside, you immediately notice the office is dark, the shades are closed, and the only light in the room is a desk lamp slightly tilted toward your boss's face, making it difficult to see even the letters of "Greg Hayen, CEO" on the large nameplate across the desk. Your boss grimaces as he sits in a chair elevated so high that he towers over the desk. The room is musty and uncomfortable with almost no ventilation. As you close the door, it creaks like two pieces of metal scraping together before slamming shut behind you with two distinct sounds. The first indicates the door has closed. The other appears to lock you into the room.

Your boss doesn't say anything to you—he simply points with an open hand in the direction of the small wooden chair sitting in front of his desk. You sit down and try to make yourself comfortable. His eyes come out of the dark and into focus. In an emotionless and hoarse tone, he says, "I need to give you some feedback on your performance." Cue the sound of thunder and flash lightning outside.

That scary situation has occurred with too many working professionals on too many occasions as they endure tough feedback in the most uncomfortable settings. Where you provide feedback can have a profound effect on how feedback is received and whether performance improvements are made.

When providing feedback, many different factors must be considered, and all those factors focus on the environment. The environment is the entire constellation of stimuli that can affect a person and change their behavior, including the temperature and lighting of the room, the placement of seating, the smell, and everything else you can imagine. The environment is especially important when receiving feedback. There is nothing too minor in the environment to examine when considering the impact that it might have on the success of your feedback delivery—even the color of the walls could make a difference. When considering where to provide feedback, consider at least the following three main aspects:

1. Whether the environment is public or private.

2. Whether the environment is casual or formal.

3. The physical organization of the environment.

The goal is finding just the right atmosphere to help you evoke the

KNOW OUR JARGON

Evoke: increase the momentary probability of the behavior. If a behavior is "evoked", it is more likely it will occur right then in that moment.

right type of performance from your employees, and achieving that begins with examining each of the three key areas.

Public vs. Private

Whether you provide feedback in a public or private environment can make all the difference when determining how your employee's behavior will be impacted. As the old saying goes, "Praise in public, punish in private." However, feedback, like other aspects of human behavior, is not that simple. Feedback requires analyzing individual preferences and contingencies instead of utilizing a "one rule for all" approach. In order to determine which is best, you have to first know your performer's preferences and learning history.

Let's start by defining the two concepts:

Private feedback is feedback given in a manner that cannot be heard, seen, or read about by anyone except the original performer at any time before, during, or after the feedback has been delivered. It is between you and the person you are providing feedback to, no one else. If in person, this means that only you and the performer are present. If sending an email or text, it means a private exchange between the two of you.

Public feedback, on the other hand, is feedback that is observable by people other than the recipient. Public feedback can be provided in a group (large or small), posted somewhere public (e.g., a breakroom bulletin board or office corridor), sent out through company email, or posted on social media. Public feedback also includes feedback provided to one person in a group chat or email with several recipients. And keep in mind that bcc'ing someone on an email still makes the feedback public, even if the performer doesn't know you've made it private (which could introduce a whole different set of things to consider, but we won't get into that right now).

Remember that each employee may respond differently to private and public feedback in different situations. Knowing your employees' preferences and their motivations for better work are essential components to effectively delivering feedback. However, both types of feedback have their benefits.

The Benefits (and Problem) of Privacy

Benefits

Providing feedback privately is the safer choice. While we recommend to sometimes provide positive feedback publicly, providing it privately does two things. First, it has a positive effect on the performer. When done correctly (by following our formula), positive feedback increases and maintains good performance. Thus, when the feedback is given privately, you are ensuring that the performer's work continues. While most of us like to be recognized publicly as well, there are two things that can backfire. First, some get embarrassed when recognized publicly. If this happens, the performer may begin to do things to avoid this embarrassing recognition, having detrimental effects on performance. Second, if another employee did a similarly great job and was not recognized, that person could become disgruntled, not understanding why they did not get recognized while the other person did. This can have an equally detrimental effect on that person's performance.

When it comes to corrective feedback, most of the time, employees do not enjoy being singled out in front of their colleagues, especially for incorrect performance. This not only has the potential to de-motivate the individual performer but also may create a sense of sympathy for the performer among their peers, which ends up de-motivating the entire group. If you don't know the individual's preferences or, more importantly, what will positively impact their performance, providing feedback privately will help you err on the side of caution. Providing negative feedback in a public location can model inappropriate behavior for your staff and create a culture of punishment instead of reinforcement. When considering positive feedback, then, it may still be more beneficial to provide the feedback in private. Providing this feedback in private allows for more specificity. Additionally, there are some who do not like to be highlighted in public, in front of their peers. When this is the case, providing public feedback can actually be punishing, and you may see the employee begin to do less to ensure they are no longer recognized in public. Thus, whether it is positive or corrective feedback, providing it privately is always the safer choice. However, there are appropriate times to provide positive feedback in public. These will be discussed later. To illustrate this point, let's look at the following example of another *feedback f!@#up.*

Joe, a manager in the delivery department, conducts a daily meeting to review progress toward reducing the number of traffic-related incidents with his team of drivers. During the meeting, Joe points out two employees. Theresa and Terry are both drivers on the team. Theresa has shown excellence in following the GPS instructions and always completes her routes on time. Terry, however, recently took a bad route and did not follow the GPS instructions for the safest and most efficient route to reach his destination. Joe praises Theresa and says that she is the model driver that all should succeed to match. He then scolds Terry, pointing out that this is not the first time something like this has happened. He gives notice that, if Terry's performance does not improve, his job could be on the line. The next morning, Terry and another driver, Martin, hand Joe letters of resignation. Martin states that he is tired of not being recognized for doing the exact same thing that Theresa does and thinks that Joe plays favorites. On Facebook, Terry also posts a video taken by another employee showing the feedback interaction. His post includes a disconcerting comment about the company and Joe's managerial style. Later that month, Joe notices not only that Theresa has been late on some of her routes but also that other colleagues are belittling one of their coworkers for missing a turn on the delivery route. When questioned about their behavior, the colleagues explained they thought that was how things worked at the company. This situation could have been avoided if Joe would have erred on the side of caution and provided feedback to both Theresa and Terry privately.

Let's examine how this might have gone if feedback was provided privately. There were several things wrong about how Joe provided feedback to Theresa and Terry; however, we are only going to examine the difference between public and private settings. Joe, Theresa, Terry, and the rest of the staff were in a meeting where Joe was reviewing progress toward reducing the number of traffic related incidents. Joe provided the overall progress of the team toward the goal and stated that he would follow up later in one-on-one meeting with each individual regarding their specific progress toward the goal.

During the meeting with Theresa, Joe told her that she was doing an excellent job of following the GPS and completing her routes on time or ahead of schedule. He also noted that she had zero traffic incidents. He thanked her for her hard work and asked her to continue her excellent service. Theresa, excited to hear that she was doing so well, continued her excellent work.

During the meeting with Terry, Joe told Terry that he went off route and did not follow the GPS. He stated that this has happened before and that it needs to be corrected or Terry's job would be on the line. Terry explained why he went off-route and did not follow the GPS as there was an accident and the road was closed, so he could not continue the path outlined by the GPS. He stated that he didn't know how to update or alert the GPS when this happened. Joe and Terry then discussed what to do in the event this occurred again in the future, and Terry thanked Joe for listening and helping him determine the best course of action.

You can individualize feedback more effectively in private because not everyone's feedback needs are the same. In a private meeting, you can provide specific details about the performer's tasks and results, as well as the behavior that produced them, in an intimate setting without publicizing information other employees should not hear. We have already discussed that feedback should be specific and will discuss this in even more detail later. For now, just remember that providing *detailed* feedback enhances the impact of the feedback. Why? It allows the performer to understand exactly what they did correctly or what they need to change and how to go about changing it. Let's see how this works with our next characters, Aileen and Gabriela.

Aileen, a retail supervisor at a high-end clothing store, passes the store breakroom and sees Gabriela, a sales representative who works in her department, and walks over to talk with her. Gabriela is talking with her

FEEDBACK F!@#up!

If there is a behavior that you want one person to do in a specific instance or set of circumstances, feedback should always be provided in private. You never want others to overhear this and think they should do it too.

colleagues when Aileen walks over. Aileen immediately begins discussing a difficult customer Gabriela dealt with earlier in the week and then provides Gabriela with feedback on her interaction with the very difficult customer. On several occasions, Aileen mentions Gabriela should have given the customer a discount that can only be used with managerial approval, and not all sales associates are aware of the discount. Later that week, two other sales associates working in Aileen's department call her on the intercom system explaining they have promised a customer the same managerial discount Aileen inadvertently told them about during her feedback session with Gabriela.

Let's examine what might have happened if this feedback were provided in private. Here, the result of Aileen providing feedback in public to Gabriela was that the other sales associates began offering a manager's discount when they likely should not have. Additionally, the sales associates learned about providing the discount as a way to de-escalate a customer, but were not provided any formal training on how and when this discount should be offered. As a result, discounts are being offered at a rate that is much higher than acceptable at the store. Had the feedback been provided in private, the other sales associates would not know anything about the manager's discount and would not offer it to de-escalate sticky customer situations. Additionally, Aileen could provide exact training should this discount be offered on a wider scale to ensure that all staff provided it only at the appropriate times.

Private feedback is better for open dialogue. Many people can be averse to public speaking, so when a leader provides feedback to a performer in a group setting, the performer may be hesitant to ask follow-up questions or even acknowledge they understand the given feedback. This is often the case with many employees (or people for that matter) because the employee's behavior has been punished in the past for questioning a course of action made by an insecure boss. Providing feedback privately allows the leader to watch for mannerisms indicating understanding (or lack thereof) and prompt the performer to ask questions or simply acknowledge they understand the feedback. More importantly, private feedback allows the leader to reinforce question-asking behavior. This process often creates a safer environment for performers to express their views and engage in meaningful dialogue with the leader. Consider Darjennys, an HR manager at a chemical company. She is leading an in-service training for plant engineers on the importance of safety while handling dangerous chemicals. Darjennys presents a group of over 100 employees with step-by-step guidelines to avoid safety hazards and with performance data for the entire company. Darjennys lists every department with a high number of safety incidents in the past week and provides feedback to those groups about how they can perform better. When she finishes, she asks if anyone has any questions. A few people respond, and Darjennys asks, "Does everyone understand these guidelines?" The crowd responds back with mostly nodding heads. The *feedback f!@#up?* Darjennys has placed herself in an environment where she can only confirm a superficial understanding of a very important training class with a large group of employees.

Let's consider how this could be done privately to check for actual understanding. It is likely unrealistic to think that the training could be provided in a private setting with each plant engineer. However, Darjennys could do two things that might help ensure that each engineer and group of engineers understand exactly how to perform the step-by-step guidelines to avoid safety hazards. First, Darjennys could meet with each group of plant managers separately so that the groups are smaller and more intimate, making it easier for questions to be asked. Second, and even better, Darjennys could provide a short one-on-one meeting with each engineer who exhibited the most problematic performance; she could then review safety guidelines and ensure understanding either by asking the individual to state the guidelines in their own words or by asking questions. This private setting would allow Darjennys to assess the individual's behavior to ensure understanding of the guidelines and what that person needs to change to meet the standards.

Corrective feedback usually works better privately. Providing corrective feedback publicly can be very problematic for individual performers. Corrective feedback given publicly is likely to embarrass the employee, who will likely focus on the shame of being corrected in front of others rather than listening to and applying your feedback. The employee's comfort level is imperative in ensuring they absorb the content of your feedback. Keeping employees calm lowers the risk that they will be become defensive or reactive to corrective feedback. We'll warn you, another *feedback f!@#up* is about to happen.

Yeneiri, a cellular manufacturing plant manager, goes down to the plant floor and notices Sal, a production line worker, incorrectly installing faceplates on cellular phones. She immediately walks over and begins chiding him for poor phone assembly. During the exchange, three other plant employees stop their work and begin watching the interaction. During the interaction, Sal looks around and sees his coworkers watching and begins to sweat nervously and feel his face flush. When Yeneiri finishes her feedback, she asks Sal if he understands what she communicated to him. Sal simply shrugs and turns away to wipe away the sweat and shame. Chances are that Sal still does not know how to put the face plates on correctly, but it will also take him a bit of time to get over these feelings of embarrassment and get back to work. Additionally, those who watched may continue to be off task while they offer comfort to Sal for the reprimand he just received.

What if this feedback was provided in private? Had Yeneiri asked Sal to step away for a moment and provided the feedback in a private setting, several benefits may have occurred. Yeneiri could have shown Sal exactly what he was doing incorrectly and how to fix it. He may have even been provided the chance to practice it to ensure that his placement of the face plate was correct. The other workers would not have stopped working, which keeps production moving. Finally, workers may not see Yeneiri as a negative, mean manager as they did not witness a public humiliation of one of their coworkers. Workers having such a view of Yeneiri would keep morale up and production high.

Problems

There is only so much time in the day. We do understand that there is only so much time in the day—1,440 minutes to be exact. With that, there is not always time to provide every single employee with private feedback every single time feedback should be provided. However, there are some ways to provide feedback privately while saving a bit of time. Especially when providing positive feedback, use email and instant messages to save some time. It is far more efficient to send an email than to schedule a face-to-face meeting. You can also work feedback into regular meetings. If you have a weekly, biweekly, or monthly meeting, make sure that you save a lot time to provide feedback. This approach will save you from having to schedule another meeting specifically for feedback. Finally, you can ask the person to stay 5 minutes after a meeting. Once the room clears, you can provide the feedback. And if you start ending meetings after 45 minutes instead of 60, you can use 10 minutes for feedback sessions and still have 5 minutes to run to the bathroom!

While the general rule of thumb is to provide feedback in private whenever possible, considering it is not always possible, let's look at the benefits and problems of public feedback.

The Benefits (and Problems) of Publicity

Public feedback can be *beneficial* as well as *problematic*:

Benefits

Important for pivot praise. If your employees are underperforming and you are struggling to find appropriate behavior to reinforce, using pivot praise might be a good alternative. Providing positive feedback to one employee in front of their peers could serve as an antecedent for the entire group to show the type of positive reinforcement available if they perform up to standard. Pivot praise can also be used to recognize several individuals in the group who are performing well.

KNOW OUR JARGON

Pivot praise is a behavioral strategy used in groups when trying to avoid providing corrective feedback in public. Instead of highlighting the incorrect behaviors, the individual focuses on the positive things others are doing and provides positive praise for that. The intent here is to bring attention to the correct behaviors, provide feedback (and hopefully reinforcement) for them. Those who are performing incorrectly will observe this, making it more likely they will also begin engaging in the correct behaviors.

In a professional development meeting, the school principal reviews progress toward a literacy initiative. One goal in this initiative is to have a specific setup of the classroom board. Prior to the meeting, the principal tours several classrooms and takes pictures of the boards that reflect exactly what's expected. In the meeting, the principal reviews progress toward this goal by stating that, while he did not yet tour every single classroom, he wanted to provide some preliminary data on what he has found thus far. While reviewing the data, he shows several examples of boards that are organized as outlined in the goal.

In this example, the principal provides a disclaimer that he has not reviewed all classrooms yet to ensure that any teacher whose board is correct but not presented as an example would not feel left out. Hopefully, they will assume that their board was not yet reviewed. He then provides several examples of the performance he expects as pivot praise. Knowing that he will be reviewing the rest of the boards and not knowing which boards were already reviewed creates motivation for all teachers (except the ones who recognize that their boards were displayed as the models) to ensure their boards meet the standard.

Additional and varied positive feedback. Providing positive feedback to an employee in public can often result in additional instances of positive feedback for the performer's behavior from their peers. This feedback is also likely to be varied as some people will pat the performer on the back, others will offer vocal praise, and some will simply send a congratulatory text message. Additionally, the feedback will likely not all come at once because others who were not present or didn't get a chance to say something in the moment may provide positive feedback later in time. When a performer receives positive feedback from multiple sources, it helps extend the likeliness the behavior will not only continue but also happen in other environments and with other people.

Mason and Paul work at a credit card company and focus on getting Fortune 100 companies to adopt the credit card as their business card. The two men recently closed one of the biggest accounts for the credit card thus far. In the next staff meeting, their supervisor announces the closing of the deal and praises Mason and Paul for their hard work. Others in the meeting clap, some pat the men on the back, and others shake their hands. After the meeting, a few colleagues congratulated them. Later in the day and for the next week, other colleagues stop by Mason's and Paul's offices to provide a positive word. Some even asked for help with learning how to close such huge deals.

Problems

Loss of control over how others respond. Even positive public feedback can cause problems, and not all of those problems will be known to the leader. It is very difficult to predict how the rest of the team will respond to an individual employee being praised publicly, even when they are praised with the best intentions. We mentioned earlier that, when positive praise is given to one or two while there are three or more who have done the same, the others who are not recognized may feel their hard work is going unnoticed. At the very least, this will result in disgruntled and demotivated employees. At most, they will begin gossiping and making claims of favorites and unfair treatment. Additionally, those who are working hard but not getting the same results may also become disgruntled and begin gossiping or making negative statements about those receiving praise.

MISCONCEPTION

People often discuss the person's intent of their behavior and account for behavior based on why they think the behavior occurred. This is a tricky and problematic thing to do, as we often don't know why a behavior occurred. We tend to assume negative intent when things go wrong and positive intent when things go right. However, this is not always the case. It is better to focus on the consequences and environmental contexts surrounding the behavior rather than attempting to determine intent.

Aubri is a manager of a retail store. Lately, sales have been down, and there has been an initiative to increase sales. At the last staff meeting, Aubri recognized the team for the hard work they have been doing and pointed out four of the staff members whose efforts had paid off. During the meeting, others congratulated the four staff who were recognized; however, later in the breakroom, Aubri overheard two of the staff discussing how two of the recognized staff were *always* being recognized and that they were Aubri's favorites. The staff in the breakroom also added they might as well give up on trying to increase sales as their hard work would never be recognized.

Demoralizing the performer. Providing corrective feedback publicly can also be demoralizing to the performer. Many individuals have a difficult time accepting corrective feedback due to negative histories with being corrected. Providing it publicly can embarrass the performer in front of colleagues. As with positive public praise, public corrective feedback can also open the individual up to receive negative feedback from colleagues. No employee should be singled out as an underperformer; we all make mistakes from time to time.

There are two situations in which corrective feedback can be provided without negative effects. The first is when the corrective feedback is provided to the entire group without singling out any one individual. This can be done when there is an error that more than half of the group is making. You would provide corrective feedback to identify the error and correct it for everyone in the group. The second situation is when feedback is a natural part of the interaction. Group training is an excellent example of this. Here, the focus is learning and practicing new skills, and feedback is provided to improve skills, not as a corrective or punitive measure. Additionally, while corrective feedback may be given to each individual one at a time, all are receiving feedback on their performance. The trick to doing this well is to balance the corrective feedback with positive feedback and ensure that no one person receives a significantly more feedback (positive or corrective) than the others. Let's examine an example to see how this works.

At basketball practice, the coach is teaching the team a new defensive play. The coach instructs the team on the play and then asks them to run it. They begin. and the coach provides positive feedback to two of the players who ran it perfectly. He then makes small corrections with the other three players. They run the play a second time, and the coach provides positive feedback to the three who were just corrected. The players give each other high fives and congratulate one another on their quick learning.

Leaderboards are trouble. Leaderboards have become commonplace in many companies. So much that many software programs offer opportunities to display employee performance ranked against their peers. While a good thought, this type of intervention comes with all the same problems of public feedback, only worse. The thought behind leaderboards is that they create competition and motivate employees to perform better. While leaderboards do create competition, they do not result in the motivation they are thought to. The competition created is not healthy and instead creates a culture where only a few deserve to be recognized. This type of competition can lead to unethical behavior as the focus becomes making the leaderboard, rather than the actual performance of the individuals. Those who perform well but are not top performers are likely to be demotivated as they may feel that they will never reach the board. Additionally, low performers will likely stop performing altogether as their chances of receiving public recognition are even more slim. Remember that all can perform well, so positive feedback should not be limited to only the very top performers. The following example will illustrate this.

A life insurance company recently adopted a leaderboard system. It provides a running total of sales for each agent and displays the top five performers for each month. At the end of each month, these five performers are provided a bonus. There are 30 people on the team. The first month, three of the five top performers outperformed all team members by at least twice as many sales. Seeing this, the other 27 people on the team (yes, even the other two who initially reached the leaderboard) stopped trying as hard to make sales, feeling that they will never catch the leaders. Additionally, the top three performers relaxed a bit, thinking they would still make the leaderboard with half the effort (knowing how many more sales were made). The next month, sales were down across the board. And even though five new individuals made the leaderboard, sales continued to decrease each month.

Public Feedback for Groups

Posting group performance can also be a double-edged sword. Posting group performance increases reinforcement between members of the group and invites reinforcement from other teams, departments, and so on. However, this can create competition between departments or teams, resulting in an unwanted **intra**-company rivalry where you really want an **inter**-company rivalry with your external competitors.

The lesson? Create as little competition between individuals and groups as possible. The key to high performance is not competition; rather, the key is providing positive feedback for continually increasing performance.

Let's recap the decisions involved in whether to provide public or private feedback by reviewing the decision tree below.

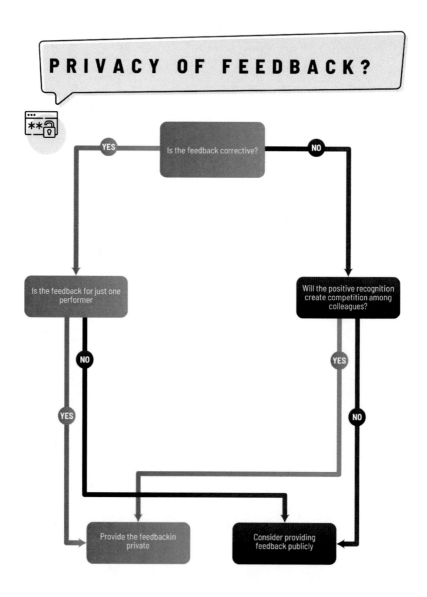

Our formula now includes consideration of privacy when delivering feedback. Let's look at it.

EFFECTIVE PERFORMANCE FEEDBACK =
(The Behavior/Action/Outcome) + *(The Person)* + *(The Number of People)* + *(The Type of Feedback)* + *(The Temporal Location)* + *(The Medium)* + **(Privacy)** + *(x)*

Now that we know when feedback should be private and when it is okay to provide feedback publicly, let's examine the next decision regarding where to provide feedback: the formality of the environment. After that we'll investigate the final component of the "where" question by discussing the physical aspects of the environment that should be considered.

Casual vs. Formal

Casual wear refers to the clothes we wear every day and feel the most relaxed in. This style focuses on comfort, recreation, and informality. Casual wear is designed more for function than aesthetics, and it can include a variety of different pieces and styles. *Formal wear* refers to clothing more appropriate for formal events, such as weddings, balls, and formal dinners, among other events. Formal attire is designed for aesthetics rather than function. Somewhere between the two is *business casual*, where the attire is somewhat formal but still comfortable. It is the best example of clothing that fits both aesthetics and function.

Yes, we know: This book is about performance feedback, not clothing. However, the point we're making is that providing feedback can be done in a casual environment as well as a formal environment, depending on your goal—just like deciding on the outfit you are going to wear. Having said that and continuing with the analogy, consider choosing the environment to be similar to choosing the clothing you will wear each day. The choice should fit the setting. In general, just like with clothing, we recommend a somewhat formal environment when providing feedback (you don't want to get too casual and look like you wore your favorite sweatpants with the hole in the leg to work). In general, more casual environments create a friendly and inviting atmosphere. Meanwhile, more formal environments can create anxiety and put employees on defense.

Before we examine what situations call for more formal settings, let's discuss what makes the setting formal. In general, the more you have to plan, schedule, and prepare for something, the more formal it is. Here are some other considerations that can make a setting more or less formal:

- **Medium.** We discussed the different mediums that could be used when providing feedback. Here, we want to note that, in addition to the considerations already mentioned, certain mediums are more formal than others. Face-to-face meetings are more formal than emails, for instance; however, providing a quick statement of praise while observing an employee on the floor can be just as informal as a text message.

- **The office.** No, not the TV show. Your actual office is what we're referring to. Meeting in your office can reinforce hierarchal roles, which increases the formality. There are situations where this is appropriate. However, we all know what it feels like to be called into that scary office of Greg Hayden, so keep this in mind when scheduling formal office meetings. When the conversation needs to reinforce the hierarchical relationship between you and the performer, schedule an office meeting. However, if that isn't necessary and you have other locations at which to meet, try to avoid the office meetings when possible.

- **Language.** The language used can create a more or less formal situation. While certain language and terms are rarely used in a work setting, consider the type of language used when providing feedback. Use more formal language when you need to create a more formal setting. However, if formality is not necessary, it's better to use some language that's more informal (but still business appropriate).

- **Seating.** The most formal situation is created when you call an employee to your office and sit across from them with your desk between the two of you. There is nothing more formal than this. This seating also reinforces the hierarchical structure. While meeting in the office is still more formal than meeting elsewhere, you can create a more casual environment in the office by sitting next to your employee or sitting at a table together. If your goal is to create a casual environment, join your employee on the other side of your desk.

Now that we know what to consider when creating a more or less formal environment, let's discuss when the environment should be formal versus casual. In general, we recommend a business casual environment. Here's why:

- **Casual environments are more about dialogue than meetings.** The best feedback (as we will discuss soon) is provided as a dialogue. Dialogue opens discussions, encourages honesty, and increases the chances your feedback will be incorporated into later performance. It also creates an environment where feedback can be provided continually rather than having to wait for just the right moment or a formal meeting to be scheduled.

- **Casual environments create openness for employees to respond.** Feedback goes both ways, but as we have mentioned, at least at first, most employees find it difficult to provide their supervisor with feedback—especially the corrective kind. A more relaxed feedback session creates openness and allows the opportunity for you to request honest feedback from your employee.

- **Casual environments grow the relationship.** The best way to show you care for someone is to remember something important to them or to provide specific details about their performance. Casual feedback creates a conversation, which both allows for you to provide specific details and creates an opportunity for small talk to learn about what's important to your employee. Beginning feedback sessions with chatter regarding important happenings in your employee's life both grows the relationship and sets the stage for a successful feedback session. It shows you care, and any correction provided is more likely to be interpreted as care for them and their performance rather than picking on them.

- **Casual environments are easier.** If you have to wait for a formal environment, you may have to wait a long time. We are all always strapped for time. That's why we all dread those ridiculous annual evaluations. They take up a lot of time—time that we don't have. However, when we master providing casual feedback—through a variety of different mediums—we decrease both the time it takes and the difficulty of providing the feedback.

The business casual approach to providing feedback keeps in mind that feedback is still a semi-formal thing. There are still rules to follow. You can't just let loose like you do with your friends. However, this approach reminds us that it's okay to have fun, be relaxed, and create an inviting setting. We recommend using a business casual approach in most situations. There are a few instances in which formal feedback should be provided, however. Here are three such instances:

- **Regulatory, legal, safety, or compliance purposes.** There are times that corrective feedback needs to be provided regarding more serious matters. In these situations, errors in performance could result in larger problems for the organization and/or the employee. In worst-case scenarios, errors could result in injuries or lawsuits. For these matters, formal feedback should be provided to ensure the message is taken as seriously as possible.
- **Corrective action.** Any time corrective action is taken, formal feedback should be provided. In these situations, follow the company's policies, which usually includes some form of documentation. Because corrective action is a formal procedure, our recommendation is to match the feedback to that context and keep it formal.
- **Performance reviews.** We did say to throw away annual performance reviews. However, that does not mean to throw out *all* performance reviews. The purpose of this book is not to provide details regarding these reviews; however, if following best practices, performance reviews should be provided monthly or quarterly. Performance reviews are formal and often tied to bonuses or other reinforcement systems. As a result, this creates a more formal setting.

In summary, the general rule of thumb is to provide feedback with a business casual formality unless the situation calls for a more formal setting. Use the following flowchart to help you decide.

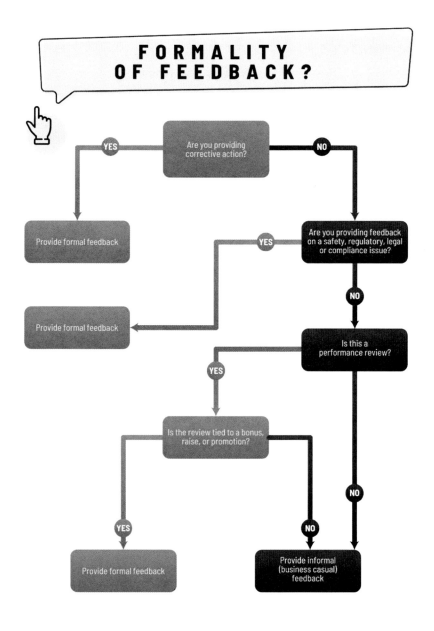

Let's update our formula:

EFFECTIVE PERFORMANCE FEEDBACK =
*(The Behavior/Action/Outcome) + (The Person) + (The Number
of People) + (The Type of Feedback) + (The Temporal Location) +
(The Medium) + (Privacy) + **(Formality)** + (x)*

We have thoroughly discussed privacy and formality. It is now time to discuss the third element of the "where" – the physical environment.

The Physical Environment

The physical environment is an area comprising objects and other stimuli that can affect someone's performance in any way. The physical environment can range in scale—from microscopic to global—and just about anything can be a part of the physical environment. Here, we separate out and talk about the physical environment as its own category to consider. Why? We have found that it is an often-overlooked part of the equation. We often do not give enough credit to the power of the environment. Yet the physical environment in which someone delivers feedback can help or hurt their efforts. Accordingly, special care should be taken when considering where you will deliver feedback.

In behavior analysis, we know that the environment is responsible for shaping and maintaining behavior. Extending this knowledge to the workforce, we know that the environment is largely responsible for why people perform (or don't perform). We tend to give the credit to many other factors, including internal motivation, training, employee mindset, and so on. While all of these do play a factor in whether an employee performs well, the most important variable is the environment—or really, the relationship between the individual's performance and the environment.

What do we mean by that, you ask? Great question! Consider this: You are in a workshop focused on feedback. This is something that you have been looking forward to for a long time, so you are excited to see what the presenter has to say on the topic. The morning starts off amazing! The room is well set up in a U-shape to encourage discussion and interaction between participants. The speaker is inviting, funny, and engaging. And the activities are crafted so that they allow humor to be used as part of the learning. Over lunch you discuss how awesome the workshop is with several other attendees. When you return from lunch, it's like entering a completely different world. It feels as though someone has turned the heat up. The room is so warm that you almost immediately remove your blazer. The lights have also been dimmed, so you find it hard to see the pages where you took notes. While walking to your seat, you also notice that the tables have been rearranged. They are now set up classroom style and separated, only allowing two people to sit at each table. You wonder what happened and why such drastic changes have occurred. As the afternoon drags on, you look at your watch several times. It seems that the day will never end. You find yourself doodling to keep from falling asleep. By the end of the day, you're so glad that the workshop is over that you've forgotten about how great the morning was. You are now thinking you should have gotten your money back.

While we would ensure this never happens during one of our workshops, hopefully this example helps illustrate how the physical environment can affect behavior. Warm rooms have been shown to decrease interactions. The arrangement of tables can increase or decrease discussion and participation. Being full makes it more likely you will fall asleep. And on and on the list goes with all the variables in the physical environment that can affect the outcomes of performance.

The other thing that happens is that the environment gets paired with the results of the interaction. Think about a time that something awesome happened. Maybe it was a proposal or birth of a child, the day you graduated, anything! If you close your eyes, can you remember what it felt like to be in that moment? Most of us can remember the sounds, what we saw, where we were, and the smells when we think of our greatest moments in life. And for most of us, if something associated with that memory comes into our environment—a song on the radio, someone wearing the same scent, returning to the same location—we are taken right back to that moment in time. This happens because the stimuli in the environment get paired with the event. And any time we come into contact with the stimuli paired with the past event, we are taken back to that moment. The same is true for our worst moments.

While the pairing is often not as strong for less emotional moments, it can become just as strong with repeated exposure. One bad interaction in your office usually does not make your office a negative place for your employees. However, repeated negative interactions in your office might.

Similarly, the negative aspects of the environment can affect the outcome of your interaction. The outcome of a difficult conversation taking place in a dark alley where someone was robbed last week will likely be very different than that same difficult conversation taking place in your living room under soft lighting while sitting next to one another on the couch.

All of the above emphasizes that, if you consistently meet with an employee in a dirty, dark, noisy, foul-smelling environment, there's a good chance they will associate your feedback with the other aversive stimuli in the room, effectively making your feedback aversive. Once this happens, it is extremely hard to reverse.

Moral of the story? If you haven't thought about it before, start thinking about the environment and the effect it might have on your delivery and the reception of feedback. Here are some of the most important aspects to consider:

1. **Natural lighting.** Darkness is especially aversive to workers, especially during a meeting, and artificial lighting can cause headaches for many people. Several studies have shown that natural light improves performance and positively impacts other biological processes, such as the circadian rhythm (sleep cycle), hormone release, and body temperature, among other important factors. Thus, choose a location that provides plenty of natural lighting. If such a location isn't available, choose a location that has soft lighting. Avoid fluorescent lights as much as possible. If you work in an environment that only has fluorescent lights, consider investing in a lamp or two. You might be surprised at the huge difference it can make.

2. **Objects (i.e., distractions).** Too many or too few objects between you and the person accepting the feedback can impact the success of the feedback session. Entering an office with a messy desk, books and papers piled on the floor, and coats in the chairs makes it more difficult to receive feedback (both positive and corrective). However, a completely sterile environment can do the same (think about those houses that are so clean you can't touch anything). Find a balance of having some objects in the environment to make it inviting, but not so many that people have to step over, move, or sort through objects to sit down and focus. We have also found that

making available small objects that individuals can "fidget" with (such as fidget spinners, putty, and so on) creates a more inviting environment and provides nervous employees something to do with their hands, removing the focus from all the "stop looking nervous" thoughts and placing it on your feedback.

3. **Proximity.** Consider the proximity of you to your employee and the proximity of objects in the room to your employee. In general, the more objects between you and your employee (desk, keyboard, monitor, papers, phone, etc.), the more formal and less inviting the environment. Even for formal, across-the-desk meetings, it is better to move everything else out of the way so that there's a clear path between you and your employee. Additionally, if sitting next to the performer to create a more casual environment, keep in mind that everyone has different "bubbles of personal space." A great way to help create an environment where the performer is seated at a comfortable distance from you is to already be seated prior to the performer entering the environment. Then ask the performer to take a seat by bringing their chair over to you. This allows the performer to place the chair at a distance that is comfortable to them without creating any awkwardness.

4. **Open doors.** Open doors are inviting. Closed doors are not. Why do we know this? When we leave our doors open, people walk right in. A great way to cut down on interruptions is to close the door. Unfortunately, the same is true when giving feedback. A big part of effectively delivering feedback is creating a safe and comfortable environment for the person accepting the feedback. Doors can be tricky as they sometimes need to be closed for privacy. In these circumstances, ensure the performer is seated between you and the door so that you're not creating a situation where it feels like the jail door is shutting and you're the warden sitting between your performer and freedom. If the feedback does not require complete privacy, leave the door open (at least a crack). This is not customary in the workplace; however, open doors send the signal that the performer is not in trouble and that they can leave at any time.

5. **Room temperature.** No one likes to shiver during a meeting. Plus, heat literally can bring out the worst in people, so make sure to consider the temperature of your office. If your employee is freezing,

they will spend most of their time rubbing their arms, shaking, or drawing their folded arms into their body. Conversely, if they are hot, they will be more focused on how much they are sweating in front of their boss, and their body heat could be amplified by nerves. Given that our ability to focus on things is limited, if the individual is focused on how uncomfortable they are, it leaves little capacity to focus on the message you're delivering. It has been found that a slightly cool environment is best. Given that all have slightly different interpretations of what "slightly cool" means and are comfortable at different temperatures, try setting the thermostat to a degree or two below room temperature. If you are not able to control the temperature, invest in a small, quiet fan. This not only allows you to cool the office when needed, but provides some air circulation, which you will see is our next item.

6. **Air quality.** Temperature is not the only factor related to air. The quality of the air is important, too. This includes the way the air smells, the stuffiness or dust in the air, and the circulation of the air. While most of us cannot control the overall air quality (the weather and ozone have more to do with that), there are things we can do to create the best possible air quality in our environment. Small things like emptying your trash cans, clearing all food from the area, and ensuring there are not overpowering air fresheners are easy to do. Larger things, such as investing in a small fan or air purifier, are also helpful. Finally, we almost hate to say this, but consider your own scent as well. There is nothing worse for a nonsmoker than coming into contact with someone who just finished a cigarette. Similarly, the scent of strong cologne can be just as overpowering. The last thing you want to do is create a headache for the person receiving feedback. In general, we recommend trying to maintain a soft, clean scent in the office and circulating air when possible.

7. **Sound.** Yes, even sound can be distracting or create an aversive environment. Ever enter a noisy restaurant and try to have an intimate conversation? Doesn't work too well, does it? Receiving feedback in a noisy environment can be equally distracting and make communication messy. Not only will parts not be heard, but eventually one of the two of you will get tired of saying things like "What?," "Excuse me?," "Can you repeat that?," and so on.

Eventually whomever is asking will stop asking, not because they can finally hear, but because it's exhausting and frustrating to not know what the other person is saying. One of you will give up and start looking for an escape. Plus, the whole point of performance feedback is communicating how the performer can improve their performance; if they can't hear your feedback, you might as well just send them an email. On the other end of the spectrum, a completely silent environment can be unnerving. The quiet is important, but so is having some type of pleasant ambient noise. Consider playing soft music in the background (think of the music you might hear at a spa) or a white noise machine. Others prefer introducing pleasant natural sounds, which can be done by opening a window, taking a walk, or sitting outside on a bench. The sounds of nature can be very calming (given they're not drowned by construction, police sirens, and traffic), allowing both parties to focus on the content of the feedback.

8. **Organization (i.e., more distractions).** Messy offices are typically aversive and synonymous with a-lot-of-stuff-to-do scenarios. This can make a simple feedback session feel like an external audit or like an internal inspection is forthcoming. Organizing your office and cleaning up your desk (even if not meeting at it) can send the message that things are under control. Disorganization, on the other hand, sends the message that you have so much to do that you don't even have time to figure out where everything should be placed. While this may be true, it is less likely that feedback of any kind will be well received when your staff think you can't handle the workload yourself. Organization is also paired with productivity (or the impression of productivity). In general, we tend to think that those who are organized are more productive and more successful than those who are not. The more productive and successful you are, the more credible you become. And the more credible you are, the more likely it is that your feedback will be incorporated into performance. Finally, messy and disorganized environments can create safety issues. The last thing you want to happen is that someone twists their ankle, sits on a pin, or gets a mouthful of dust that sends them into an asthma attack while you're giving feedback.

9. **Choices.** The power of choice is not often discussed in business settings. However, as behavior analysts, choices are used all the time. Choices are powerful, and offering choices can have very positive results. Here, we recommend providing the performer the choice of where to meet. We will repeat this concept until we run out of space in this book: **comfort and safety matter when deciding where to provide feedback**. The easiest way to provide a comfortable space for the session is to allow the performer to choose it. You can provide an open-ended choice (e.g., "Where would you like to meet?"), a forced choice (e.g., "Would you like to meet in your office or mine?"), or even a yes/no choice (e.g., "Would you like to do a walking meeting today?"). These choices allow the performer to decide on the environment that makes them feel most at ease.

10. **Prior history.** Picture this: You have worked under your current supervisor for the past year. You still remember the first day when you were excited about the change in leadership and that you were identified as the person who would serve as the "right hand" to the new leader. Your excitement changed quickly, however, when you were called into the office and given a long list of tasks. The excitement changed to fear on the second day when you were yelled at for not completing the never-ending list of what seemed to be tedious and meaningless tasks. Day in and day out for the past 365 days, you have been called to the office and provided negative feedback for trivial things. You can't remember the last time you were told you did something right. The result? Every single interaction you've had in that manager's office can be defined by a bombardment of negative feedback and nothing else. What kind of effect do you think the simple sight of that manager's office has on you, let alone actually being in it?

Thus, history with the environment and the person are important. Even if you're new, if the previous manager (whose office you now have) had a long history of yelling at people or being negative, you might want to avoid providing corrective feedback in your office for a while. Instead, focus on calling people to your office to discuss the positives to unpair the aversiveness that has likely occurred. Choose a neutral location, such as a breakroom or conference room, to provide the corrective feedback.

There is a lot to consider when thinking about the physical environment, and it can be overwhelming, especially when considering all of the other components of feedback. Fortunately, we created the following checklist to help you out.

PHYSICAL ENVIRONMENT FOR FEEDBACK

QUESTION	YES	NO	IF YES, THEN	IF NO, THEN
1 — **Did you ask** the performer **where they want to meet?**	○	○	You came out of the gates rocking it! Now, let's check the chosen environment to make sure it's ready	This is a great place to start. Decide what kind of choice you want to provide and ask the performer where they want to meet.
2 — Is the chosen **location associated with** positive or neutral things?	○	○	Very good. You can keep this location and keep moving forward.	This is surprising, considering the performer chose the location (unless you skipped step 1...in that case, return there and start over). You can consider a different location or go with it. Since the performer chose it, maybe it's not as negative as you thought.
3 — Is there a lot of **natural lighting?**	○	○	Great work! Move to question 4.	Find a location that has natural lighting or lamps. Avoid fluorescent lights.
4 — Have you **removed distrobjects?**	○	○	Nice! You're ready for question 5.	Remove papers, books, folders, etc. from your desk (even if not meeting there). Turn off your computer monitor. Put your phone in your desk.
5 — Do you have **seating that is not across** the desk from one another?	○	○	Awesome! Use that seating. Move to the next question.	Either consider another location, talking a walk to provide feedback or moving your chair to the same side of the desk as the performer's chair.
6 — Can you leave the **door open?**	○	○	Check! Keep moving ahead!	Make sure that the performer is seated between you and the door.
7 — Is the **temperature comfortable?**	○	○	Excellent. That is probably nice for you as well!	If you can change the thermostat, do it now. If not, find a fan or space heater (depending on what direction the temperature needs to go). If all else fails, find a different location.
8 — Is the **air quality good** (meaning free from smells, dust and stuffiness)?	○	○	You are moving right along! You're almost ready - just a few more.	Consider a clean scent plug in (turned to a low setting), a small fan, and/or air purifier
9 — Is it **pleasantly quiet?**	○	○	Wow! Look at you perfecting the environment! Please proceed.	Try turning on soft music in the background or investing in a white noise machine.
10 — Is the **environment organized?**	○	○	Super. This saves you a lot of time. Job well done at staying organized! Your environment is thoroughly prepared for an effective feedback session.	If you can't quickly organize (even if it means throwing all those papers stacked on your desk in a drawer), consider another, more organized location.

And finally, to close out the chapter, here is our updated formula:

EFFECTIVE PERFORMANCE FEEDBACK =
(The Behavior/Action/Outcome) + (The Person) + (The Number of People) + (The Type of Feedback) + (The Temporal Location) + (The Medium) + (Privacy) + (Formality) + **(Physical Environment)** *+ (x)*

Thus far, we have discussed nine of the 11 components of effective performance feedback. If you have made it this far, you are dedicated to providing the most effective performance feedback possible! We would like to commend you on both your dedication to your workforce and development as a leader, and for the distance you have traveled on this journey. The final two components include the frequency of feedback and the content of feedback. We saved these for last as they are the two most important characteristics. In fact, they're so important that you could likely fail at several of the first nine components, but get these two correct and still have a positive outcome. And yes, we purposely saved them for last as, if we told you this up front, you would have just skipped to the next section without reading the rest. We told you: We know behavior.

7

SCHEDULING FEEDBACK

"Take care of the minutes and the hours will take care of themselves."

~Earl of Chesterfield

The Frequency Conundrum

We just mentioned how far you've come in your feedback journey and how you have learned a lot about the useful tool of feedback! We saved this component—scheduling feedback—as one of the last as it truly is one of the most important characteristics of feedback. You've already shown your dedication to leadership and improving your employees' performance; you've come this far, after all. Your reading this book and working through each step of effective performance feedback shows that you want to do all you can to improve their performance. And because you have come this far, we're ready to tell you one of the best kept secrets of all time! Ready? Excited? We know—we can't wait, either!

One of the most effective ways to increase and maintain performance is to provide feedback frequently.

Disappointed? What, you thought that we were going to tell you something that wasn't so obvious? Sorry, not sorry. The truth is, many of us know that providing frequent feedback is important. Most of us have overcome the old thinking that people should just do what they are supposed to do because they want to do what's right and never need to be told they are on the right track. However, there's a glaring problem: It turns out that leaders everywhere have *many more* responsibilities *besides* providing feedback. The more employees and responsibilities leaders have, the more difficult it is to provide feedback frequently and consistently, resulting in the minimal improvement of employee performance.

Well, that stinks. Here we are teaching you about a tool that seemed so easy (and essential) to use, but one that grows exponentially more difficult to practice over time. I guess that ends our feedback coverage…

But wait! What if we could find a solution to this conundrum? Hear us out. It's time to pull some more science out because, next up, we'll be exploring the concept of finding the right times and the right balance to how often feedback should be provided.

Your Regularly Scheduled Programming

KNOW OUR JARGON

Target behavior(s): the behavior(s) that have been chosen for increase, continuation, or decrease. Target behaviors are the behaviors we are trying to change in some way.

By now, you may have gotten the impression that, to be an effective leader, you should be handing out large amounts of positive feedback to your employees. However, think about what that would look like. Let's say that you've honed in on one target behavior with an employee, Louis. We'll say you're targeting her timely submissions of a daily report. Each time Louis submits her daily report on time, you immediately send her a descriptive "thank you" email. Assuming that your email functions as a reinforcer (meaning it increases her performance in the future), Louis's timely submissions are more likely to occur in the future.

BEHAVIOR

CONSEQUENCE

Louis submits her daily report **ontime**

You send Louis a **"thank you"** email

RESULT: Louis is more likely to submit her daily reports on time.

At first, this may be beneficial, especially to ensure that this behavior keeps happening in the future. No problem, right? What happens over time, though, when the "thank you" messages start to pile up? *Feedback f!@#up!*

That's *a lot* of "thank you" notes. Have you ever heard a boss say "great work" so many times that it got old? There are times when the feedback occurs so often that it comes across as meaningless, feeling more like a habit as opposed to a well-thought-out message. This phenomenon is likely to happen in this situation. The emails probably initially had an effect on Louis's behavior, but she might just ignore the emails after a while. In fact, Louis might start to find them annoying. Over time, your frequent feedback, no matter how positive and behaviorally specific, starts to lose value and also results in you wasting your own time that could be spent on other activities.

I'm sure you're thinking, "Wait, you first told me to provide feedback all the time. Now you're telling me that providing all the time can get old. What in the hell am I supposed to do?!?!?!" Don't worry: Just stick with us, and we'll explain it all. The simple answer is that, for new behaviors or behaviors that have recently been corrected, feedback should be provided as often as possible. However, for those behaviors that are well established and happening consistently, feedback should be provided less often. In other words, you're changing the frequency at which you provide feedback based on the need.

The frequency at which to provide feedback can be thought of on a continuum with no feedback on one end and feedback every time the behavior happens on the other. We call this the Feedback Frequency Continuum, and it's illustrated below.

Now let's think about each of these frequencies and their impact on employee performance. Think about the boss who *never* gives feedback. Unfortunately, most of us have had a boss like this and know how frustrating it can be. You show up at work day in and day out and assume that you are doing well enough because no one is saying anything to you. The only time you know you're valued and doing things well are when you happen to come into contact with an outside source; maybe you closed a sale or finished all tasks early for the day, or received a positive comment from a colleague.

The problem with this *feedback f!@#up* is twofold.

First, there's nothing in place to increase or maintain the behaviors that are important for high performance. Second, reinforcement is left up to the environment, which means the wrong things could be reinforced. Think about Jacques, the employee who spends the entire day goofing off in the breakroom. Chances are, Jacques did not start off spending all his time in the breakroom. Rather, this behavior was likely shaped slowly over time due to a lack of feedback from his supervisor and positive feedback from his colleagues every time he visited the water cooler. When there is a lack of feedback for the right behaviors, people rely on the environment to get feedback elsewhere, and chances are, that feedback will be for the wrong behaviors.

On the other end of the continuum is constant feedback. Here, feedback is provided each and every time the skill is demonstrated. This is useful when establishing new skills or when a skill has recently been corrected. However, as we illustrated earlier, when used too often, feedback loses its effect on behavior.

Finally, in the middle, we have the large area of everything between never and always, or the "sometimes" region. Determining how often to provide feedback is an often-overlooked component of feedback and one of the reasons that feedback often fails. Finding the right balance can be difficult if you don't know the rules, so below are some guidelines to help you navigate these challenging waters.

<u>Teaching New Skills—Provide Feedback Always or Frequently</u>

We've all been there before: the dreaded day one of a new job. Unless you were fortunate enough to step into a job where you naturally excelled from the get-go, odds are, you probably struggled like the rest of us. If you worked in an industry where you dealt directly with customers, the first customer with a complicated request probably triggered a cold sweat and a stutter. A similar feeling would haunt a teacher or professor stepping in front of their students for their first time, or a police officer pulling over a car on their first patrol. The point is, day one can be daunting for the simple reason that you're in a new situation and have yet to receive any feedback regarding your performance or preparedness to perform.

This situation is when frequent feedback is needed the most. Whether it's during training, once training is complete, or when a new employee is first demonstrating newly learned skills, frequent feedback is necessary to increase these behaviors and ensure they become well established. Frequent feedback not only reassures the employee that they are doing things right but also ensures anything done incorrectly will be corrected immediately.

Maintaining Existing Skills—Provide Feedback Sometimes

Now think back to how you felt after the first 6 months on the job. Everything seemed easier, didn't it? By this point, the employee will have settled into the position and, if given the right feedback up front, will be performing at high levels. Now feedback is not needed as often. You can start to scale back your feedback to every other time or every third time, and continue to decrease your frequency as long as employee performance remains high.

You may be thinking, "How do I know when to start scaling back, and how quickly can I scale back? More importantly, how can I keep track of all of this?" Don't fret: While there is no set rule that tells you when to start scaling back and how quickly to decrease the frequency, you can figure this out based on the employee's performance. The general rule here is that, if you start to see performance decrease, you probably faded too quickly. No worries. Just increase the amount of feedback you are providing, and you should see performance increase again.

Long-Term Performance—Provide Near Zero, but Never Zero Feedback

When an employee has mastered a task and achieved fluency, it is easy for a leader to simply stop providing feedback for that behavior. For example, an expert salesperson is unlikely to need much feedback for their sales behavior that has presumably seen much success thus far. However, not needing *much* feedback is not the same as *no* feedback. As employees become comfortable in their roles, leaders should continue to monitor even their expert employees' performance to ensure that variables like quality and safety are maintained over time. Additionally, you want to be sure that your top-performing employees don't get left by the wayside. They deserve feedback just as much as your new and struggling employees, so continue to provide feedback for their jobs well done, too.

Different Behaviors, Different Frequencies

Now that we have discussed how often to provide feedback in relation the newness or fluency of a skill, you may be thinking that not all employees reach the same level of performance across all facets of their jobs at the same time. And you're right! Most employees don't master all skills at the same time or reach the same levels of proficiency in everything. We all have different strengths. You may have a chef who can masterfully cook all items on the menu, but takes too long to chop the ingredients. Or you may have employees who perform well when everything goes as planned, but decrease in performance when faced with different challenges, such as malfunctioning equipment, staff callouts, a sudden rush of customers, or an overhaul of the menu. Even the most skilled programmers are bound to run into new obstacles, bugs in the software, or maybe a desire to learn new skills to expand their repertoires. Or another scenario may be that a longstanding employee one day decides they'd like to go into management themselves, creating a whole barrage of leadership skills to learn before they are ready to take on those responsibilities. No matter the situation, more often than not, employees' skills on different tasks will vary from one employee to the next.

In these situations, the leader should focus on providing more frequent feedback on the skills that are still emerging, new, or more difficult while fading the feedback provided for the more advanced or well-established skills.

We know that trying to decide how often to provide feedback for all of the different behaviors that people do each and every day at work can be a little overwhelming. Not only are we asking you to be aware of the learning continuum of each and every important work behavior, we are asking you to provide feedback at different frequencies for each as well.

When you have one employee, this might not be so overwhelming, but when you have 1,000, the story is a little different. Here are some additional tips that will help put it in perspective.

Act Naturally

When you think about it, the frequency to provide feedback is pretty natural. Think about a child learning to talk. When that child says their first word, everyone goes crazy. It's a party. That party continues every time the child says something new and continues until the child begins talking frequently. Then, the child receives less feedback for the words they are saying all the time, but there's still a party any time a new word is learned. Employee skills are similar. When employees are learning new skills, more frequent feedback should be provided. However, once those skills are learned, feedback is faded for that skill.

Leaders can fade feedback either by providing the feedback less often for the behaviors that are well established or by refocusing feedback delivery on more complex behaviors. Let's examine what this might look like by using two examples:

- **Example 1:** Rochelle has just started a new position as an administrative assistant. She is fluent with the software used in the office and proficient in dictation. However, one of her responsibilities is talking with outside vendors to ensure orders are placed correctly. Rochelle does not have much experience in this. Initially, Rochelle's supervisor, Jeffrey, provides Rochelle with feedback about her performance and daily follow-up with vendors. Jeffrey notices that Rochelle's skills are developing, and he has provided only positive feedback for the past week. The next week he provides feedback only on Monday, Wednesday, and Friday, and Rochelle's performance continues. He fades his feedback again the next week and again the following week as Rochelle continues to maintain her performance.
- **Example 2:** Timothy, another new employee, has just been hired as a safety manager. He is responsible for ensuring his teams follow the complex safety protocols and that new staff are trained in how to maintain safety while working. Martina, Timothy's supervisor,

understands the complexity of the position and the many tasks that Timothy will have to master. Initially, Martina provides feedback on each step that Timothy completes correctly. Once Timothy has mastered each individual component of his complex tasks, Martina begins to pair them together and provides feedback after he has completed the more complex task.

In both of these situations, the supervisors decreased their feedback as their employees' performance increased. However, Jeffrey simply

KNOW OUR JARGON

In behavior analysis, we refer to this as "reinforcer potency", which indicates how effective the reinforcer is in that moment. Reinforcer effectiveness can increase and decrease depending on the difficulty of the task, how recently it was contacted prior to the current delivery, or how easy it is to contact the reinforcer outside of the current context. For example, if you skipped breakfast this morning and it is now one hour before lunch and your supervisor walks by and says "lunch on me if you finish that report before lunch", chances are you are going to work really hard to get that report finished. Why? First, chances are your supervisor does not offer to buy you lunch very often, making this a unique opportunity. Second, you have not eaten today, which likely means you are hungry. Time without food makes food more reinforcing. If you eaten a large breakfast and another snack five minutes before your supervisor offered to buy lunch, you would be less likely to work as hard to finish the report. Food is not as potent of a reinforcer when you are not hungry.

decreased the frequency in which feedback was provided, while Martina increased the amount of work that had to be completed, or the complexity of the skill.

Another thing that leaders can do to help maintain employee performance while fading feedback is to tell the employee that feedback will be faded once they demonstrate proficiency. Being transparent with staff can help temper any expectations that the level of feedback will remain the same. Such transparency can also serve as an additional reinforcer as the employee now knows less feedback equals better performance. Be careful with this, however, as you don't want it to backfire and for your feedback to become a negative as your employees are wondering why you haven't faded yet.

Variation to Maintain Potency

There is another continuum that is important to consider, called the *Effectiveness Continuum*. The Effectiveness Continuum relates to how often someone contacts a specific item or stimulus and how effective it will be as a reinforcer. Items that we have not contacted recently are more likely to increase and maintain our behavior. However, those items that we have all the time or that we have had large amounts of recently are less likely to affect our behavior. This is important when considering feedback or, more specifically, the type of feedback we provide. Leaders vary the type of feedback they provide to ensure that their feedback remains highly effective. The following are examples of how to vary feedback to ensure it remains potently effective:

1. **Vary praise statements**. Instead of using "Great job!" all the time, be specific about what you are praising and change your words often. Here are some examples of varied feedback:

    - "I was really impressed with how you thanked the customer and walked them out the door. Well done."
    - "Your performance in putting together sales and productivity reports has been outstanding lately, especially the formatting and grammar of the documents."
    - "You did amazing work on the software development project. A lot of employees have talked about how much its implementation has made their jobs easier."

2. **Provide feedback using different mediums.** Yes, we know we spent an entire chapter discussing different mediums for feedback. We bring them up again here to remind you that you can use a variety of different mediums to increase both the ease of providing feedback and its effectiveness. Variation is not just for the words used when providing feedback. Leaders can introduce variation in the medium in which feedback is provided as well. An email may be sent one day, while in-person feedback could be provided the next. There are several different modalities that can be used, but here are some of the most common:

    a. **Email:** Provide a quick email regarding the skill that was demonstrated. Emails allow for feedback to be private and can sometimes build the bridge between more immediate feedback and a longer delay when you can't talk with the person directly in private.

    b. **In person, formal:** Formal, in-person feedback is always the preferred method; however, we know that this is impossible to do all the time. Yet leaders should be sure to periodically call employees into their office to provide more formal feedback. This approach not only ensures that feedback is something positive but also sends the message that employees are highly valued.

    c. **In person, informal:** Feedback can be provided informally as you are passing an employee in the hallway. A brief statement like, "Excellent presentation yesterday; you were really well spoken and communicated the points effectively," or, "Got your email; thanks for the information—it was really helpful," are easy to provide and don't require extra time or planning. Make it a point to walk through the office a few times a day to provide feedback to your employees. This not only increases their behavior but also makes your presence more preferred. If you haven't done this yet, don't get discouraged if your employees run the other way at first. It takes a bit of time for your employees to learn that you are not making rounds to see what's going wrong if that used to be your pattern. Remember Greg Hayden and his dark office? He had to walk around the office for months before people stopped running!

d. **Text or instant message:** Most offices now have some sort of instant-message chatting software where everyone can send a quick note to one person or a group of individuals. These messages are used often to get questions answered quickly or exchange information between meetings. Sending a quick "thanks for that response" or "appreciate your thorough answer" is another great way to provide feedback. Just make sure you always spell check before you hit "send". There is nothing more embarrassing that to review the text you just sent to find out you sent "please be *intimate* tomorrow" instead of "please be *on time* tomorrow".

High-Frequency Feedback

Providing effective feedback has one critical component—frequency. When it comes to employee engagement, the more feedback, the better. That means meeting with employees at least 2–3 times per week, if not daily, to better understand their unique challenges, the tasks they avoid, and their important reinforcers. We refer to this as *high-frequency feedback*.

Receiving high-frequency feedback can work well as a reinforcer, especially for 21st-century employees who are used to receiving immediate reinforcement through digital and societal mediums. High-frequency feedback has MANY benefits and should be implemented regularly with team members. Below you will find a long list of benefits from providing high-frequency feedback:

1. High-frequency feedback increases a leader's opportunities to provide positive reinforcement in the form of praise and acknowledgement for work well done. It also provides learning opportunities to correct areas in which the employee needs improvement.

2. By receiving high-frequency feedback, employees receive an immediate explanation of the desired behavior and expected outcomes—details that can then be utilized to create their own performance intervention plan.

3. High-frequency feedback allows managers to hone their skills through the multiple sessions in which they provide feedback.

4. High-frequency feedback eases the manager's preparation for formal performance reviews (if you have them) as the manager has completed most of the work and simply needs to collate the information rather than recall it.

5. Feedback interactions between employees and managers are critical in establishing instructional control between the manager and the employee's behavior, which can ultimately improve engagement among the parties.

6. High-frequency feedback helps build a culture of trust by shaping and maintaining an open forum of communication. Such a forum reinforces the verbal behavior of employees and encourages the discussion of issues and successes in a safe environment.

7. High-frequency feedback models and reinforces coaching behavior throughout the organization.

8. Continuous performance measurement helps ensure the validity of the data being collected and analyzed.

9. Coworkers have more opportunities to give each other feedback, and delivering feedback in the moment is better than developing feedback at a later time.

10. If you give positive feedback more frequently, your constructive feedback will seem more credible.

11. High-frequency feedback helps to shape new skills and results in more efficient training. People learn faster with high-frequency feedback because more opportunities exist to reinforce or correct their behavior.

12. High-frequency feedback turns behaviors into habits, making employees proficient in their tasks.

The Goldilocks Zone of Feedback

Now that you have successfully mastered how often to provide feedback, there's one more component to consider: the ratio of positive to corrective feedback. We discussed earlier that positive feedback is used to strengthen or maintain skills and that corrective feedback is used when things are not being done correctly. While both types of feedback are needed, there is a science behind how much of each to provide.

In astronomy and astrobiology, "The Goldilocks Zone" refers to the area around a star where temperatures are not too hot and not too cold, allowing for a potentially habitable planet. We'll borrow this concept in terms of feedback. Here, you are the star (of course!) trying to find a healthy balance between providing too much feedback and providing too little. Remember, though, there are multiple types of feedback. We'll focus on the two that strive toward improvement: positive and corrective feedback.

The frequency of feedback and the ratio of positive to corrective feedback are both critical. We already know that not providing enough feedback is detrimental; however, having the wrong balance of positive and corrective feedback, what's known as the *habitable zone*, will also slow or pause employee performance. We call this sweet spot the *Goldilocks Zone of Feedback*.

Let's slightly alter our feedback spectrum visual to fit both positive and corrective feedback. The grid below illustrates the Goldilocks Zone of Feedback.

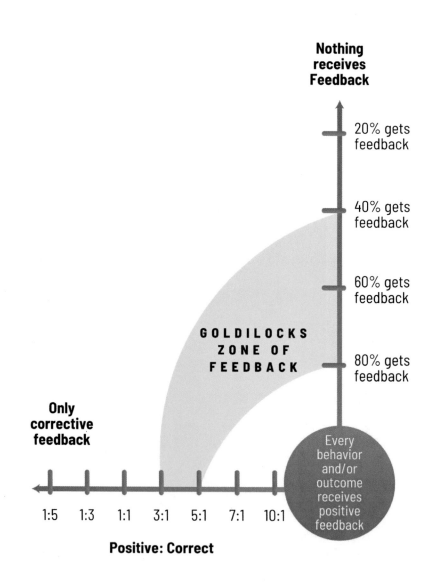

The recommended ratio of positive to corrective feedback is typically set somewhere between 3:1 and 5:1 (positive to corrective). To simplify, we will simply recommend that you attempt to average a 4:1 ratio of positives to correctives. The ratio is not a mandate, but more of a guideline for making your presence in the work lives of your employees more reinforcing. Following this guideline helps you stay out of the other not-so-Goldilocks-ish zones, such as when managers are seen by their employees as aversive, only remarking on their errors.

Deciding how often to provide positive feedback in relation to negative feedback is often very difficult for managers, especially when they're also considering whether a behavior warrants frequent or less-frequent feedback. Managing the many different behaviors of each employee is a large task, and missteps are bound to happen. The trick is to both catch errors as quickly as possible before they become a serious problem and to ensure positives flow freely.

FEEDBACK F!@#up!

This is a common feedback f!@#up that we see across all industries and levels. We tend to fall into that "if it ain't broke, don't fix it" mentality and stop providing feedback to our employees who seem to always do well. The problem? Just like we need to perform maintenance on our cars before they break down, we need to provide feedback to our employees before their performance decreases. Remember, periodic feedback maintains the good behaviors that we want to continue. Don't get stingy with your feedback when performance is high!

Consider the following example: Sally is a good worker. She shows up on time, does her work well, and does not complain. She is ambitious, learns quickly, and would like to move up. She receives feedback for her work, both good and bad, about once per month. However, Sally would like more feedback to grow, but she doesn't know how to get it. Instead, she continues to do exactly what she's always done, and sometimes even less because she feels no one will notice.

In the example above, a lack of feedback stifles Sally's potential. With the right feedback, Sally could become an even more valuable asset to the company. Instead, Sally responds with a less desired behavior due to not receiving enough feedback to maintain her high performance.

Remember that the 4:1 ratio is simply a recommendation meant to highlight the importance of providing more positive than corrective feedback since providing too much corrective (and negative) relative to positive feedback can be seen as aversive to employees. You may find that some employees will prefer corrective over positive feedback. In these cases, you may hear an employee state, "That's great that I am doing well, but I want to know how to improve." Our argument here is that this occurs because we're not providing enough behaviorally specific positive feedback. By increasing your focus on stating exactly what's being performed correctly and being intentional about correcting mistakes, you will help make the employee confident that their supervisor is not overlooking areas in which the employee needs to improve. Remember, employees want to thrive and are looking for feedback that tells them they are in fact thriving or, if not, how to fix it so that they *can* thrive.

The Feedback Bank

Over the years of consulting, we have found that one of the best ways to think about positive-to-corrective feedback distribution is to compare it to a bank account. Positive feedback is money going into the account, and constructive feedback is money leaving the account. Just like with your money in the bank, you have to budget and manage the feedback bank to ensure you don't go into debt. Real monetary bank debt doesn't just come with a negative balance, but also the additional negatives of bank fees or other interest charges. And just like with a bank account, going into the negative with feedback has additional negative effects for employees.

Additionally, when you have so much of something, losing a bit of it is no longer important. For example, when you have millions of dollars saved, you might not think much of a $10 debit or overage charge. Similarly, when you provide positive feedback too much, the corrective feedback does not have as much of an effect. Then, the final consideration is the number of transactions that occur. The more transactions that occur, the more work that's needed to keep track of everything. Similarly, as we discussed before, providing too much feedback can have detrimental effects as well.

So just like with a bank account, with the feedback bank, you have to manage what comes in, what goes out, and how much debt you take on. Leaders are tasked with regularly balancing their feedback checkbooks to ensure they don't overdraft when interacting with their employees.

Consider the following *feedback f!@#up* example.

Stephan is learning a new job and feels confident in his skills. However, his boss constantly supervises him and provides positive and corrective feedback about every aspect of his job. He is frustrated and feels on edge. He barely listens to what his boss says anymore because it's too overwhelming to sort through all the feedback.

In the previous example, Stephan no longer trusts his boss's feedback because of the amount of feedback he receives. As employees gain more experience, they can't possibly need or comprehend feedback on every task, nor do they need constant supervision. To gain an employee's trust, then, we need to give well-thought-out, clear, and concise feedback. It needs to make sense to the employee without causing them to feel overwhelmed.

Let's look at another example. Emilio has been on the job for about 3 months. Initially, he received feedback on several aspects of his job, and most of it was positive. But as he advanced in his skills, he began making more errors. Feedback from his supervisor quickly changed from mostly positive to mostly corrective. Now, 3 months into the job, Emilio is feeling discouraged and as though he can do nothing right. He eventually stops trying because he thinks he will never again receive the positive feedback he got when he first started.

In this example, the supervisor started out correctly. Positive feedback was provided frequently and at the correct ratio as Emilio was learning new skills. However, it is likely that the supervisor faded the positives for the easier tasks too quickly as Emilio took on new, more difficult tasks. The supervisor made several deposits into Emilio's account early on, but then made too many debits, going into debt. As employees take on new tasks, continue the balance of an average of 4:1 positive to corrective feedback to ensure the employee remains encouraged and successful.

Quick Chats

One of the leader's primary responsibilities is ensuring their employees achieve goals by the scheduled deadlines. To accomplish these goals, managers often have to spend more time interacting with their staff to understand the barriers employees encounter; leaders can then provide solutions for those problems. However, working with each employee on the many different issues that arise during the day takes time out of the leader's already busy schedule.

This is where high-frequency feedback becomes extremely important. Leaders can provide a series of "quick chats" with employees that help leaders understand and address the needs of their team in real time. Employees engage in work behavior, and leaders can use quick chats to reinforce or correct those behaviors accordingly, making the employees better at their job and able to produce more efficiently for the company.

In basic terms, more positive interactions between leaders and their employees leads employees to feel more connected to their work. From the employee's point of view, leaders are paired with positive interactions, making them a conditioned reinforcer and creating more employee engagement. Leaders who incorporate efficient, daily meetings with their employees will produce higher engagement with their teams, which usually results in better outcomes for the company. Does this mean leaders need to set aside an hour each day to meet with their staff in the conference room and discuss the happenings of the work day? Absolutely not. To stay engaged, leaders should quickly stop by an employee's office to answer any quick questions they might have, or send an email or direct message when they have some free time. These interactions are meant to be informal and maintain a high level of ongoing communication.

The delivery of performance feedback is something that should be worked into our daily operations, not a project that we plan out (and likely end up putting on a shelf because other, more-pressing issues arise). To help with this, we have created a daily operations feedback checklist to help you remember to incorporate feedback into your daily operations. We encourage you to spice this up a bit and put it on your wall to serve as a reminder. You might also get creative and work it into your daily operations checklists (if you have them).

DAILY OPERATIONS OF FEEDBACK

ITEM	FREQUENCY	COMPLETED	NOTES
Provided at least **4 positive feedbacks** for **every corrective feedback**	Average across the week		
Provided **positive feedback** at least **once to every staff** who directly reports to me	Minimum: monthly Goal: weekly		
Provided at least **one handwritten note** of **positive feedback**	Weekly		
Ensured **positive feedback** was provided at least **3 times this week** to **all new employees** (those present for 3 months or less)	Weekly		
Observed employees **providing one another positive feedback**	Weekly		*If not observed, create a strategy that will increase this.
Provided **feedback** using at least **3 different mediums**	Weekly		
Feedback has become a natural part of my language	Weekly		
Provided **more feedback** for new skills and fewer instances for mastered skills	Weekly		

We have now reviewed every component of feedback except one: the content of feedback. Yes, we know, it is the most important. And I'm sure you are thinking, "Get on with it already!" We will not make you wait any longer, but first, we want to do a quick review and update our formula. Be sure to review it carefully as we didn't just add on another characteristic. Frequency operates a bit differently. It is not just something to consider when actually delivering feedback; rather, it determines how effective it will be and operates exponentially. Here's our updated formula:

EFFECTIVE PERFORMANCE FEEDBACK =
[Frequency] * ***[****(The Behavior/Action/Outcome) + (The Person) + (The Number of People) + (The Type of Feedback) + (The Temporal Location) + (The Medium) + (Privacy) + (Formality) + **(Physical Environment)** + (x)]*

SECTION III

HOW TO

8

THE CONTENT AND DELIVERY OF FEEDBACK

"Whatever you do in life, there is content and form; only those two put together create special meaning…" —*Itay Talgaim*

Everything we have discussed in this book until now is important; however, it can all be thrown out the window if you do not follow the guidelines and suggestions in this chapter. Thus far, in line with the quote above, we have largely focused on the form of feedback. We have set you up for success to deliver what should be the most well-received and readily incorporated feedback that one can offer. However, for lack of a better analogy, if you tell a basketball player how to throw a football, it doesn't matter how great your form. It will be useless, and you will forever be discounted as that crazy coach who doesn't even know what sport you're coaching.

Okay. Maybe not quite that dramatic. But it's seriously close. The content of the feedback provided is one of the most important aspects of feedback. It may seem obvious that the content of the feedback is the performance being discussed; however, what's included is where it can get tricky. The good news is, if you follow a few simple steps, you will ensure that your content is just about perfect.

Wait!!!! I'm getting confused. Can we go back to the basics for just one minute?

Of course we can! We know that we have thrown a lot at you, and honestly, we even have to remind ourselves just what we're talking about. Let's quickly review our definition of performance feedback. This will help us determine what content should be included and what should be saved for other times.

Performance feedback is information transfer from a mediator to a performer about their behavior/action (or a result of their behavior/action) that will affect the outcomes of their future work in some way. Let's break this into its parts for a bit of simplicity. Performance feedback is...

1. Information transfer: Here, there are two things at play. One person delivers a message, and the other person receives that message. Essentially, one person talks to, emails, sends a text, and so on to another person.

2. From a mediator to a performer: This is simple—the mediator observed the behavior or outcome of the behavior, and the performer is who did it.

3. About the behavior/action: The topic of the information is the actual behaviors or performance.

4. Something that will affect the outcomes of the performer's future work in some way: The performer will change or maintain the behavior.

We like to drive points home, so let's see if we can state it even more simply: *Performance feedback is information that effects performance transferred from one person to aznother.*

Ah! Got it! So the content of performance feedback should be focused on the behaviors and actions that led to the outcome being discussed. That's simple (in theory at least). Let's look at the following examples to determine what should be included in the content of feedback.

Leslie has worked at an insurance company for about 15 years. She works in the risk assessment division, where she has been for almost 5 years now. Leslie is a consistent and reliable worker. She shows up on time, she works hard, and she always finishes her tasks. Linda, her boss, really enjoys working with Leslie and loves having her on the team. However, as the end of Leslie's fifth year approaches, Linda reflects on why Leslie has not yet been promoted. Most team members in this division are promoted or make lateral moves after 2–3 years as the work in this department gets repetitive and old rather quickly. Leslie has not made mention of movement, which seems contrary to her strong work ethic and motivation to do well. Upon further reflection, one thing stands out as a potential reason Leslie has been consistently passed up for promotion. Linda decides she will provide Leslie feedback regarding this in hopes of increasing Leslie's chances for promotion.

Now that we know the situation, let's determine what content should be included in Linda's feedback. The goal of the feedback is to increase Leslie's chances for promotion. Thus, content should only include information about how to accomplish this goal. Everything else should be excluded. Pretty easy, right?

Let's look at one more example to make sure you've got it.

Paige is the director of clinical services at a behavior health center. She is young and moved up very quickly. Paige has a lot of really amazing qualities. She is brilliant, and her clinical expertise is largely unmatched. She is excellent with both the patients and their families. The staff all seem to love her. Additionally, she has great ideas for new services and research, fulfilling the vision of the company to both expand and add to the research within the field. Being young, Paige also seems to have boundless energy and is often the first one in every morning and last one to leave at night. There is no doubt that Paige is on the fast track to becoming CEO or executive director of a similar company (or even this one) within the next 5 years.

Let's stop for a moment. We all want a Paige on our team, right? And if we have a Paige, we want to be sure to keep her. It is likely Paige does not need a lot of feedback for her to continue her stellar performance. However, remember that even our top performers need feedback from time to time. To ensure that Paige remains motivated and engaged in your company, you decide to provide her some positive feedback. What will you include?

If you said something about her strong work ethic, her creativity in suggesting new services, or her dedication to adding to the field, you are spot on! All of those would be excellent content to include in the feedback. Here, the focus is on Paige's discretionary effort (her willingness to go above and beyond). We want her to continue this, so the content of feedback should be focused on these behaviors. The things that she does that are excellent, but part of her regular everyday tasks should not be included.

KNOW OUR JARGON

Discretionary effort is the level of effort someone puts into their work that is above and beyond what is require to meet the performance standard. Discretionary effort is the result of truly enjoying your work, making the completion of that work reinforcing. Many employees learn to do just enough to not get into trouble. They meet the minimum performance standard and so continue working according to the status quo. However, when positive reinforcement (or positive feedback) is used, the work tasks that resulted in positive reinforcement become more reinforcing to complete. Thus, discretionary effort is developed through the use of positive reinforcement – or, in our case here, positive feedback.

Sometimes there are several things that could be included in feedback, and it's difficult to decide whether all should be included. This is especially important when you have an employee like Christina, who seems to be doing everything wrong. Let's take a look.

Christina has been working as a gas station attendant for 3 months now. She has been through training twice already. She still works with a shadow, and customers actively get out of her line at least four times an hour when it's busy and once at lower demand times. The gas station is consistently busy, so the attendants must work efficiently. While Christina is really nice and pleasant to be around—everyone seems to like her— she consistently pisses the customers off, which, in turn, pisses off her colleagues. Robin, being a stellar shift manager, has taken the time to provide Christina feedback consistently from the beginning. Robin has really focused on providing positive feedback to ensure that Christina's day is not filled with too many corrections. Unfortunately, Christina is not improving. Robin decides she will spend an hour observing Christina and documenting exactly what happens to try to pinpoint the problem. Below is what Robin observes.

A customer enters the store, grabs a soda, and gets in line. Christina is restocking the cigarette shelf (something that's supposed to be done periodically throughout the day between customers) and doesn't see the customer waiting in line. After approximately 45 seconds (which seems like forever when you're the customer and waiting on someone to look up and provide service), the customer says, "Uh, excuse me...can I get some help?" Christina looks up and smiles pleasantly. She has three cartons of cigarettes in her hand. She looks at them and back at the customer and says, "Yes, of course. My apologies. One second." Christina then stocks the three cartons of cigarettes in her hand, after which she finally attends to the customer. By now, the customer is quite aggravated and a bit rude to Christina. Christina remains pleasant and wishes the person a nice day, apologizing again for the wait. As soon as she is finished with the customer, Christina begins looking around for more stocking that needs to be done, missing the person who is standing in line waiting. In fact, there are now three people waiting in line. The next customer, not nearly as nice or patient as the first, slams their items on the counter and says, "Hey miss, I'm in a hurry here. Can you please come check me out? Or are there more pressing things that you must do rather than provide good customer service?" Christina looks up and apologizes to the customer, stating, "Yes, of course you are the most important thing I have to do. I am so sorry for making you wait. I didn't see you standing there." The customer retorts, "Wow...forget your glasses today?" Christina, a rather soft-spoken woman, forces a smile and again apologizes, "I'm sorry, sir. Really I am. I am new at this and keep seeming to screw up. I hope I didn't cause too much of a wait and that you have an excellent rest of the day." The customer grunts while paying and then walks out. Paying close attention to the growing line, Christina calls the next customer up. Nervous and a bit frazzled, she rings everything up incorrectly. The customer points out the error and rolls their eyes.

Robin planned on observing for an hour, but has had enough. Poor Christina is really struggling, so Robin jumps in to help out before the customers not only tear Christina apart but also decide to go somewhere else. However, before Robin jumps in, she notes one very important thing. She writes the following note to herself in all caps, underlining it three times:

"NO MORE FEEDBACK FOR STOCKING SHELVES!!"

Why did Robin write this? Because she realized that the content of her feedback was actually one of the reasons Christina was failing so miserably. In search of positives, Robin's ***feedback f!@#up*** was consistently providing feedback on Christina's attention to ensuring the shelves behind the counter were fully stocked. Robin provided so much positive feedback on this, in fact, that it was now working against Christina's performance as she was distracted and too focused on restocking the shelves. Restocking now took priority over checking for customers, and Robin was to blame for it all (at least in part). Fortunately for Robin, she knew what to do.

Choosing the right content is not always as simple as it appears to be. To ensure you include the right content, focus on the outcome of the performance. If the feedback is positive, what behaviors and actions led to the wanted outcome? These behaviors and actions should be the content of the feedback. If you're providing corrective feedback, the content should include the incorrect behaviors and actions, the impact they had, and how to correct them. Including information regarding unrelated behaviors and actions or events that have nothing to do with the performance should be eliminated from the feedback. This includes small talk. The more extraneous information included in feedback, the more diluted the message. Feedback is meant to effect performance, so the message needs to be clear. One of the best ways to do that is to keep the content focused and specific.

There is no need for a flowchart or checklist here. There is only need for one simple question.

"Is what I'm about to say directly related to the performance being

discussed?"

If the answer is yes, let it roll off your tongue. If not, save it for a different time.

It's not <u>what</u> you said; it's <u>how</u> you said it.

We've all heard this a time or two before. We are at the end of an unnecessary argument over what we thought was a small thing, and then the person we argued with tells us that it was all in our tone. They had no choice but to respond defensively because our tone of voice, our facial expressions, or our language all sent the message that they were being attacked. They had no choice but to defend themselves.

While we know this is not entirely true—the other person could have chosen to give you the benefit of the doubt or respond without being defensive, but we're not focused on them. We are focused on you and what you can do to deliver feedback effectively. Now that we have ensured our content is focused on the performance, there are a few things to keep in mind when actually delivering the feedback. Ready? Let's dive into them.

It's all in your tone.

Have you ever said something and gotten a completely different reaction than you expected? Maybe you said something meant to be funny, and the other person started crying instead. Or possibly you were trying to be sarcastic and got yelled at instead. Whatever the situation, we have all encountered a time when we were told our tone of voice somehow changed the entire message. While we might not have been aware of it at the time, the other person tuned in to something we did not account for. And that something made all the difference.

We would like to think that we're all masters of the tone and inflection of our voice. Unfortunately, if we're being honest, that's pretty far from the truth. There are times we get excited, passionate, or angry, and as a result, the volume of our voice increases unintentionally. There are other times that we're distracted in our thinking, and our tone of voice is muted or with low inflection, signaling we're upset. Whether we like it or not, our tone of voice sends a message that is usually much louder than the actual content in the message. Because of this, we must be aware of our tone, volume, pitch, and rate when providing feedback.

- **Tone.** The Merriam-Webster dictionary defines *tone of voice* as the way a person is speaking. Doing a deeper dive into what tone of voice is provides one with a lot of very subjective interpretations, including deep tones, harsh tones, and even pleasant tones. While these may all bring images to your mind, these definitions are rather mentalistic. As behavior analysts, we always strive to define terms objectively, clearly, and completely. Thus, we will define tone of voice as follows:

  - The sound or pitch of one's voice, as determined by the rate of vibrations emitted by the vocal cords. A neutral tone of voice is emitted when vibrations are equivalent to that of the sound of middle C on a piano. An increased or high pitch of voice occurs when the rate of vibrations increases, resulting in notes or sounds higher than that of middle C. A low or decreased pitch results from a lower rate of vibrations, resulting in sounds lower than that of middle C.

  The tone of one's voice tends to increase (resulting in higher pitches) when emotions are increased. Thus, when delivering performance feedback, your tone should be neutral, equating the rate of vibrations equivalent to middle C. When your tone of voice is higher than that of middle C, it's often interpreted as though you're excited or angry. Similarly, when your tone of voice is lower than that of middle C, it may be interpreted as sad, depressed, or disinterested. Maintaining a neutral tone of voice reduces the potential of your employees to interpret you as having negative emotions toward them or the feedback being provided.

- **Volume.** While it is funny to watch shows where bosses yell at their employees, in real life, it sucks to be yelled at. And while it might not make you feel like a peon, not being able to hear you because you're speaking so quietly is equally frustrating. The goal here is to have a conversational volume at all times when providing feedback. In objective terms, conversational volume is about 50–55 decibels, or if you're like us and that means nothing to you, it's loud enough to be heard within 10 feet of distance, but not so loud that someone 15 feet away can hear you.

Let's look at the following example to see how tone and volume alone can change the meaning of a statement. For this example, read each sentence aloud, speaking the word in *italics* slightly louder and with an emphasis. Make note of how the meaning changes as you do. If you want to make it really fun, read it aloud to someone else, and ask them how your message changed.

- o "I never said you are a lousy employee."
- o "*I* never said you are a lousy employee."
- o "I never said you are a lousy *employee*."
- o "I never said *you* are a lousy employee."
- o "I *never* said you are a lousy employee."
- o "I never said you are a *lousy* employee."
- o "I never *said* you are a lousy employee."

Hopefully this little exercise shows just what a small change in the tone and volume of your voice can do and just what can happen to the message being received. This is why you should be aware of how you're using your voice when providing feedback.

- **Pitch.** Pitch refers to the "highness" or "lowness" of your voice. Some people are described to have "squeaky" voices, while others may be described as having a "baritone" voice. These are descriptors of pitch. While voice pitch is largely determined by throat anatomy, there are times that we are squeakier than usual. Research on pitch and leaders has found that we tend to select those as leaders who have lower-pitched voices (Klofstad et al., 2016). While you can't change the entire pitch of your voice, the message here is to refrain from using your "high" pitch when providing feedback.

- **Rate.** Rate refers to how fast or slow you talk. In general, conversational rate ranges from approximately 120–160 words per minute. When providing feedback, aim to keep your rate within this window, with focus on slowing it down a bit. Speak fast enough that the conversation flows, but not so fast that the performer has a difficult time ingesting everything you're saying. Pause when necessary to allow time for processing.

Keep in mind that these variables are still included even when our message is written or typed. We all know that using ALL CAPS means someone is yelling, and <u>underlining</u> and *italicizing* are used to emphasize a word. However, even without these prompts, the person reading our messaging is incorporating their own tone, pitch, volume, and rate when they're reading your words. This is why it's even more important to ensure the words you use are considered carefully when sending a written message.

Think (and write) before you speak.

Just like any other skill, providing effective performance feedback takes practice. Most of us stumble at least a few times before we perfect it. The words we use when providing feedback are just as important as the content behind the words. Even slight variations in words can change the meaning drastically, so be thoughtful about the words used when providing feedback.

Think about the following two statements:

- "Did you mean to overlook the deadline?"
- "Were you aware of the deadline?"

While the content of the two statements is largely the same. We can conclude that the employee missed a deadline and that the supervisor is trying to determine why the deadline was missed. However, the first statement points the finger toward the employee and looks for blame, while the second attempts to identify a potential error that can be corrected. While the differences may be slight, the choice in our words can drastically change the meaning.

Let's look at a few more examples.

For this example, we look to ourselves. Think about which of the following statements you would prefer to hear from one of your employees.

- "You're a great boss."
- "You're a great manager."
- "You're a great leader."

If you're anything like us (and we think you are!), you would prefer to be called a "great leader" above all else. While bosses, managers, and leaders all play similar roles in a company, the meaning and differences of each label are slightly different. Leaders don't have to be in leadership positions—leadership is a reflection of their behavior and the effect it has on their followers. Great leaders are those who inspire and get people to rally behind them. Managers and bosses are much more tied to their positions and are not always referred to in positive tones.

When you are first practicing providing feedback—both positive and corrective—we recommend writing out the words that you will use. Examine them, and consider whether they are sending the message you intend. Remember, feedback is the delivery of information, so you want to be sure that you get the information right. Refrain from words that have powerful undertones, and instead choose words that are positive or neutral in nature. Also, be careful of saying things like "I understand what you're saying *but*..." The word "but" negates everything that comes before it. Thus, if you're saying "I understand *but*...," the message you are sending is that you really don't understand. One exercise that we use with our leaders is to practice saying "and" instead of "but." We tend to use "but" as a filler word and distort its meaning in the process. The problem is that the receiver has not distorted the meaning and receives the "but" as it is grammatically intended—to negate everything before it. When writing the words you intend to use, write the entire statement, and then practice saying it. Writing helps organize and provide time to reflect, correct, and perfect. Once you have the words right, practice articulating them aloud to ensure your tone, volume, pitch, and rate of your speaking voice is consistent with the message you intend to send.

Following a recipe out of order ensures disaster in the kitchen.

Have you ever tried to add the cheese to the macaroni before draining the water from the noodles? Us either, yet we can imagine how gross that would be. When you do things out of order, you can ruin the entire recipe, or end up with a completely different item than intended. Recipes, like instructions, are written in a specific order because order matters. And like with a recipe, the order in which content is delivered is important.

When delivering positive feedback, the recipe is simple:

1. Begin with a positive descriptor, such as in these examples:

   - "It is really great that..."
   - "I appreciate how you..."

- "Thank you for…."
- "That presentation was amazing!"

2. Describe the action and/or outcome specifically and objectively. Adding on to our examples above, results in these examples:

   - "It is really great that you scored 90% on the audit review."
   - "I appreciate how you turn in your reports on time each week."
   - "Thank you for the kind words you provided to your colleague."
   - "That presentation was amazing! The graphics were engaging, you explained everything thoroughly, and you got great audience participation."

There are a few more steps when providing corrective feedback.

1. **Thank the person for meeting.** No one wants to enter a room and have the first statement made be about how you screwed up. If you are entering this meeting, your performer already knows corrective feedback is going to be given. However, two things are important. First, those who avoid confrontations tend to make nervous small talk to avoid jumping into the task at hand. This not only creates awkwardness but also delays the inevitable and can increase the anxiety of the performer, leading to less receptiveness on their part. Second, thanking the person for the meeting acknowledges that this might not be comfortable for them, but that you appreciate their willingness to meet (even if they had no choice—though, technically, they could have called in sick). Beginning the session with a quick thank you sets a positive tone and provides a lead-in while avoiding the distracting small talk.

2. **State the error clearly, specifically, and objectively.** State exactly what happened using objective language. Provide specific details, including time, location, and what each person involved did. Refrain from making subjective statements or labeling the person's inferred emotions.

3. **State the observed or common antecedents and consequences of the error.** The goal of providing feedback is to identify how the error occurred in the first place. We know that behavior

is controlled by the environment or, more specifically, by the antecedents and consequences surrounding the behavior. Thus, note what happened just before the error and what the outcome of that error was. If you didn't observe the error directly, state likely antecedents and consequences that you have observed in the past in similar situations.

4. **State the impact the error had on the company, team, or client (whichever was affected).** Simon Sinek is famous for his "Start with Why" TED Talk©. The reason for that is that people connect to the why behind the behavior. It not only provides understanding and justification but also creates motivation. Most can understand that what they did was wrong. However, many do not immediately connect how a small error (or even a large one) negatively impacts others. Even if it is completely obvious to you, don't assume it is to your staff. Stating the why also shows that the error is not just about the employee following the rules, but instead shows that the rules are in place to provide the best outcomes for all involved. Understanding how a behavior impacts others and how it ties into the company's vision is one of the best ways to motivate employees to perform in ways that will actually accomplish the goal. Don't underestimate the impact of the "why."

5. **Tell the employee how to correct the mistake.** This is an often-overlooked component of corrective feedback. We mentioned it when we discussed the difference between negative feedback and corrective feedback. Negative feedback simply tells the performer that they were wrong. Corrective feedback provides the performer with the information necessary to fix the mistake. Thus, the key to success in this step is to use the same clear, specific, and objective language as you did when describing the mistake. Don't just tell your employee to "make the customers happier" or "be more pleasant." Tell them exactly what they can do that will result in those things happening. Examples might include "be sure to smile when you first greet a customer" or "ask about the customer's day to show interest in them."

6. **Model.** Provide examples of the correct behavior. You can do this through modeling, role play, video review, or permanent product (a sample of the correct finished product). While explaining the

correct behavior is important, as we said before, "a picture is worth 1,000 words." Learning increases with each different modality used to instruct. Thus, tell the performer how to correct a behavior and then show them what the correct performance looks like.

7. **Allow time for practice.** Don't expect that the performer will immediately correct the behavior without having time to practice it. So many people believe that people will perform differently simply because they were told to do so. Performance issues occur for many reasons, most of which are not because people were never told the right thing to do. To increase the effectiveness of your corrective feedback, provide your employee an opportunity to perform the correct behavior.

8. **Provide feedback on the performance.** Immediately provide feedback on the practiced performance. This is one of the most important steps in providing corrective feedback; if the performer demonstrates the skill, yet still does it incorrectly and no one tells them, they will likely just continue on doing it incorrectly. Therefore, find what the employee did correctly and anything that needs to be corrected. Repeat this at least a few times (or until they demonstrate it fully correctly if possible).

9. **Follow up.** Once you have confidence the performer can demonstrate the correct skill, be sure to follow up. You can do this both formally and informally, and it is best to do both. You should follow up soon after the feedback was provided to ensure maintenance of the newly corrected skill.

Let's look at an example of how it looks to follow these steps. You can practice writing out your feedback to practice as well!

In this scenario, the inventory manager, Craig, did not complete the monthly inventory report on time, which is 5 days after the end of the month. His supervisor, Mindy, is not sure why the report is late, but she knows this past month was especially busy and that Craig was out for a week on personal leave. Mindy wants to provide feedback and ensure this does not happen again. Given that she is still learning this new order of steps for providing feedback, she follows our advice and writes it out first. This is what she wrote:

1. **Thank the person for coming in:** *Craig, thank you for coming in*

to meet with me.

2. **State the error clearly, specifically, and objectively:** *I have not yet received the end- of-month report for last month. End-of-month reports are due on the 5th of the following month; however, it is now the 10th.*

3. **State the observed antecedents and consequences:** *I know that you were out for several days and that this was an especially busy month, increasing the amount of inventory and the time it takes to complete the report. In the past, reports have always been submitted on time or a day or two late, and I have never given feedback about that.*

4. **State the impact the error had on the company, team, or client:** *Not knowing the status of our inventory makes it difficult to plan for the month ahead. We want to always be sure that each department has the materials it needs to provide their services. Unfortunately, we don't know whether we need to reorder or keep a bit more in stock if we don't know what we used and reordered in the month prior.*

5. **Tell the employee how to correct the mistake:** *Please complete the report today, and moving forward, either complete the report no later than the 5th of the month or, if you will not be able to do this, please notify me prior to the end of the month. This will allow me to problem solve with you.*

6. **Model:** *For example, if it is three days before the end of the month and you think you might not be able to complete the report on time, please come to me and say that you will not be able to meet the monthly report deadline. You can also send me an email if I am unavailable.*

7. **Allow time for practice:** *(??? How does he practice this right now? I will ask him if he can have the report finished today, though I don't think he can, so this will allow him to practice telling me he can't finish it!) … Will you be able to complete the report and submit it to me today?*

8. **Provide feedback on performance**: *(If he tells me he cannot finish, I will provide positive feedback about the fact that he told me he couldn't finish it and then offer help to get it finished; if he says he can complete it, I will ask him if he really only has 1 more hour of*

work left on it. If not, I will tell him that he should tell me that he can't finish it today.)

9. **Follow Up:** *(I will schedule a follow-up meeting with him in 2 days after I review the report and again on the 6th of next month so that I can provide positive feedback for meeting the deadline.)*

Mindy, you rocked it! Mindy identified all of the steps to providing corrective feedback and found solutions to each step. As you can see, thinking about each step and writing down her actions and words helped her problem solve when the action was not immediately recognized.

Another Quick Note on Feedback Sandwiches

Don't do them. Yes, we know we already said this, but we know repetition leads to learning and we really want to make sure you remember this!

If you want to know why, check out our explanation in the "Special Considerations" chapter. What we want you to know and remember right now is that we hate them so much (because they are so ineffective and do so many detrimental things) that we simply say **DON'T DO THEM!** (Yes, we were just yelling. Sorry. We got a little carried away right there. We are a bit passionate about this.)

And now......

Drumroll please! *(Long, dramatic pause here...we're literally waiting for you to make a drumroll sound...)*

We have just finished the last step of the Performance Feedback Formula! WHAAATTTT?!?!?!? HELL YEAH! You did it! If you have made it to this point, you have completed the entire formula.

Here it is:

EFFECTIVE PERFORMANCE FEEDBACK =
[(Frequency) * ((The Behavior/Action/Outcome) + (The Person) + (The Number of People) + (The Type of Feedback) + (The Temporal Location) + (The Medium) + (Privacy) + (Formality) + (Physical Environment)]] / (Content + Delivery)

To finish it off, we have provided you with a checklist to ensure you follow the right recipe, perfecting your content and delivery of performance feedback.

CONTENT AND DELIVERY OF FEEDBACK

ITEM	COMPLETED	NOTES
Identify the most important behaviors and actions related to positive performance.	○	
Practice using a positive or neutral tone of voice. You may record yourself and play it back to make sure you are delivering feedback with the right tone.	○	
Keep your volume conversational. Someone more than 10 feet away should not be able to hear you.	○	
Try to keep a consistent pitch in your lower range. Squeaks should be avoided.	○	
Aim to speak at 120-160 words per minute.	○	
Choose your words carefully. If providing feedback verbally, write them down first and review them. Are they free from subjective judgement and blame?	○	
Follow the recipes:	○	

A. Positive

Begin with positive descriptor	○	
Describe the action and/or outcome specifically and objectively	○	

B. Corrective

Thank the person for meeting	○	
State the error clearly, specifically, and objectively	○	
Provide an empathetic statement	○	
State the impact the error had on the company, team, or client	○	
Tell the employee how to correct the mistake	○	
Model	○	
Allow time for practice	○	
Provide feedback on the practice	○	
Follow Up	○	

9

FEEDBACK ALONE ISN'T ENOUGH

"Great things are done by a series of small things brought together"

~ Vincent Van Gough

Throughout this book, we have introduced you to several behavior analysis terms and explained the how's and why's of our recommendations based on how they will affect employee performance. We have also argued that feedback is the most powerful tool that you, as a leader, have to change the performance of your followers. However, the one thing we have not yet discussed is that feedback alone is not actually enough to truly increase performance to optimal levels.

Feedback as a Reinforcer

Before you get upset and start yelling at us, wondering what the point was in learning the entire formula, we do want to stress that feedback *is* the most powerful tool you have to change behavior. That still holds true, and all of the learning and practicing you have done thus far was not in vain. However, to explain why we now say it's not enough, we must first turn to the definition of reinforcement and how reinforcers are established.

There are some items in this world that are reinforcing without learning, meaning that their positive qualities and their effect on behavior happens even without previous experience with that item or activity. Food, shelter, clothing, and sex are examples of these unconditioned reinforcers— or those reinforcers that require no previous experience. However, the rest of the items and activities in the world—including social interactions, praise, money, games, raises, and time off—become reinforcing through our learning history.

KNOW OUR JARGON

Unconditioned Reinforcers: Those items and activities that serve as reinforcers without a prior learning history. These items include food, shelter, clothes, and sex.

Conditioned reinforcers become reinforcers through their pairing with unconditioned reinforcers. In other words, we learn that money is a good thing, and we will work for money because money has been paired

---

KNOW OUR JARGON

Conditioned Reinforcers: Items and activities that are neutral are paired with reinforcing items and activities. Through this pairing, the neutral items and activities adopt the positive qualities of the reinforcing items and activities. This pairing is called conditioning. It is the same principle as Watson used with Baby Albert, except here we are focused on pairing positive things (not things that cause fear, as Watson did).

---

with food, shelter, and clothing. When previously neutral items are paired with highly preferred and reinforcing items, they adopt the same properties and become reinforcing. There are a few things that are important to note about conditioned reinforcers:

1. **These items only become reinforcers after close and repeated pairing with other reinforcers.** This pairing process consists of presenting the neutral item/activity with the reinforcing one. For example, when you were young, your grandfather might have given you a nickel. This nickel meant nothing to you at first. However, your grandfather then took you to the candy store and told you to exchange the nickel for a piece of candy. He continued to do this each day for a month. At the end of the month, you completed chores to earn the nickel. The nickel became reinforcing due to its pairing with candy.

> ### KNOW OUR JARGON
>
> Pairing/Conditioning: This is the process of presenting a neutral stimulus with a reinforcing or preferred one. The two items are presented almost immediately with one another several times, resulting in the neutral stimulus becoming preferred or reinforcing.

2. **Once the conditioning process is complete, the conditioned reinforcer can be used alone, but slowly loses its reinforcing properties each time it is presented without the unconditioned reinforcer.** Going with the same example above, each day you complete a chore and receive a nickel, but are not taken to the candy store. In fact, the candy store closes down, and there are now no candy stores in your town. As a result, you keep earning nickels, but cannot ever spend (or exchange) them for candy. You slowly stop doing chores each day as the nickels are no longer as reinforcing; they no longer lead to the candy.

What does all of this have to do with feedback? Again, amazing question! Feedback is a conditioned reinforcer. Feedback alone is not reinforcing; we learn it is reinforcing because, in the past, it has led to other reinforcers (like money that we can then use to buy things). When you first meet an employee, your feedback is likely a neutral consequence, not having much effect on the employee's behavior. Your feedback must be paired with preferred items both when you first begin interacting with employees and then periodically after that to ensure that your feedback adopts reinforcing qualities and maintains those qualities over time.

Let's look at the following example. Remember Emilio and Azumi? Let us refresh your memory. Emilio was the manager of the four new wait staff. Azumi was the third new staff member of Emilio's focus. When he first interacted with Azumi, Emilio provided her immediate and behavior specific feedback on *everything* she did. We noted then that the feedback was ineffective because Azumi did not *value* Emilio's feedback. We explained earlier that one of the reasons was that Emilio had not interacted with Azumi much during her first 4 months of work. Behaviorally, Emilio was not paired with or conditioned with any reinforcing stimuli. He was simply neutral, or possibly negative, in that he was paired with negative outcomes rather than positive ones.

Until Emilio was a preferred person, his feedback would continue to be ineffective. Thus, Emilio had to do other things to pair himself with more positive things.

To initially pair yourself and your feedback with already-established reinforcers, we provide the following recommendations:

1. **Initially pair yourself with positive items and activities.** This may include having a bowl of candy on your desk, remembering an important detail about the employee, or providing helpful information that makes the employee's job easier. When it is time for bonuses and raises or promotions, be the one to give them; don't pass it off to Human Resources (unless you are Human Resources, of course, and then pass it off to yourself!).

2. **Pair your feedback with positive items and activities.** Give your employees a high five or thumbs up. Throw a piece of candy to the staff who offered an answer during a staff meeting. Give out gift cards or entries into a drawing for a gift card for completing reports on time. Whatever you do, this pairing process will ensure

your feedback adopts the positive qualities of these reinforcers and becomes a conditioned reinforcer.

3. **Provide positive feedback often and corrective only when necessary.** Just like with the conditioning of reinforcers, the conditioning of punishers can happen. If you read our tidbit about Watson, you will know that Watson conditioned previously neutral items with a negative stimulus (the clinging of two pipes together), and the startle response that occurred when the pipes were hit together transferred to the neutral items (including a white bunny). The white bunny became negative, and Baby Albert began to cry any time he saw it. Just like that white bunny, you too can become a stimulus that your staff avoid. This happens when you are paired more often with negative stimuli (like corrective action, yelling, docks in pay, firing of employees, etc.) than you are with positive ones. Thus, you always want to be sure that you maintain a ratio of positive to negative such that the positive is always winning. This concept ties back into the Goldilocks Zone of Reinforcement in that you want to provide about four times more positive feedback and have four times more positive interactions than negative feedback or interactions.

4. **Continue to periodically pair yourself and your feedback with unconditioned or powerful conditioned (e.g., money) reinforcers.** To ensure that you and your feedback remain conditioned reinforcers, you must periodically deliver more potent or unconditioned reinforcers. This means that you may sometimes bring candy to meetings and pass it out when staff members offer answers, but not always. It could also mean that sometimes timely reports result in you saying "nice work" and delivering a gift card, and other times you simply say "nice work."

Feedback Is NOT Training

We have heard many managers and supervisors say "but I told them what to do" when describing their frustrations regarding performance problems. As behavior analysts, we know that providing feedback, or simply telling someone what to do, is not enough. Have you ever heard the saying "just because they know it doesn't mean they'll do it"? We take this one step further and add "just because you said it doesn't mean they know it." Thus, you have two problems that could arise if you use feedback as your only performance improvement tool. Let's look at each statement.

"Just because you *said* it doesn't mean they *know* it."

We have defined feedback as an information transfer, meaning that the message sent is the same message received. When you follow our formula, this will happen. However, when training occurs, we do not typically check to ensure the information being trained is the information trainees actually receive. Instead, training often consists of a trainer talking, lecturing, providing videos, and when they're really good, demonstrating the skills we want the trainee to learn. Most trainings, however, do not include the trainee practicing the skills and receiving feedback on their performance. Instead, trainees are expected to take in the information offered and then go perform at high levels. Unfortunately, this does not always happen.

To ensure trainees actually learn the information and can perform the skills to expectations, we recommend including a behavior skills training (BST; Miltenberger, 2004) model in all trainings. BST is a four-step teaching strategy that has been proven to work across industries and with individuals of all types. Here are the four steps:

1. **Instruction:** Provide a description of the skill, its importance, when to use it, and when not to use it.

2. **Modeling:** Show the trainee how to perform the skill, or provide a sample of the end result of the skill (e.g., a completed report).

3. **Rehearsal:** Allow the trainee to practice the skill. It's best to have the trainee practice the skill in-situ whenever possible.

4. **Feedback:** The trainer provides positive feedback for correct responses and corrective feedback for errors. (No, we didn't add this step—it's actually part of the model!)

As you can see in the training model, feedback is only one part. If you want to ensure the information sent is actually the same information received, use a BST model in all your trainings. This practice will ensure that, "when you say it, they know it."

Now that we're certain the employee has indeed mastered the skill, the second statement becomes relevant.

"Just because they **know** it doesn't mean they'll **do** it."

We all know people or have had situations where the individual can tell you and show you exactly what was supposed to be done, yet that specific action was not done. *Why?* This is where we, as behavior analysts, tend to stand apart from most other professions. It is easy to hypothesize

FEEDBACK F!@#up!

If you caught this one – great work! The problem here is that when Luke demonstrated the correct behavior, there was no positive feedback. Remember that positive feedback needs to be provided at a higher frequency when establishing new behaviors.

about why an individual did not perform as they knew they should. It could be because they are lazy or don't care about their job or just maybe don't like to do things that way. These are all mentalistic interpretations of what is happening; they don't lead to the best solution. As behavior analysts, we know better. We know that behavior is controlled by the environment— and the behavior itself does or does not happen due to the antecedents and consequences that occur.

Let's look at the following example. Here we have Bo and Luke. Bo is Luke's manager and has become quite frustrated with Luke's tardiness when returning from lunch. Bo has read this book (up until this section, of course) and has provided Luke with performance feedback. Unfortunately, Bo's behavior has not changed—at least not long term. On the first 2 days after receiving feedback, Luke did come back from lunch on time. However, no one seemed to notice. Luke, who actually skipped eating so that he could return to work on time (he usually went to visit his daughter who was in daycare up the street), was frustrated that he made such an effort to return on time, but no one noticed. Thus, the next day, he came in a few minutes late. Again, no one seemed to notice. The next day he was a few more minutes late. This continued until Luke was again arriving about 15 minutes late from his lunch break.

What happened? In this example, the problem is both the antecedents and the consequences. Let's look at the antecedents first. What is happening prior to Luke's return from lunch? While we don't know all of the antecedents, we know two things: (a) he is with his daughter, and (b) he has not eaten. Both of these antecedents likely work against Luke's return to work. We can assume that he would probably prefer to stay longer with his daughter *and* get something to eat.

Now let's look at the consequences. When Luke arrived back to work from his lunch break on time, nothing happened. When he was a few minutes late, nothing happened. It is only when he arrives 15 minutes or more late that a consequence occurs. Based on this pattern, it is evident that Luke's tardiness is not because he doesn't care about his job—rather, it's because he prefers his daughter, is hungry, and nothing happens when he does arrive back from lunch on time.

What can Bo do to turn this around, you ask? It's really quite simple. Bo can ensure that he provides positive feedback to Luke when he arrives back from lunch on time. This consequence will ensure the target behavior (arriving to work on time) is reinforced, rather than going unnoticed. As we have stated before, positive feedback for the wanted behaviors is the best and strongest way to increase and maintain high levels of performance.

Feedback is ultimately the most powerful tool that leaders have to effect the performance of their team. However, without ensuring feedback is paired with unconditioned and/or potent conditioned reinforcers, providing effective training, and ensuring the right antecedents and consequences are in place, the feedback will not obtain the desired results. Be sure that you take the time to pair feedback so that it becomes reinforcing, that you train to mastery of skills, and that you follow positive behavior with positive feedback. These steps will take your feedback to another level and ensure all of the hard work you have done thus far is not wasted!

10

HOW TO TAKE DATA

"In god we trust, all others must bring data"

*~ **W. Edwards Deming***

Behavior analysts focus on data a lot. It's how we know whether what we're doing is actually having the effect we intend. Data are so important to us that it's easy to lose sight of the fact that we went to school for years and practiced all the different ways to collect and interpret data. Data create a rabbit hole that is so big that we can't help but to jump in.

When we first wrote this chapter, we literally wrote over 20 pages detailing the different types of data and methods of data collection and interpretation you can use to monitor your feedback. However, as we edited and reviewed (and received some feedback), we realized that we lost the message in the thick of all those words! Even we can improve our performance through feedback. Thank goodness!

This chapter is not meant to make you masters of data collection or even provide training in data collection. Rather, the goal of this chapter is to highlight the importance of data collection in regard to measuring the effectiveness of your feedback and to provide a few strategies to help incorporate this into your regular routine.

The Importance of Measurement

By now, you have been providing feedback for a while and using all of the different techniques and tips we have discussed thus far. Employee morale has seemingly improved, you are providing information to your staff on what they should do more and less of, and just as importantly, your organization is reaching its goals…or is it? Are you certain that your feedback is changing morale and performance, or is your viewpoint skewed because you have put in so much time, energy, and work to perfect your feedback-delivery skills?

It's usually easier to observe changes in behavior when you are not involved in the day-to-day changing of that behavior. When you are up close and personal with the treatment plan (or in this case, the delivery of performance feedback), two things can happen. You can either be so involved and close to the daily performance that you don't notice the continual, small positive changes that are occurring, or you can be so invested that you begin seeing positive change where there really is none. Neither of these are accurate measures of your efforts.

Knowing how well your efforts are working can act as a reinforcer that will help continue your hard work. There is nothing better than knowing that all that hard work, blood, sweat, and tears paid off. Conversely, there is nothing worse than to feel that you put in all this effort for little to no gain. To remedy this, measure the effect of your efforts.

Data are not just important for you and your efforts, but are also important for the performance of your staff. Like you, they are also putting in effort to improve their performance. Providing them with objective information (e.g., data) on how their efforts are paying off can be equally reinforcing, helping to continue their hard work as well!

Finally, in case you're not quite convinced that data are important, think about this: Data can provide you the evidence and objectivity that is sometimes necessary when providing corrective feedback. It is far better to show the objective data on performance than it is to say "I feel like you're not improving." Data not only provides objectivity but also provides evidence that is hard to dispute.

First things first—what are you measuring?

Performance of course! The entire point of performance feedback is to increase performance. Thus, any data collection that occurs should be on the actual performance or performance outcomes. When choosing what to measure, follow these three rules: identify, objectify, and specify. Let's dive more specifically into each.

Identify the target. Performance is the result of specific behaviors and actions. One of the first things discussed in this book was how to select the right target for feedback. We gave four rules. The first two are important here: (a) provide feedback on accomplishments and goals, and (b) provide feedback on the behavior or the results of the behavior. The target that you will measure is the exact behavior, accomplishment, action, goal, or outcome that you are providing feedback about.

One quick note about behavior—us behavior analysts like to do a **dead person's test** to determine what's behavior and what isn't. The test? It's simple. Ask this question: Can a dead person do it? If the answer is yes, it's not behavior. If the answer is no, it's behavior. As an example, do "stay in work chair" or "stay off social media" pass the dead person's test? Nope. They sure don't. Dead people can stay in a work chair (if they're put there first, of course), and dead people stay off social media. Take these off your target list. Instead, include things like number of sales calls made, length (or duration) of total interaction with a customer, time it took to complete a task, number of breaks taken throughout the day, total dollars of revenue generation, or scores on customer service surveys. These are all behaviors, accomplishments, and outcomes that can be measured.

OBM Tidbit

Target behaviors should be tied to outcomes
and accomplishments that move the
organization toward realizing its vision.

Objectify the target. By *objectify*, we mean define objectively. This can be harder than it sounds and often takes years of practice to perfect. An objective definition for a target behaviors is evident when two or more people can *agree* that the performer is carrying out the target behavior or has completed it. The trick to objectifying is to include only things that are observable and that do not require interpretation in the definition. The difference between "smiles" and "is happy" illustrate our meaning. Everyone can agree when someone smiles. However, not all would agree if someone is happy. Happy is an interpretation of the actions or behaviors one makes. Similarly, completing a task after a deadline is objective, while scoring someone's laziness is highly objective.

As an example, the recent conversation described here captures how two people may disagree on a definition. A manager asked an outside consultant how quickly he usually responds to emails. The consultant's response was "very quickly." The manager, not knowing exactly what this meant, asked the consultant to clarify, stating, "What exactly do you mean by 'very quickly'?"

The consultant replied, "That is obvious; when I am working, I usually respond very quickly, meaning that I usually respond within a few minutes."

The manager responded "Wow! That is very quickly. I thought you meant within the next 24 hours."

This simple example illustrates how terms and definitions can be taken for granted, that we can assume all understand a definition in the same way. That's why we always recommend that you ask two or more people to tell you exactly what your definition is or to show you what the target behavior looks like. That way you can be sure that you have defined it clearly.

You're thinking, "But I really do just want them to be more productive while doing their jobs." While that may be true, you must define the target behavior the performer should increase or reduce by being specific and clear: describe what you want them to do more of and what "being productive" looks like for a given team member's individual responsibilities. It's also helpful to include a nonexample of the target behavior because behavior that might be appropriate in one context may not be in another. Let's look at a few examples:

- Think about those annoying marketers who call right around dinner time. These peddlers are hired to sell products or services over the phone, and they do a fantastic job disturbing the peace, don't they? In their industry, the number of products or services sold is most certainly a highly prioritized target, but it starts with making a phone call. Imagine how many numbers these marketers have to dial before they actually get someone to (a) pick up, (b) listen to more than three words before hanging up, and (c) actually buy what they're trying to sell. Given all of that, it makes sense to conclude that an initial target to reach could be *increasing the number of phone calls made.* In a general sense, this target behavior can be defined as "every instance of using a phone to dial a number provided on a phone list" or, more specifically, "any instance of using a phone to dial a number and hearing the voice of the receiver on the other end." Nonexamples of this definition could include making personal phone calls to persons such as family and friends.

- Defining "on-task" behavior can be a little trickier because it is a much broader area, but it can be done! For example, during a computer-based activity, "on-task" behavior can be made observable by defining it as "eyes open and oriented toward a computer with only windows and/or documents relevant to the assigned task open on the screen, which may be accompanied by a motor movement (e.g., typing, clicking the mouse)." A nonexample here might be when more than a minute elapses without an active motor movement. Let's apply this example in a more specific setting. "On-task behavior" for a restaurant server or bartender may include executing one of the following tasks relevant to their job position: interacting with customers, retrieving food items, ringing in orders, cleaning/bussing tables, or completing a drink order within a certain amount of time. A nonexample of on-task behavior might be chatting with coworkers about non-work-related activities or going outside for a break.

Specify the target. This goes hand in hand with objectify; however, the focus here is providing enough detail that someone who is provided the definition or specifications about the target, and nothing else, could still pick out the behavior or accomplishment. Specificity can make the difference between why someone rates the completion of a report as satisfactory, while someone else states that the report needs improvement. If the instruction is "score the completion of the report," one may have taken the target at face value and scored whether the report was complete. However, the other person may have interpreted "complete" to mean that it was both finished and did not need any revisions. In other words, leaving out important details about satisfactory performance not only leads to inconsistent feedback across personnel, but it also makes data collection very difficult.

Selecting and Designing a Data Collection System

This is where the rabbit hole can get muddy. As a leader, you have many things on your plate, and the last thing you need is to have the new task of designing a complex data collection system that allows you to monitor your feedback effectiveness. Whether you're a long-time pro or a novice at data collection, we recommend keeping the system simple. It is highly unlikely that you will know the effects of every single feedback provided; however, you can monitor your overall efforts.

The best way to do this is to have a performance monitoring system. These systems usually include scorecards that have identified the key performance targets for each employee. Employee progress toward these targets is then monitored at least monthly, and if you're really good, the overall performance for every target is tied to a pay-for-performance system. Unfortunately, we don't have time to discuss these systems in detail, but we do encourage you to dive into them by reading *Pay for Profits* by William Abernathy. If you have a performance monitoring system, mark when you began providing feedback regarding specific goals and targets, and then review the data before and after this mark. If you see performance improving, keep going. If not, review what you are doing, then make some changes.

If you don't have a performance monitoring system, don't fret. You can still monitor the effects of your feedback on your employee's performance. Once you have identified, objectified, and specified your target, you will know the best way to measure it. If you are trying to increase billable hours, you will likely measure the number of hours billed. If you are focused on increasing the number of calls made, you will count the number of calls.

If you want to look at the length of interaction, measure the number of minutes of the interaction. In other situations, you might not be able to easily observe performance, but can review the outcome of performance. Here, you can measure the number of errors in a report, the number of tasks completed on time, or even the quality ratings from consumers. The key here is to make it easy, and the best way to do so is by looking at what you are already measuring. The case with many leaders is that they're not always aware of the many things already being monitored. The reason for this is that we often have technology that we use for one thing and have not yet discovered it can be used for other things as well. For example, several scheduling software programs measure the number of billable hours of each employee. Simple reports can be generated with a few clicks of a button, but many leaders are unaware of this as they have used the technology only to schedule hours, not to monitor how many are actually billed. Investigate what measurements are currently being collected, and first use them to measure the outcome and effect of your feedback.

If, after investigating, you determine that nothing of importance is being measured, create your own system. When doing this, start with something that is hugely impactful, such as gross revenue or direct sales. Chances are, you're measuring some things about the outcome, but not the direct impact of the behaviors you're trying to increase. That's okay. Everyone has a starting point, and the key here is that you want some objective data to provide information about your feedback (i.e., you want feedback about your feedback). And if all else fails, ask your staff. Check in with them to see if your feedback is making a positive impact. While this is subjective, gaining information about your feedback directly from your staff is a great measure, at least for their morale and perceptions.

11

GENERATIONAL FEEDBACK

"People try to put us d-down (talkin' 'bout my generation)

Just because we get around (talkin' 'bout my generation)"

~ The Who, "My Generation"

"You see us as you want to see us—in the simplest
terms, in the most convenient definitions."

~ The Breakfast Club (1985)

We've learned about the great impact that feedback can have on employees and supervisees and that a good leader will strive to tailor feedback to employees' individual needs. But does all this seem too good to be true? The most skeptical of leaders may be thinking, "There has to be more. This can't possibly work with all my employees. What about these new interns we just hired or those employees who have been with the company for decades?" This brings us to yet another piece of the puzzle. The elephant in the room that we have yet to address, and it is one that has become a hot-button issue in the organizational world today: generational differences.

As of this writing, there are currently three major generations and a micro generation in the workforce: Baby Boomers, Generation X, Xennials (the microgeneration of those who grew up like Gen X but were young enough to catch the technology wave of Gen Y), and Generation Y, also known as Millennials. It's difficult to pinpoint exactly when these generations begin and end as there isn't much consensus between researchers, but it's generally believed that a generation can be divided by the notable things that the people of those generations experienced while growing up.

Baby Boomers were born sometime in between the mid-1940s and mid-1960s, living through events such as the Civil Rights Movement, the Cold War, and the first moon landing. Generation Xers were born between the mid-1960s and the early 1980s, and their generation is defined by events like the fall of the Berlin Wall, the Challenger disaster, the Watergate scandal, MTV, and the first personal computers. Millennials were born between the early 1980s and the early 2000s and experienced events like the Columbine shooting, 9/11, and the rise of the Internet and social media. Those in the new microgeneration, the Xennials, were born from 1977 to 1983. This microgeneration (called this because of the small window) is characterized by the unique technology wave that has shaped Millennials and stumped Generation Xers. Xennials are the ones who remember the good ol' days of no technology, yet spend all of their time keeping up with the latest technology trends. You could call it the best of both worlds (or the bias of the person writing this). All these happenings undoubtedly shaped the people in their respective generations, but the extent to which they shaped individuals within each generation is hard to say. This chapter will look to examine these potential differences and look at how leaders can address them.

Findings from a Pew Research Study conducted in 2015 suggest that, in the United States, Millennials have overtaken Baby Boomers as the largest living generation (as cited in Fry, 2016). As more Millennials enter the workforce, will managers of older generations have to drastically alter the way in which they conduct their businesses? There is no easy answer here. A quick search on the Internet will yield a plethora of strategies for how a leader can manage their older employees while mitigating the rising tide of the younger generation, but what we want to examine is the utility of these separations by labels. By now, we know better. An individual's environment shapes their performance, but how these environmental variables affect that performance is mostly idiosyncratic. Therefore, are these generational labels worth panicking over? Let's examine this.

The Label Problem

Are labels helpful? They can be. In the search for ideal employees, employers are on the hunt for a prospect labeled as a "team player" versus a "spectator," a "go-getter" instead of a "loafer," or a "seasoned veteran" versus a "young upstart." At the same time, if you were to get a handful of these labels, what do they really mean? Take a look at some common adjectives often thrown in résumés:

- "Hard-working"
- "Detail-oriented"
- "Creative"
- "Strategic"
- "Eager to learn"
- "Passionate"
- "Dependable"

If you slapped these words on a whiteboard and asked 100 people how they would describe them, you're likely to get 100 different responses (kind of like asking the definition of the word "feedback"). Even worse, they may describe these labels with words that seem like satisfactory definitions, but are they really? If we define a "creative" person as someone that "thinks outside the box," have we come closer to an objective definition? Is a manager who yells at their employees "passionate" about the job? Is an employee who turns in subpar work but always on time "dependable"? Is an intern who asks question after question "eager to learn"? Labels can be useful, but the danger lies in when we use a label as a sole explanation for someone's behavior.

Let's say we are working in an office setting, and we have Phil from the accounting department. Phil has the reputation of being "lazy." Before we go into what Phil has done to earn that reputation, what behaviors come to mind? Does Phil procrastinate? Does he delegate frequently rather than doing the work himself? Does he complain that he is entitled to a year-end bonus regardless of the quality of work that he has done? It could be any or none of these. The point is that he has done something to earn the reputation of being "lazy."

You can probably think of a few of your own co-workers who have similar reputations or maybe even better ones. Anne from Human Resources is "friendly" and "caring." Jorge from the upper management team is "stubborn," yet "efficient." Hugo from IT is "aloof" and "in his own world." What's the problem with all these labels? Aside from the fact that we don't know how accurate these labels are, they ultimately place the source of all the behaviors on the individual, completely taking the person's environment out of the equation and creating the logical fallacy of circular reasoning. Take a look at this sequence of thoughts:

Phil is "lazy." How do we know that Phil is lazy? He doesn't do anything at work. He just shows up and immediately starts goofing off. Why doesn't Phil do his work? It's because he's lazy!

Did we ultimately discover something about Phil? Other than "he is lazy," nothing was added in terms of finding an explanation for his behavior. There could be numerous explanations, but let's give "Lazy" Phil a bit more of backstory at his current job.

When Phil shows up to work, he needs to complete a series of tasks, but mostly is left to his own devices. Phil finds it a lot more reinforcing to goof off, scroll through social media, and watch funny cat videos on the Internet. If Phil's job was paying for his time rather than for his effort, it's no wonder why he would choose to do anything else! When his deadlines get closer and closer, Phil begins to work "harder and faster." That is, with the looming threat of missed deadlines coming up, Phil waits until the last possible moments to start putting effort in, and when he can't meet the deadlines, he begs his boss for an extension. Phil's coworkers see this and feel this is "Phil being Phil" and discretely label him as "lazy."

By this point, we're hoping that you're thinking, "Well, what kind of feedback does his supervisor give him? How often is he receiving feedback for his work? Is the supervisor making sure to allocate reinforcers for turning in work on time?" In which case, job well done! Labels can be harmful and distracting, but they may point to the very fact that there is a problem that is worth addressing. In other words, what are the factors that are responsible for Phil's "lazy" behavior? It's when we use a label to simply brush away a problem that labels become useless. Instead, follow the guidelines in this book, and look to the organizational environment for the answers.

Generations—Another Label

Not much will change in the previous scenario by calling Phil a "Millennial" even if we were talking about different behaviors or "common traits." Millennials, for example, may be referred to as "entitled." That is, members of this generation supposedly feel that certain things are "owed to them," including benefits, raises, or high-paying jobs with little experience. If this is your view of the "typical Millennial," then it may shock you to learn that very little research can back up such claims. If you're thinking, "Well, I know Millennials just like that!" That may be true, but do you know other non-Millennials that engage in the same or similar behavior? Would a Baby Boomer or Generation Xer object to the claim that, after working at job for many years, they would be entitled to a raise or benefits that other workers are receiving? After earning a degree, would a Baby Boomer or Generation Xer object to the claim that their higher education would open the doors to a higher-paying job?

Let's now apply the *label problem* to generational differences using three examples of employees: Mark, Li, and Juan.

Mark is a Baby Boomer. He's a workaholic and strongly believes that the more you work, the more that gets done. He puts in 50+ hours a week every week and likes to excel. However, he gets frustrated when he sees younger workers moving up the ladder, but putting in fewer hours. His solution is attempting to come in even earlier and then leave even later to prove his dedication. As a result, Mark's bosses see him as someone who can always be counted on to meet the fluctuating needs of their customers.

Mark looks forward to his annual performance review, but was blindsided when his supervisor told him he'd like to see him have more work–life balance and reduce his hours to no more than 45 per week. Mark was also confused by feedback regarding his need to be more of a team player. His supervisor would like to see him pitch more ideas that involve teamwork. Mark's experience has led him to believe that the more you can do on your own, the more respect and better opportunities you receive.

Li is a Generation Xer. She likes work, but views it as a means to an end. She works to provide a better life for herself and her family. Her dream is to become an entrepreneur and open her own business one day, but until then, she works on building her career and résumé. She likes to challenge people to produce the best ideas and views, even if that means occasionally challenging those in leadership roles. She likes receiving feedback and will ask for it if necessary, but is uncomfortable if her boss gives her feedback on a weekly basis. She feels she needs a little more room to do her work on her own without constant supervision. She tends to give her supervisees monthly feedback, unless issues pop up that need to be dealt with immediately.

Juan is a Millennial. He has been in his chosen field for about 5 years and enjoys the fulfillment he gets working for a nonprofit organization. He is goal oriented and loves to work as part of a team. Juan seeks frequent feedback from his superiors and often feels lost if he doesn't receive feedback weekly—even if the feedback is just to let him know he is doing well. He is not afraid to ask his manager for feedback, but when he does, he typically gets something like "you're doing great" and struggles with where he should be making improvements. Recently, his boss gave Juan feedback that he needs to be more independent, but he's not sure how to apply that feedback to his daily performance at work.

If you're thinking, "Well, this perfectly describes each one of these generations," take a second look at each one of these examples. Each of these labels may paint a picture of a person based on what is "typical" of that generation, but do these labels actually help us solve each of these problems? By calling Mark a "Baby Boomer," Li a "Generation Xer," or Juan a "Millennial," did a solution magically appear before your eyes? We'll hazard a guess and say no.

But what can we do? We've learned a lot about feedback, and it clearly seems that each of these hypothetical employees would benefit from some sort of feedback. We'll start by breaking down each of these scenarios and sort out all the helpful information with the "not so helpful."

We'll start with the labels: **Mark is a Baby Boomer. Li is a Generation Xer. Juan is a Millennial**. We're leaving the Xennials out because no one has quite figured them out yet, and hopefully you will get our point with the other three. No offense to the Xennials. Remember, at least one of the authors of this book is one of them, so we're leaving ourselves out, too!

These labels essentially just tell us around the time each of these employees was born and maybe even how long each of them has presumably been in the workforce. Sure, the labels tell us what historical events these individuals may have been around for, what music was popular during their time, and maybe even what TV shows and movies entertained the masses. However, the labels themselves do not tell us *how* or even *if* these events affected each individual.

By highlighting their ages, the labels open the door to other presumptions as well: The older the individual, the more experience we assume they have. This might create a situation where "working a long time" is erroneously assumed to be the same as quality experience. We might also presume the opposite, where the younger individual is presumed to have a lot less experience. Either of these statements could be true, but could just as easily be false.

In these descriptions, there is also some information that we *can* work with, including information on each employee's potential reinforcers:

[Mark] puts in 50+ hours a week every week and likes to excel. – From this, we have information about the amount of time Mark works during a given week, 50+ hours. He also "likes to excel," which could tell us that seeing progress on tasks and projects is a strong reinforcer for him.

[Li's] dream is to become an entrepreneur and open her own business one day... She likes to challenge people to produce the best ideas and views, even if that means occasionally challenging those in leadership roles. She likes receiving feedback and will ask for it if necessary. – Li has a long-term goal of eventually opening up her own business. This fact tells us that she may value information, advice, and yes, feedback that will get her closer to that goal.

[Juan] has been in his chosen field for about 5 years and enjoys the fulfillment he gets working for a nonprofit organization. He is goal oriented and loves to work as a team. – Juan values working in a nonprofit organization and enjoys working as part of a team. While this is general information, Juan's supervisor could look deeper into what aspects of working in a nonprofit and working as part of a team Juan finds reinforcing.

We also learn a bit about what each of these employees does not like, or what would function as a punisher for them:

[Mark] gets frustrated when he sees younger workers moving up the ladder, but putting in fewer hours. – It is aversive for Mark to see others who do not put in 50+ hours a week receive reinforcers like greater positions in the company or additional compensation.

Mark looks forward to his annual performance review, but was blindsided when his supervisor told him he'd like to see him have more work–life balance and reduce his hours to no more than 45 per week. – Mark likes putting in additional hours, but his supervisor has decided to remove this reinforcer for what they *believed* to be a reinforcer for Mark.

[Li] is uncomfortable if her boss gives her feedback on a weekly basis. She feels she needs a little more room to do her work on her own without constant supervision. – Li finds frequent feedback aversive, which would be in contrast to what we have been advising. This would be worth looking into for Li's supervisor as Li might have had a previous history of receiving poor feedback frequently.

[Juan] feels lost if he doesn't receive feedback weekly—even if the feedback is just to let him know he is doing well. He is not afraid to ask his manager for feedback, but when he does, he typically gets something like "you're doing great" and struggles with where he should be making improvements. – Juan is motivated by knowing he completes work that others recognize as excellent. His supervisor assumed that because Juan is consistently being told he is doing a great job that Juan is receiving the feedback that will continue his performance. Unfortunately, what the supervisor is missing is that Juan is seeking out the feedback instead of the supervisor providing it freely…and of course the feedback is not specific, which might make it come across as ingenuine.

Finally, each of these employee's profiles also tells us a bit about what each of their supervisors can do moving forward:

[Mark's] solution is attempting to come in even earlier and leave even later to prove his dedication. As a result, Mark's bosses see him as someone who can always be counted on to meet the fluctuating needs of their customers. – Mark's willingness to work additional hours presents itself as an opportunity for him to not only contact additional reinforcement by completing tasks and projects, but also to provide a benefit to the company.

Mark was also confused by feedback regarding his need to be more of a team player. – Mark's supervisor could have done a better job of providing Mark with specific feedback regarding what behavior to engage in. Remember, feedback needs to be understandable to the employee and must point to objective and measurable behavior. Otherwise, you risk a situation where the employee could potentially become defensive.

[Li] tends to give her supervisees monthly feedback, unless issues pop up that need to be dealt with immediately. – It may be worth asking how Li's supervisees are responding to infrequent feedback. This could present itself as a teaching opportunity to teach Li useful leadership behaviors like assessing the effects of her feedback on employee performance and the importance of providing feedback in the moment or immediately after behavior.

Recently, [Juan's] boss gave him feedback that he needs him to be more independent, but Juan is not sure how to apply that feedback to his daily performance at work. – Juan, and all employees out there, would benefit more from detailed feedback that tells them what behavior to engage in.

In these examples, we have hopefully demonstrated the utility of not focusing so much on labels but rather focusing on what employees are *doing*, how we can determine potential reinforcers, and how we can create plans of action to shape our own behaviors as effective leaders. While you might not be sold yet on giving up on labels altogether, it is worth noting another potential pitfall.

More Harm Than Good

When you think of a Baby Boomer, Generation Xer, or Millennial, what do you think of? Is your image of a typical member of each generation a positive or negative one? If you find yourself thinking that it might be the latter, you're not alone.

For example, whenever the term *Millennial* is brought up, it seldom feels like it's being brought up in a positive light. "Ugh, Millennials are entitled." "Millennials are lazy." "Millennials lack work ethic." When is the last time you heard an employer say "I wish all my employees could be like Millennials"? It seems like this word alone is enough to immediately evoke eye rolls everywhere from people who can't stand whoever they define as Millennials or a self-identified Millennial simply looking to go about their day. A recent journal article even discussed the possibility of unfair reverse age discrimination against younger employees stemming from the Millennial label.

Ultimately, the problem with these labels is that pop culture uses them to paint a negative picture of the members of those generations. In fact, if you were to look up old magazine covers, you'll see that at one point or another Baby Boomers, Generation Xers, and Millennials were all labeled as the "Me Generation." Thus, it is best to keep in mind that we are all not only products of our environment, but also products of our time. Economies rise and fall, government regulations change, and technology develops—all creating new and evolving sets of contingencies that we either grow up in or adapt to.

Products of Our Time

Our intent in this chapter is not to completely dispel the idea of generational differences; after all, there may very well be significant differences between each generation. A generation that grew up during wartime may see things a lot differently than a generation that grew up at a time where the major headlines were more about technological advancements. For example, the typical Millennial likely grew up at a time when the Internet was beginning to boom. With home computers becoming more of a norm during the mid- to late-nineties, the advent of email and instant messaging emerged. At their fingertips, Millennials had access to endless streams of positive reinforcement and even reinforcement we ultimately don't have to do much work to acquire (we'll call this non-contingent reinforcement).

What's the problem with this constant access to reinforcement? One could argue that we come to expect it all the time. In fact, we may start to develop the idea that this is the norm. The biggest problems with non-contingent reinforcements are that they tend to decrease behavior over time or, at the very least, maintain it at low rates. If Millennials don't have to work very much to contact reinforcement, then what incentive is there to go above and beyond? Is this where the typical Millennials' entitlement comes from? It's difficult to say because, again, not everyone will experience life the exact same way. From the aforementioned examples, however, it can be seen how a major event can shape an entire group of individuals.

On the verge of entering the workforce are members of Generation Z, meaning those born in the early- to mid-2000s. This is a generation of people who will never know a world without technology; who from an early age learned to use tablets, laptops, and smartphones; and whose childhoods will be easily accessible on social media. In other words, this is a generation born and raised in a world where they quickly learned to use technology and tools that gave them access to both immediate social reinforcement and immediate social punishment. How this affects them as they enter the workforce is difficult to say, but just as every good leader should know to do by now, the answer lies in the environmental contingencies and the feedback formula.

Managing Differences

One of the biggest challenges in today's workforce is managing different people who not only come from different generations but also come from different histories of reinforcement. Leaders need to tailor to the needs of each individual, but some managing strategies can be used to simplify the gaps regarding feedback and used to our advantage as leaders.

While managing individuals and improving feedback culture, focus on the five key strategies below, as derived from the previous chapters:

1. ***Attend to the frequency of feedback.*** For some, feedback is best given in person, but for others, it may need to be more frequent. If this is not possible, leaders may consider providing additional feedback through electronic means, such as videoconferencing or email.

2. ***Focus on clear goals and the steps needed to meet the goals.*** In behavior analysis, tasks are broken down into manageable steps, and these steps show a clear path to reaching a goal. When writing a performance improvement plan, keep the steps clear, concise, and focused on the end goal.

3. ***Set up mentoring programs.*** Encourage employees to provide each other with feedback.

4. ***Practice what you preach.*** Invite your employees to give you feedback by asking for it directly AND apply this feedback when relevant. Employees learn by example.

5. ***PRACTICE!*** In behavior analysis, repetition is an important part of learning and eventual fluency. Practice giving feedback to different people from different generations, and find what works. Keep in mind that everyone is an individual and learns in a different way or at a different pace regardless of their generation.

12

HOW TO RECEIVE AS WELL AS GIVE

"To get the full value of joy you must have someone to divide it with."

~ Mark Twain

The Gift That Keeps on Giving

Today is the day—the day I'll get everything I wanted. I don't need an alarm clock for this day—no, not today. Today, I want to wake up. I want to meet the day and take everything it has to offer... because today... is... Christmas.

Adam, one of our authors, shares this story with us.

These were my thoughts as a child every year on December 25th. I loved Christmas and everything that came with it. Racing out of my room each Christmas morning, I passed footprints my dad made on the carpet by cleverly putting talcum powder on his work boots and walking back and forth between the front door and Christmas tree to simulate Santa tracking in snow from his sled. Such is life in the snow-less sunshine state of Florida.

As a child in the '80s or '90s, you saw Christmas as the only day of the year that seemed like you could order almost anything you wanted in the days leading up to the holiday, and it would magically appear underneath the tree right as the clock struck midnight on the 25th. It was like a once-a-year Amazon Prime before the existence of Internet.

As I dove underneath the Fraser fir Christmas tree and into boxes wrapped in brightly colored, decorative paper to unveil my gifts every year, my mom stopped to remind me we should take turns opening gifts because everyone (including my brother and sisters) gets presents. She explained that gift giving is a show of appreciation, thankfulness, and love that allows you to single someone out in a positive way to make them feel important. She also taught me that receiving a gift makes you feel special because someone was thinking of you. Therefore, the gift-giver should be shown gratefulness and appreciation in hopes the behavior would be maintained and generalized to others. Most importantly, she reminded me of the importance of giving in addition to receiving, highlighting the bidirectionality and importance of the exchange.

It was challenging to learn this skill, especially when I received an awkward-looking sweater I would never ever use from a distant relative. At first glance, I would scoff, let out a huge disappointed sigh, and throw it to the side in search of more boxes with my name. Sometimes my uncle would put a baseball-sized gift inside a box, wrapped inside another box, wrapped inside a larger box, and then placed it inside a box the size of a new bike that I really wanted just because he felt it would be funny. When I uncovered the gift at the bottom of the box to be a bottle of hair gel purchased in hopes of straightening my helmet-hair mullet, I was not amused, nor appreciative. I didn't know it at the time, but lessons could be learned from both circumstances.

So why did we just discuss Christmas day, gift giving, and holiday protocol? And what does that have to do with feedback? The answer to that question is simple: feedback is a gift.

Feedback is usually given with the intent to make someone better at something. We expect that by now you're providing feedback to others with that intent—you want to improve their performance. We also expect that you have run into a few instances in which your feedback was not well received. Just like kids on Christmas morning, our staff want as many gifts (pieces of feedback) as they can get their hands on. To accomplish this vision of unlimited feedback gifts, we need to also teach how to accept gifts (even when they are those boxes that, at first glance, are not what we included on our list to Santa).

This chapter is unique in that the information presented can be useful for both the individual delivering the feedback and the individual receiving the feedback. While this book is not focused on how to accept feedback as the leader, we do recognize this is a skill many leaders must also learn (chances are, there will be a book about this soon). Thus, the information provided in this chapter can also be used as a way to increase your acceptance of feedback from your staff.

Consider the following two examples. First, a clinical manager at a rehabilitation facility, Marty, is meeting with a newly hired, yet highly experienced and trained therapist, Trish, who will be taking over group sessions. Marty developed the format for the groups 5 years ago when Marty opened the treatment facility. He has trained Trish in the protocols and has observed her implementation of the sessions for the past 2 weeks. Marty and Trish are now meeting to review any last questions prior to Trish taking over. During this meeting, Marty provided the following feedback: He states that he noticed that there are times that Trish launches into an explanation and seems to lose the group members. He observed that over 50% of the members start to look away, look down at their hands folded in their laps, or start side conversations any time Trish talks for more than 2–3 sentences at a time. Marty suggests a slightly different format to the groups to increase engagement from the participants.

Here, Trish has two choices, and the choice she makes is likely the result of how well she receives feedback. If she is receptive to feedback and sees it as a gift, she will likely take Marty's feedback and incorporate his suggestion. If not, she will likely reject his feedback and offer an explanation about how she has been doing this for years. She could also make some other justification that maybe the protocol is outdated and needs some updating and revisions.

Now let's look at how to help an employee accept feedback. An administrative assistant began working for an executive about 3 months ago. Overall, things have been going well and the administrative assistant is doing an excellent job. The executive initially provided high rates of feedback in the form of positive praise for the things they did correctly. The executive pointed out when the administrative assistant went above and beyond, completed tasks in less time than expected, and handled calls correctly (based on the executive overhearing the calls). Three months into the position, the administrative assistant made an error in the executive's schedule, causing the executive to miss an important meeting. It is time to give some corrective feedback. How do you think it will be received?

Hopefully the executive knows the answer to this question already because, while providing feedback all along, they have determined how well the assistant accepts feedback. Now let's explore all this a little more.

An Ounce of Prevention

There is an old saying that goes something like this: An ounce of prevention is worth a pound of cure. The gist of this saying means a *little bit* of preparation is better than *a lot* of cleaning up. This basic tenant holds true with the delivery and acceptance of feedback since accepting feedback can be a sensitive situation (to say the least) for most people. In the past, people have been given feedback incorrectly (the performer did not learn much and felt very uncomfortable during the process, or worse, their character was questioned for a small mistake), and the mere mention of the word *feedback* has become a *conditioned* aversive for most performers. This typically results in the performer shutting down and becoming closed off from hearing any helpful information offered. For most leaders, this means the first time you give anyone feedback, you will likely have a steep hill to climb in dealing with the damage done by previous mediators before you can gain the performer's trust. You can thank all of our parents and teachers for that!

Have you ever walked up to someone and said, "Can I give you some feedback?" Chances are, you probably then watched them take a long, deep, uncomfortable sigh. Eventually, they then respond with "Sure, go ahead," in a sarcastic and unappreciative tone, almost as if they are daring you to fight with them. If you've ever had such an experience, you probably don't want to experience it again.

In fact, even as we are writing this book, one of the authors can recall a conversation that began exactly this way. Her supervisor walked into her office one day and said, "I want to give you some feedback." This took place over 5 years ago, but the image is still clear in her mind. She remembers her heart rate increasing and cautiously saying "of course" (as if she had any other choice) as her boss sat down opposite her. She sat there staring at him as he spoke, not knowing exactly what he said. When he stopped, she waited for him to say the next thing.

When he didn't say more, she asked, "What's the feedback?"

He laughed and said, "I just gave it to you."

Shocked, the author remembers trying to remember what her supervisor said. He said several positive things, but she was so focused on bracing herself for the negative comments that she thought were going to follow the infamous "Can I give you some feedback?" statement. As a result, she missed out on all the good. Embarrassed (and now disappointed in herself for not listening better), she thanked her boss, stating that she thought he was going to tell her what she did wrong. Even all these years later, this moment sticks with her as she really wishes she knew what positive things he said. It also serves as a lesson for her as a supervisor, reminding her that sometimes the word *feedback* can be so negative that its mere utterance can create an environment of deaf ears. Now it's a lesson you can draw on, too.

If you want feedback to be successful, it's a good idea to teach people how to receive, process, and apply the feedback BEFORE you actually give it. In other words, show people how you want them to behave before placing behavioral expectations on them. This approach helps prevent uncomfortable situations resulting from the delivery of feedback and ultimately improves the behavior of the person receiving the feedback.

Consider this example: Elaina is a receptionist at a large law firm. She is an excellent employee, and everyone loves having her in the office—staff and clients alike. She scores high on all performance reviews, and there really isn't much that ever needs to be corrected. It's time for her quarterly performance review, and her supervisor has scored her as high as is possible. To give a bit of background, there are six ratings, and the scores can be 1, 2, or 3. A score of 1 means there is room for improvement; 2 means that the employee is performing exactly as expected; and 3 means that the employee is going above and beyond expectations. Elaina has been given five scores of 3 and one score of 2. The score of 2 is on her adherence to the dress code, and the goal is written clearly (score 1 if dress code is not met; score 2 if dress code is met; do not score 3). Gladys, Elaina's supervisor, sits down with Elaina and gives her the paper that documents her scoring. Before anything is said, Elaina tears up. Not understanding what is happening, Gladys asks, "What's wrong?"

Elaina becomes very silent and points to the "2" glaring back at her from on the page and asks, "What did I do wrong? I thought I was doing well." While the instructions clearly stated a score of 3 was not even an option, to Elaina, just seeing the score of "2" indicated sub-par performance. And as shown through the tears in her eyes, she had not learned to accept corrective feedback of any kind.

Accepting feedback is one of the most challenging aspects of the performance feedback process. Not only is it difficult for most people to hear difficult feedback about themselves, but everyone is different, meaning they receive and apply feedback differently. Being an effective leader involves the ability to work with all different personality types (i.e., behavioral repertoires), but it doesn't hurt to give everyone a leg up and teach them how to receive feedback appropriately. If fact, it is crucial if you don't want your feedback to fall on deaf ears.

Equally important is being aware that you too have a history of receiving feedback that is likely just as negative. Because of this, leaders must be even more aware of and proactive in learning how to accept feedback. Many leaders also have the unique position where they have to accept feedback from both sides—their supervisees as well as their supervisors. This can be draining or intimidating at times, which is why it is just as important for leaders to master the skill of accepting feedback as it is for them to master providing feedback.

In light of all of the above, this chapter includes ways employees and managers can become better at receiving feedback, as well as ways leaders can improve on this. As we discuss each point, we will provide examples for how to teach this skill and how to master it yourself. This process begins with defining what acceptance actually means.

Defining Acceptance

As with any behavior, *acceptance* can be defined functionally and structurally. As behavior analysts, we know that functional definitions are the most important, so we will provide you with that here. The functional definition of accepting feedback is this: Feedback has been accepted if the performer's behavior changes in the way in which the feedback provider intended as a result of the mediator's feedback delivery.

Accepting feedback isn't just about hearing and taking in what the mediator communicates; it's about acting on it as well. Simply put, accepting feedback means behavior changes in a specific, predetermined way as a result of the feedback provided. We can measure acceptance by how much the behavior changes in the direction in which it was intended to change.

Acceptance shows the impact of the mediator's behavior (deliverance of feedback) on the behavior of the performer (acceptance of the feedback). The gradation of feedback acceptance is determined through the measures identified and the goals associated with those objectives.

Accepting Something You Don't Want, By Learning New Skills

"How the *bleep* do you accept something you don't want?" You might be asking yourself this question (unedited, of course), but the answer is rather straightforward: You learn new skills and change your reinforcers, and this process is usually done with intense training using behavioral skills training (BST). However, before you can do that, you must first identify and understand the skills you need to effectively receive feedback. Then you need to identify which of those skills you are missing or need to work toward improving.

To begin, we've organized some of the most crucial skills into four categories: preparation, listening, self-management, and reinforcing the mediator's feedback.

Preparation

Like so many activities in life, the success of the feedback session for the receiving party is determined before the session even begins. This means the performer should probably engage in certain activities before a feedback session begins in order to accept feedback successfully. Since our recommendations revolve mostly around high-frequency feedback that (hopefully) occurs throughout the day, preparing to receive feedback *before* the workday begins is a good idea. Additionally, teach your supervisees to prepare for feedback as well.

Here are some helpful tips to prepare for receiving feedback:

1. **Have the materials you need to take notes.** Paper, pencil, tablets, stylus, touchscreen laptops, a bloody finger—whatever it takes. Just make sure you have something to take notes with (but we don't *actually* recommend a bloody finger).

   To teach others to receive feedback, stress the importance of coming to meetings prepared to take notes. If they show up to meetings without a way to take notes, give them something to take notes on or make them return with a way to take notes. Do this even if you are not going to give feedback during the meeting (although chances are, if it's a meeting, some sort of feedback will be provided).

2. **Jot down questions you want to ask the other person.** This will help you focus on the feedback content in addition to (probably) reinforcing the feedback behavior of the mediator. When giving feedback to others, tell them beforehand that you will give them a chance to ask questions. Encourage them to write down any questions that come to mind while you're talking so that they do not forget them.

Listening

This is one of the most important groups of skills to develop if you want to learn to accept feedback appropriately. To properly discuss feedback, the verbal behavior involves an interaction between a speaker and a listener and really emphasizes the bidirectionality of human interactions. If one party (in this case, the listener) does not do their part to reinforce the behavior of the speaker, the speaking behavior stops, and discourse can be lost. Loss of communication is the first step toward organizational problems.

The performer's goal when listening in the context of feedback is to soak up as much information as possible about their own behavior. To help achieve this, the performer should attempt to maintain the speaker's feedback behavior (keep the feedback coming) for as long as needed to gather the information desired and ultimately improve their own performance. Therefore, if you want a behavior to continue (in this case a speaker delivering feedback to you), you should reinforce it. In fact, you should reinforce it early and often. Remember that these behaviors should be reinforced as often as possible prior to giving feedback. You can reinforce these behaviors in meetings, when you're observing employees interact with others, and during training.

Also remember that you should be focused on your own behaviors so that you are prepared to receive feedback as well. Make sure that you monitor your own listening behaviors by checking in periodically. Are you actually paying attention to what the other person is saying, or are you are more focused on what you are going to say next?

There are some specific behaviors that can be reinforced to increase listening behaviors. Let's break them down below:

1. **Active listening.** This skill set involves the listener confirming their understanding of the speaker's behavior using the listener's own behavior (e.g., paraphrasing) instead of the exact behavior of the speaker. You can teach your supervisees to engage in active listening by asking them to paraphrase what you said. You can also practice this skill when your supervisees are speaking by paraphrasing what you heard once they are done talking. If you practice doing this any time you enter a conversation, you will soon master this skill. Plus, the more often you do this, the better model you provide, which increases the chances your supervisees will begin doing it as well.

    A great way to practice eye contact is to talk with others in a group. Here is an activity that you can do to practice your listening skills or to have others practice theirs at the same time.

    - Choose a topic to discuss.

    - Have others observe those talking and listening, then create rules for their own as well as each other's behavior (instructions and modeling).

    - Interacting in groups also allows individuals to practice with multiple people at one time, which builds fluency with a variety of different people and response types (rehearsal).

- The group will provide feedback on listening behaviors. If someone listens well, the speaker will continue speaking to them. If that person does not listen well, the speaker will talk to others in the group. This type of learning often happens without being aware of it.

- At the end of the discussion, have each member of the group score both themselves and each of the other group members on their listening skills. Compare scores to determine if everyone scored listening the same way for each person.

2. **Eye contact.** Eye contact is one of those tricky things as you have to find the right balance between too much and too little eye contact. Have you ever had a conversation with someone who has just stared at you, almost as if they didn't even blink? It was uncomfortable and a bit creepy, right? What about the opposite—where you are talking to someone, and they are looking anywhere but at you? It may not be as creepy, but it is frustrating to talk with someone who is looking at everything other than you.

   To make eye contact not too creepy and not too rude, follow these basic rules:

   - Establish eye contact right away. This is a great way to begin the conversation on a positive note.

   - Some people recommend a 70% rule in which the listener maintains eye contact for 70% of the conversation. This is not necessarily a hard-and-fast rule, but more of a guideline for better eye contact and really a good place to start.

   - Maintain eye contact for 5–7 seconds, but no longer than that at any given time. Take a break for a moment or two to look up or away, and then reestablish eye contact. Do not stare. That's just creepy, and it typically makes people feel uncomfortable.

   - When momentarily breaking gaze, you can include a breath, a head nod, or some form of verbal acknowledgement, such as "Mmhmm," to communicate that you are still listening to the speaker.

   - Look anywhere but at a digital device. This includes

avoiding televisions, computer screens, iPads, and especially your phone.

- When the speaker looks away, the listener can also look away. This is a perfect time for a break in gaze because it shows that you are following along.

Eye contact can be difficult to learn because the only way to practice is working with another individual. Eye contact can also be difficult to learn because you may start concentrating so much on whether you are making eye contact at the right levels that you forget to actually listen. Like with most skills, the best way to train yourself or someone else is using BST. The following tips will help you develop good eye contact skills.

- Create instructions for the exercise, and have someone model appropriate and inappropriate eye contact.

- Rehearse. Listen to someone, and have them give you feedback on your eye contact as soon as possible. If they feel awkward or uncomfortable, ask them to tell you right away because immediacy is critical for learning. If you are teaching your supervisee about eye contact, be sure to provide feedback immediately so that they can correct their eye contact and master the skill as well.

- Have a passionate conversation with someone, whether it is an argument or a communication of your affection. Passionate discussions help hone your eye contact skills by creating motivation to establish and maintain eye contact. Maintaining eye contact is a show of strength during an argument, and deep feelings for another person are great motivation to practice affectionate eye contact. For example, tell someone you love them and mean it.

3. **Have open body language and posture**. Body posture is one of the oldest forms of communication between humans. Before we could speak, we communicated through mannerisms and body language. In fact, your body language can communicate your feelings toward a particular topic more effectively than your words. Closed body postures make both the speaker and the listener feel

defensive; open body postures are welcoming and invite feedback. The following techniques can improve body language:

- Work on limb positioning. Keep your arms open and away from your chest, and your hands should be open and relaxed. Crossed arms are an example of closed body posture. Your feet should move seamlessly with your upper body, and you should avoid only moving your torso as this is a sign of tension. If someone's feet point toward the exit but their upper body is awkwardly pointed toward you, it indicates they're uncomfortable and ready to leave, as opposed to listening closely to what you're saying. Fluid, total body movement and posture are preferred.

- The next time you have the opportunity, pay attention to your limb positioning in the following situations: when you're uncomfortable with what's being discussed, when you're angry and/or having an argument, when you're relaxed and engaging in a pleasant conversation with a friend, and when you're bored or disinterested in what the person is saying. Pay attention to how your positioning changes, and then try your best to always mimic the body positioning that you displayed when you were relaxed and engaged in a pleasant conversation with a friend.

- When coaching your supervisees, it's okay to mention their body postures. You can do this by providing a training on body postures and what they indicate, and then doing a fun activity to see if you can change supervisees' body postures based on the topic of conversation. This is a fun way to bring awareness to the subject and teach the appropriate body postures when giving and receiving feedback.

- Match body positioning and language. Most people think the best way to speak to someone is face to face, and although that technique can have its benefits, sitting side by side with someone can help reduce tension and put you on the same level as the other person.

4. **Ask follow-up questions**.

- Follow-up questions are typically short questions about the speaker's content and are used to confirm understanding. Asking follow-up questions can build and maintain engagement between the speaker and the listener.

- Follow-up questions usually involve "Wh" questions: **Wh**at task do you want me to do? **Wh**ere should I do the task? **Wh**en should this task be completed?

- When receiving feedback, ask questions about the consequences of actions. If the feedback says to do or not to do something, ask a "why" question, such as "What are the implications if I do or don't do that?" This shows interest and concern about the topic and usually reinforces the speaker's behavior.

- Tie early statements to later ones. If the speaker says, "It's important for you to dress professionally," early in a feedback session and then later says, "Don't forget we are meeting with new clients every week," the listener could step in and say, "…which is why we should always dress professionally." This process shows understanding and strongly reinforces the speaker's behavior.

- Ask only the questions that need to be asked. Overusing follow-up questions as a skill for accepting feedback can interrupt the speaker's flow and make them feel like you are interrogating them, which could eventually lead to a loss of trust. Asking follow-up questions is designed to gather more information and reinforce the behavior of the speaker, not make them feel uncomfortable.

- There are a variety of ways to teach the skill of asking follow-up questions. One way to do this is to ask if there are any questions any time you present new information. Initially, new employees may especially say they do not have any questions as, in the past, asking questions has not been a behavior that was reinforced. In this case, you can prompt the questions by asking, "Was I clear on (what to do, why we should do it, when it needs to be done, etc.)?" This type of question models the types of questions that are appropriate and signals that you welcome questions, which increases your receptiveness to feedback.

5. **Use verbal responses that indicate interest.**

- Examples of interest-confirming verbal responses include "Sure," "Uh-huh," "Got it," and "Makes sense."

- Don't use these responses for everything the speaker says. Mix them in with other skills to make the interaction come across as more natural.

- Use positive body language, such as a head nod or a thumbs up, with your words to communicate to the speaker that they have your full attention.

- This is another skill that can be difficult to teach. After modeling it, you can purposely pause while talking to see if affirmations are provided. If not, you can ask a question to check for listening.

6. **Use paraphrasing to summarize.** These statements usually begin with phrases such as "So what you're saying is...," "In other words...," or "Let me see if I understand this..." Paraphrasing can be a helpful skill when listening to others speak. Here are helpful suggestions to improve your paraphrasing skill set.

- Take notes when someone speaks to you during a feedback session. Not taking notes during a meeting can be very aversive to speakers as they may interpret a lack of note-taking to mean their instructions or feedback are not important enough to mark down for accuracy. As stated before, make sure your supervisees show up to meetings prepared to take notes as well. When in meetings, you may take notes and tell your employee to take notes as well. At the end of the meeting, compare your notes to make sure that all of the important points are not only captured, but agreed upon.

- Practice using synonyms. The use of synonyms is critical when paraphrasing as it allows the listener to say the same thing the speaker said in a different way. Prompt others to do this by having them put things into their own words or asking your employee if they can say it better than how you originally stated it.

- When restating someone's point, change the order of the words in their statement. Moving from a passive voice to an active voice is a simple and effective manner of paraphrasing.

Self-Management

Managing your own behavior before, during, and after a feedback session is critical to a successful session. Self-management assists with correcting performance errors (accepting negative feedback) while becoming fluent at generalizing and maintaining performance successes (accepting positive feedback) in order to achieve professional goals. The self-management skills discussed below can help manage behavior associated with both negative and positive feedback skill sets.

When people talk about accepting feedback, they are usually talking about receiving, processing, and applying negative feedback to effectively improve performance. Unfortunately, performers will often, for various reasons, get upset with mediators during feedback administration and blame them for how the performers themselves perceive the feedback. Performers become incensed with the messenger rather than focusing on the content of the message.

So the question becomes, what is the protocol for effectively accepting difficult feedback?

Don't Shoot the Messenger—Self-Managing Negative Feedback

This process typically begins with identifying triggers, which are things that may evoke negative emotions—such as anger, frustration, fear, or sadness—that cloud a person's ability to make good decisions. The process continues by managing those triggers and emotions before and after they occur, so the negative feedback can be applied effectively (without interference from the negative emotions) to improve performance. Importantly, as a leader, you must know your triggers; you have to not only model the appropriate response to feedback but also reinforce the times that feedback is provided—even when it's something you didn't want to hear.

Here's a breakdown of the process:

Identify triggers. A trigger is a statement at the start of a piece of writing, a video, speech, and so on that alerts the listener, reader, or viewer to the fact that it contains potentially distressing material (Dictionary.com). In behavioral terms, a trigger could be one of two things:

- A trigger could be a controlling stimulus—specifically, a stimulus that signals punishment or some kind of aversive consequence. We call these types of controlling stimuli an S^{DP} (not an acronym for anything just short hand). In other words, an S^{DP} is something that signals something else negative could happen in the very near future. Here are a few examples:

  > **Example 1**: A red light is an S^{DP} for driving through an intersection. If the driver continues through an intersection when the light is red, there is a strong possibility they will be hit by another car.

  > **Example 2**: Another S^{DP} could be hearing your boss say something like this: "We need to talk. Meet me in my office in 5 minutes." If you have said this to an employee, chances are you just set them up to NOT receive the feedback you are about to provide.

- A trigger could also be a conditioned aversive—something that has been paired with an aversive stimulus in the past and is now considered aversive itself because of the past association. Here's an example:

  > **Example**: Have you ever broken up with someone and smelled their perfume or cologne on someone else, immediately leading to you getting upset? That distinct aroma became a conditioned aversive because it was paired with your ex and now makes you upset.

While triggers can be classified by their behavioral effects, it may be equally useful to identify them by how they may creep up in feedback. There are two types of triggers with respect to feedback: content triggers and mediator triggers.

Content triggers are pieces of feedback information that are inaccurate, invalid, unreliable, or unfair. These types of triggers focus on the information being presented as not useful or invaluable to the performer.

For example, Kristin, a new operations manager overseeing the technology department, provides Danny, the head of said department, with his team's quarterly performance numbers containing two key performance indicators for his department: (a) data on technology issues resolved and (b) customer satisfaction numbers indicating how polite and respectful Danny and his team were when interacting with employees. In the past, Danny and his team have never been held accountable for the second measure as the previous managers have focused solely on how effective Danny and his team were with resolving computer problems. However, Kristin values the interactions between employees and wants Danny to focus more on being polite when servicing company hardware. This proves to be a problem when Kristin presents the feedback to Danny, who responds by taking a deep breath, sighing, and rolling his eyes as he doesn't value politeness. Rather, he only cares whether the delinquent device has been repaired.

Mediator triggers are usually people who have been paired with negativity in the past and are now a conditioned aversive for the performer. In other words, they are someone the performer does not like because the performer has had a bad interaction (or several bad interactions) with the mediator in the past where the mediator presumably presented faulty content or presented content in a bad manner.

For instance, Joe, a manager in the delivery department, yells at Samantha three to four times a week for a variety of issues and provides little to no positive reinforcement. After several weeks of this type of treatment, Joe will quickly become a conditioned aversive to Samantha.

1. **Managing triggers.** Once triggers have been identified,

performers can better manage their impact on feedback acceptance. Below are some strategies to effectively manage triggers associated with negative feedback delivery when you are the receiver of feedback.

- **Utilize deep-breathing relaxation skills.** This is one of the most commonly used and effective methods to manage triggers. Performers are usually well practiced in this technique, and it can be done before, during, or after a feedback session.

- **Request a break.** This is one of the most underutilized techniques to manage triggers. Most people feel they are stuck in bad situations and simply have to endure them. However, this is not true. Simply ask for a break to use the bathroom, get some water, or take a breather. It is hard for

---

KNOW OUR JARGON

Motivating Operations: events, conditions, or stimuli that have two effects:
They increase or decrease the likeliness of the behavior
They increase or decrease the effectiveness of the reinforcer for the behavior
For example, the absence of food for several hours is a motivating operation to eat. It increases the reinforcement of finding and then eating food and the likeliness that one will in fact find and then eat food. However, eating a large meal has an abative effect (opposite of motivation) in that it decreases the effectiveness of food as a reinforcer and makes it less likely one would engage in any behaviors that would lead to the consumption of food.

---

someone to deny those requests.

- **Beware of motivating operations, or in lay terms, watch your mood.** Don't show up to a feedback session hungry or tired. This can increase the value of eating and sleeping and can comparatively decrease the value of everything else, like being polite and patient.

When you are the provider of feedback, you can teach or prompt these skills when you see your employee is responding to a trigger. You can do this by suggesting a break, taking a deep breath yourself and pausing before continuing the feedback, and asking your employee prior to providing feedback how they are doing. If they respond negatively, you might wait until their mood has improved a bit before providing feedback. Finally, if you find that someone is not accepting your feedback, you should be honest about it and ask for their feedback in turn.

In the example with Danny and Kristin, Kristin could have said, "It seems like being polite is not of high value to you. Can we talk about that a bit so that I can learn more about your priorities when working with customers?" This approach provides a non-confrontational and non-judgmental way of discussing Danny's priorities, which gives Kristin insight into how to better motivate him and how to explain why politeness is essential when interacting with customers.

Don't Get Cocky—Self-Managing Positive Feedback

Yes, this is a skill (behaving humble, that is), and it's an important one. Too much of anything can be a bad thing—or at least that's how the old saying goes. That concept also applies to positive feedback. If you only receive positive feedback from others, you may no longer focus on what you can do better and instead simply revel in your successes. This can unfortunately lead to a decrease in performance and/or affect the performance of others. The truth is, we could all improve in at least one thing at any given moment.

Conversely, there are some who have a difficult time accepting positive feedback. This is likely due to a learning history where positive feedback has, at some point in the past, been manipulative and followed by negative feedback or some other aversive situation.

Let's review some tips you can use to ensure you accept positive feedback and ensure your supervisees accept it as well.

1. **Use polite verbal behavior.** Wait for the person to finish their statement before speaking. Create a latency period between the end of their sentence and the time you start talking. This shows maturity and professionalism. Additionally, say something appreciative, such as "thank you" or "I really appreciate that."

   When teaching others to do this, you can use various nonverbal cues to prompt them to wait until you are finished speaking. You can also provide a quick prompt for them to accept the feedback graciously by simply saying "thank you." Do not attend to statements of self-put-downs or responses that are not simple acceptances of the positive feedback.

2. **Return positive feedback with positive feedback.** When someone provides you with positive feedback, you can also provide them with positive feedback about their role in what is being discussed. For example, let's say that you are a principal and you had several teachers call out sick. One of the teachers has to manage two classes due to short staffing. You notice that the teacher appears to be overwhelmed, so you enter the classroom and begin helping out. At the end of the day, the teacher thanks you for helping out and says that you were really excellent with the kids and that working with the struggling students 1-on-1 allowed her to not only stay sane all day but also get through the lesson. You can respond by telling her that you are glad to help and that you were impressed with her composure in a really difficult situation. This shows that you recognize her work as well and reinforces the delivery of feedback to you.

   This behavior is a bit more difficult to teach; however, you can reinforce it when it occurs. If one of your employees responds to your positive feedback with a statement of positive feedback to you, accept it gracefully.

2. **Reinforce the feedback.** Feedback delivered by a mediator to a performer is behavior on the part of the mediator (assuming the mediator is a human being and not a machine). If you want that

feedback delivery behavior to continue, reinforce it often. This means the performer must have knowledge of the most impactful reinforcers for the mediator's behavior. In the case of an employee receiving feedback from theirmanager, the employee must have a good understanding of the manager's reinforcers. Here are some ways that you can show your employees what reinforcers work best for you.

a. **Use appreciative statements.** Make sure you use descriptive appreciative statements; in other words, tell them what you are appreciative for. Feel free to change up the statements and mix some statements with others. Everyone likes to be appreciated, right? Show your appreciation using these very popular statements:

> "Thank you for listening to and accepting my feedback."
>
> "I really appreciate the questions you asked when I provided feedback."
>
> "Your feedback about my feedback was really helpful."

When you are the receiver of the feedback, you can still show your appreciation of your employees' feedback. Here are some common statements to show appreciation:

> "Thank you for the feedback. It was really helpful to have insight about _____."
>
> "I really appreciate your willingness to provide open and honest feedback to me."
>
> "Your feedback was really helpful and led to us improving our process."

b. **Ask for more feedback!** Don't be afraid to say, "Please feel free to give me feedback whenever you feel it is helpful." Asking for more feedback not only shows appreciation, but also indicates you are most likely going to act on their suggestion. You can prompt your employees to be more open to feedback by asking them if it is okay to continue to provide them feedback or asking whether your feedback was helpful.

c. **Request a time to follow up.** Asking to follow up on the feedback session shows appreciation, indicates you are going to act on the feedback, indicates you would like more feedback in the future, and strongly reinforces the behavior of most mediators. Any time you are provided feedback by an employee, schedule a time to follow up on it so that you can ask for their ongoing input regarding your behavior change.

You Can't Expect Acceptance Without Training

So you want people to do well at accepting feedback, huh? Then you better train them to do just that. We have provided several suggestions throughout this chapter about how you can increase others' acceptance of feedback. We will provide you the specific steps to take to provide this training. Keep in mind that most people show up to feedback sessions (especially new hires) with their own preconceived notions of feedback. We're here to tell you that these notions are usually unpleasant notions. As previously mentioned, this is due to a long history of conditioning with bad feedback delivery. You can either blame their previous managers, or you can take responsibility for training the staff to accept feedback appropriately. If you don't, you may be wasting your time or making their performance worse.

What's the best way to insert those skills into skill repertoires of everyday employees in order to help them better accept feedback, you ask?

As we mentioned earlier, use BST…

1. **Instruction.** Break the skill sets discussed earlier into smaller, more easily understood units on how to accept feedback appropriately. You should list the steps in addition to examples of correct and incorrect behavior (behavior analysts call those exemplars and non-exemplars, respectively). By doing this, you create what behavior analysts refer to as a *task analysis*.

2. **Modeling.** Set an example by modeling correct feedback acceptance behavior. This should be done as often as possible because employees are always watching and listening, and because employees talk to other employees. As a mediator/leader, you must request feedback from your direct reports to show the importance of feedback and create a culture of feedback.

3. **Rehearsal.** Usually, you can't become very good at something without a lot of practice. Set up as many opportunities as possible for performers to practice accepting feedback to build fluency. Role-playing scenarios are an excellent way to practice because they allow the performer to practice in real-life situations without the stress of real-life consequences. It also helps the performer become more comfortable accepting feedback in low-stress scenarios overall. During these practice scenarios, the sting of negative feedback should be lessened enough for the message to get through but not completely extinguished so that the behavior still changes.

If you really want to make sure employees learn this skill as soon as they enter your organization, work these activities into new-hire training. Here is an example of what that might look like using the BST model:

1. **Instruction:** Provide the definition of feedback, when it is received and given at your organization, and the expected results of feedback. Ask employees to share positive and negative experiences with feedback, and maybe even state what they would think if someone told them, "I'd like to give you some feedback." (Hint: Most will say they would prepare themselves to hear something negative.)

2. **Modeling:** A great way to model the behaviors of giving and accepting feedback is to do role-playing. You can video tape different scenarios, or you can call in current employees to role-play some common scenarios. Role-plays can be really fun and engaging, so don't be scared to have some fun with this—especially when addressing more difficult topics. You can also provide nonexamples of what to do and have trainees identify what went wrong and how to correct it.

3. **Rehearsal:** Provide the trainees with different scenarios to role-play themselves. Have them practice in trios, where one person practices providing feedback, the second person practices accepting it, and the third person observes and provides feedback about the role-play feedback session. Make sure you have each trio practice giving and receiving each of the following scenarios: (a) positive feedback regarding performance, (b) corrective feedback regarding a slight error, and (c) corrective feedback about a commonly uncomfortable subject.

Remember practice makes perfect, so the more you can provide feedback to others, the better they will get at receiving it. In turn, the more you can get others to provide you with feedback, the better you can get at receiving it, too!

13

EVERYTHING ELSE: SOME FINAL TIPS ON DOS AND DON'TS OF FEEDBACK

"A tiny remnant of a big thing is better than a whole little thing."

~ Abraham Isaac Kook

The Gateway to Trust

In order to provide behavioral feedback, preparation and trust are both imperative. Think back: remember that great manager you had? Now recall a manager who was less than stellar. Which one did you want to perform better for? When we trust someone, we are much more likely to want to put our best foot forward. We're also more apt to trust the feedback they give us. Behaviorally speaking, trust means there is correspondence between what people say and what people do. In other words, are they practicing what they preach? The delivery of honest feedback is a powerful way for a leader to build this trust, but before we get there, we need to ensure you're ready to deliver feedback effectively.

Thus far, we've discussed many topics regarding the delivery of feedback, including when to give it, how often to give it, and even what it looks like. However, before you attempt to give feedback, we want to provide a few more "dos" and "don'ts" for you to keep in mind. Recall that behavior analysis looks at different factors and how those factors influence behavior. In this chapter, we'll look at several different factors and how to use them to create steps for influencing behavior in regard to giving, applying, and receiving feedback.

Additional Dos and Don'ts of Feedback

First, we will review some things you should avoid when providing feedback and what to do instead. Then we will review some guidelines to remember when you're providing feedback.

Don't use subjective labels to describe the problem. When you're providing feedback—whether it be positive, corrective, or negative—we have stressed to remain as objective as possible. This means focusing on observable and measurable behavior rather than talking about the person or subjective qualities of the person. It's easy to blame a person for being "entitled," "lazy," or any other label indicating that there is something innately wrong with the person rather than them simply doing something that can be corrected. Placing blame like this is problematic for two main reasons. First, it presents the situation as unchangeable. Referring to someone as "lazy" or "entitled" presents the illusion that they cannot change—that there is just something innately wrong with them. It also loses sight of the specific problem. It is difficult to correct being lazy. However, knowing exactly what was done wrong leads to correcting the problem and improved performance. Second, describing someone's mistake as a character flaw or negative label can evoke defensive behavior from the supervisee, leaving them searching for a way to defend themselves. This behavior then leads to blaming, making excuses, talking back, and denying contribution to the problem. Both of these reasons show how placing blame fails to lead to solutions, leaving the employee to continue making the same mistake over and over again.

Instead, describe the specific behavior that was incorrect. When errors are made, stick to describing the exact behavior or outcome that was incorrect. You may say "the report has been submitted late" or "you have not responded to consumer emails within 24 hours." Such specific descriptions keep things objective and helps prevent your supervisee from getting defensive.

Let's look at the following example. Charlie is Maryanne's supervisor and has been working hard on his feedback delivery skills. He has learned to think through feedback sessions as he used to provide a lot of subjective feedback. Charlie was feeling as though feedback was not important until he began reading this book! He has now learned that he was simply approaching feedback the wrong way. Now Charlie has learned the difference between subjective statements and objective, behaviorally specific ones, but he is still working to master his skills. Thus, he decided that he would plan how to provide Maryanne some feedback about her recent decrease in performance. Charlie began thinking about what he would have said in the past.

Maryanne has been working for Charlie for approximately 3 years now. Over the past 6 months, Charlie noticed some not-so-good changes in Maryanne's performance. She was not responsive to emails and was turning in reports and other tasks after the deadlines. In the past, Charlie would have most likely called Maryanne into his office to discuss the problem and provide feedback by saying something like this: "Maryanne, I've never known you to be lazy and careless, but lately I'm beginning to think that things are changing. I've noticed that you aren't doing your job as well lately and it just reeks of someone who doesn't care about their job. I'm hoping we can fix this."

Charlie remembered this **_feedback f!@#up_** and that this usually makes people defensive and thought Maryanne would respond by defending herself. He imagined she'd say something like this: "Charlie, I'm not sure what you're saying, but I know you know I'm not lazy. I work hard each and every day, and I've given you 3 years of my life—often staying late just to get the job done. I've never asked for any credit, but I am not okay with you calling me lazy." Charlie knew a statement like this would lead to him trying to defend his statement by focusing on how Maryanne has been screwing up and that all her screwups were indicative of laziness. Of course, that would lead to Maryanne becoming even more defensive. Charlie knew this would not end well.

He then decided to think through the scenario again. Remembering that feedback should be objective and specific, he decided to write down the things that have happened that made him think Maryanne was being lazy. He wrote the following items: she is not returning emails within 24 hours, reports are turned in late and with more errors, and the project deadline was missed by 2 weeks. He decided he would try to describe these things and ask Maryanne if something was going on. Ready to give it a try, he called Maryanne into his office.

"Maryanne, I want to talk with you about a few things that I have observed lately. I have observed that you have been taking more than 24 hours to respond to your emails, and both your reports and the project you were assigned to have been late and filled with errors. I want to problem solve so that this does not continue."

Maryanne responded, "Charlie, you're right. I haven't been on my A-game lately. I've had a few things happen in my personal life, and then I got sick but didn't want to not follow through on my assignments. I tried to keep working through it all, but found that it was really difficult to concentrate."

Charlie was glad that Maryanne took accountability for everything. However, listening closely, he realized that there must be a reason Maryanne didn't ask for help. He wanted her to do this in the future so that she could care for herself *and* perform better. He followed up her statement by saying, "I appreciate you working to keep your word and commitment to things. However, I also want to be sure that you are caring for yourself and not working while sick. Is there a reason that you felt you couldn't ask for help?"

Now Charlie and Maryanne are engaged in a dialogue that will likely lead to a solution. Charlie did an excellent job of avoiding the subjective labels and remaining specific and objective.

Don't be stingy! This is important! We don't believe that leaders are actually stingy people. Instead, they get busy and get caught up in their daily tasks and forget to fill up their employees' feedback banks. Leaders are used to being called upon to put out fires, so it is easy to forget to give feedback until it is time to correct something. This reality not only creates situations where employees start to avoid you since you only present corrective feedback but also stifles growth. If employees don't know what they're doing right, it's up to them to decide, and most often employees will just keep doing what they're doing, right or wrong, until someone tells them to do something different.

Instead, provide positive feedback plentifully outside of corrective feedback. Instead of attempting to find some positives to blanket on top of corrective feedback, make it a point to provide positive feedback often. Remember the Goldilocks Zone of 3 to 5 positives for every 1 corrective feedback statements (Fredrickson, 2009). Remember that, for trust to be built, employees have to know that you also notice when they do things right, not only when they do something wrong. If you see an employee do something correctly—especially if it is above and beyond what is expected—deliver that positive feedback. Everyone likes to know when they are doing things right. Even more, no one wants to be managed by someone who *only* talks to you when things go wrong. Remember the old adage here: catch 'em being good!

Now it's time for an example. Josiah has been working for the company Anytime Fidgets for the past 5 years. He was just introduced to his new boss, Amrita. Upon meeting Josiah, Amrita comments that she got to observe him while she was interviewing. "Josiah, it's a pleasure to formally meet you. I remember observing you while I was interviewing here, and I was really excited to hopefully have the opportunity to work with a team that seemed so positive. I noticed that you were smiling as you talked with both colleagues and customers, and everyone who interacted with you left smiling as well. I remember thinking to myself, 'Now, this has got to be a fun team if one person can make everyone so happy when they talk with him.'" Josiah, excited for this feedback (it was actually the first of its kind in the 5 years he had been there), thanked Amrita for the kind words. He gracefully shook her hand, smiling, and said he was looking forward to working with her.

Josiah then returned to his place on the floor, where his colleague Santiago was waiting for him. Santiago, eager to know the low down on the new boss, asked, "So is she as bad as the last one?"

Josiah smiled widely and said, "Not at all. I think we're going to like her. She actually told me that I'm the reason she wanted to come work with us. She said that everyone smiled when they talked to me. I can't believe it! No one has ever told me I was ACTUALLY DOING A GOOD JOB, let alone that I'M the reason they want to work here. I think we're going to like her."

Everyone likes to know when they're doing a great job. As this example shows, Josiah's trust in and eagerness to work with Amrita was immediately established due to her providing an immediate positive about what she had observed.

Don't assume negative intention. This one is tricky, but it seems that managers will often deliver corrective or negative feedback based on what they perceive to be the employee's "intention." That is, rather than provide feedback for actual behavior, managers deliver feedback for what they believe to be an employee's perceived purpose for a behavior. For example, a leader may assume a warehouse employee driving a forklift too fast is "due to wanting to get a job done quickly" or "because they don't care about safety." There are two problems with this. First, it assumes that errors are caused due to negative intentions from employees. While every blue moon or so employees make mistakes on purpose or because of negative intent, it is more likely that this is not the case. Second, just like subjective labels, such judgments are likely to evoke defensive behavior from employees, even if delivered alongside any sort of feedback.

Instead, stay focused on the behavior. We've already discussed how to remain objective and specific. The same holds true here. When you have to provide corrective or negative feedback, deliver it based on objective observations and information. Who's involved? What exactly did they do? What is the issue at hand? When and where did the behavior occur? What do you want to see instead? Gathering such information will equip you as a leader with the ability to deliver judgment-free feedback.

There are certainly many more don'ts that we could focus on, but just like we've been preaching, we will focus more on the positives. Let's now focus on what to do when providing feedback.

Clearly define expectations. There is nothing worse than knowing exactly what you did wrong, but not having a clue about what to do to fix it. When providing feedback on current behavior that you want to see change in the future, clarify the exact correct behavior. There are a few things to consider in addition to the exact behavior, namely your expectations regarding the targeted behavior. You can define expectations in the following ways:

- *Competency* or *Mastery*: This expectation is the minimum ability and skills needed to get the job done. It is the most basic definition of targeted behavior in that it tells you the exact behavior or the outcome of that behavior. For example, it may be that one can write a report with no grammatical errors or complete all of the steps on a checklist. Competency or mastery can be determined either by having the employee demonstrate the skill or by reviewing an outcome that is the result of the skill being performed (a report, for instance). Leaders should aim to have employees be competent in all the skills required for a job from the get go. Ensuring such competency is achieved will require frequent supervision, guidance, and of course, feedback.

- *Proficiency*: This is how well someone can do something and how many times someone can do that thing well. Ensuring that an employee can perform a skill correctly is not enough. Leaders must also ensure that employees can complete the skill no matter when they are asked to do it (Vargas, 2013). Those who are proficient in their skills don't just perform when the boss is around or only in the morning after they've had their coffee. They also don't just perform the skill in a specific situation. For example, if someone is a painter and responsible for painting the interior of houses, that person should be able to paint any kind of room, no matter the shape, size, or height. Those who are proficient in their skills do not require frequent supervision or guidance. However, remember that supervision and feedback both remain important to ensure the great skills continue; they are just needed less often when employees are proficient.

- *Fluency*: This is how well someone can do something and how many times someone can do something within a certain period of time. Fluency is a combination of accuracy and speed, common characteristics of competency (Binder, 1996). Fluency does not always have to be demonstrated for all skills required in the job; however, ensuring staff are fluent in all skills will ensure their success over time. For example, a billing auditor who is responsible for checking the billing codes prior to submitting them for payment may not have to complete a review of 25 checks per minute. In fact, it is highly unlikely that employers are putting those kinds of targets in place. However, a billing auditor who reviews 25 codes per minute is a far more skilled auditor than the one who only reviews 10 per minute. While both may have the same accuracy over time, one will complete more work. Leaders should always work to train their staff to a specific fluency to improve performance and efficiency overall.

Always be specific. We know, we've said this before, but it is really important! Whether you're providing positive or corrective feedback, always be specific. Those who are specific are seen as more genuine and are more likely to see a change in behavior when needed. Not convinced? Think about the people who tell you how awesome you are. Who do you believe? The person you barely know who says "you're just so awesome!" or the one who says "your awesomeness shines through every time you help me because you seem to always know where to find the answers I need." Follow three rules when being specific: Be complete. Be objective. Be easy to understand.

Use effective listening. We discussed active listening when we discussed accepting feedback. Effective listening is similar in that it means that you heard what the other person was saying and understand their intended message. Effective or active listening is important not only when accepting feedback but also when providing feedback. When providing feedback, especially when providing corrective feedback, most leaders tend to focus on what it is they have to say—how they will identify and then correct the problem. There are times when it feels like the person who erred provides excuses or tries to reason their way out of the correction. In those instances, make sure you listen and receive the message the performer is sending. After all, this is still behavior, and if you want the performer to not provide excuses when receiving correction, you have to identify it as a behavior to change and provide feedback regarding it. The other important reason to listen effectively is that performers will often identify other antecedents and/or consequences that you were unaware of.

Let's look at the following example for perspective here. Terrance met with his supervisor Katerina to discuss some concerns he had. When asked to put his concerns into his own words, Terrance stated, "I don't feel like we're a team here. I feel isolated and as if I don't know what's going on. I think that you hoard information. I understand the hierarchy and that you are not my direct supervisor, but it would be nice to be kept in the loop."

Katerina, thinking that she had been open and communicated transparently with her staff, was taken aback by Terrance's words. Initially, she wanted to react by rebutting what Terrance stated, but luckily, she read this book and remembered to first ensure she listened effectively. Katerina responded to check whether the message she received was what Terrance intended. She stated, "I want to be sure I heard you correctly and received what you intended. Can I state what I heard back to you to make sure it's correct?" After Terrance affirmed, Katerina stated, "You are upset because you think that I don't share information. This isolates you and makes you feel that you're not part of the team. Also, you think in general that we don't operate as a team here and that everyone operates in silos, working independently of one another."

Terrance frowned and stated, "That's not really what I meant. I do think that everyone is a team here, and I do feel that I know about all of the projects that are happening. I think that I have felt a bit isolated lately because I have been working on an independent project. It would be nice to have another project or some different tasks where I get to work with other people and not by myself all the time."

Katerina paused for a moment, thinking that was not the initial message she heard at all. She decided to check for understanding again. "So let me see if I get it now. You are currently feeling isolated due to working on this independent project and would like to get involved in a team project. But outside of that you feel that communication is transparent and that we are working well as a team. Is that right?"

Terrance smiled and responded, "Yes! That's right! Is there something I can get involved with?" Katerina smiled and nodded, thinking of two projects that might be perfect for Terrance's wants and skills.

In this example, Katerina's check for understanding likely prevented what could have been a blow up. It is easy to feel defensive when someone tells you that you're not doing a good job. However, Katerina's check for understanding not only showed her that her initial perception was not correct but also helped Terrance focus more on exactly what was bothering him. We know that not everyone has read our book, so they don't all know that being specific and sticking to the actual behaviors is the way to go when providing feedback. But by asking questions and checking for understanding, you can help others get more specific, leading everyone to higher levels of success!

Find points of agreement. It is going to be a fact of any job that sometimes the manager will not be around to observe the employee engaging in certain tasks, and there will be disagreement about what really happened. When this occurs, the challenge becomes how the leader can best deliver feedback for behaviors that they didn't witness. The first step in these situations is not jumping to conclusions and instead asking the employee what happened. Listen for key details, such as when and where the incident occurred, and determine whether you can both agree on any facts. Start by saying "it seems that we can agree on…." This will show that you are searching for agreement and not simply jumping to conclusions. If you have cultivated a culture where honesty is reinforced rather than punished, you will find that these conversations are not as difficult as others make them out to be. People will share with you what went wrong, and you will easily find a place of agreement.

Consider your own contribution to the problem, instead of finding someone to blame. Everyone has some contribution to the problem, and as the leader, you're ultimately responsible for the actions of everyone following you. As such, it may be that you need to adjust your technique in order to better lead the employee. Keep in mind that everyone is different, and a flexible leadership style is necessary to bring out the best in everyone. You might have overlooked something or made assumptions. Or possibly, you used a management style that works well for you but not for your follower. Blame is about judging and finger-pointing, and contribution is about understanding; blame looks backward, and contribution looks forward (difficult conversations). It isn't difficult to figure out that understanding contribution is more effective than finding a scapegoat.

Present the "why" behind the need for the behavior change, and allow for questions from the employee. While it may seem like common sense to you, it is our experience that not everyone understands the why behind the feedback. Understanding what you did specifically, as well as the effect it had on others, is important—it links the behavior to the outcome. This is true for both positive and corrective feedback. Think about the following example with a disgruntled customer.

The customer service representative answered the phone and said,

"How are you today?"

The customer retorted, "Not good. I wouldn't be calling if things were great."

The customer service agent, not skipping a beat, said, "I'm sorry to hear that. I realize that you wouldn't be calling if there was not a problem; however, I do hope that other things are going well today."

The customer, caught off guard by this, replied, "Well, actually things are pretty okay. The weather is good at least."

The agent smiled and then asked, "So what is the problem? Let's see if we can get this corrected, so you can focus on having a great day." The call proceeded, and unfortunately, the agent could not fix the issue. However, the agent continued the entire phone call with the same statements, never allowing the customer's negative statements to change the tone of the conversation. Upon ending the call, the customer replied that, even though they were disappointed the problem was not fixed, they really appreciated the agent for trying.

The supervisor, who observed this call, approached the agent afterward and said, "Nice call there! I really like how you remained positive and asked specific questions that focused the customer on the positives. You also asked questions to show that you were genuinely interested in the customer and their problem. This is the reason that the call went so well and ended with the customer disappointed that the problem was not fixed, but not upset or ready to leave the company. Your style is excellent customer service and the reason we get such great reviews!"

Here, the supervisor's feedback tied the agent's behavior directly to the outcome for the company. It shows the value of the agent's work and provides an explanation for why her role and work are so important to the company.

Understanding the why behind the behavior not only reduces the "because I said so" style of leadership but also builds value in the employee and ties their job directly to the vision of the company. This approach is even more important for corrective feedback as employees also need to know how their errors can negatively impact the company and/or its consumers. If you cannot provide an explanation at the moment, inform the employee that you will speak about it when it is more convenient for both of you. Remember, though, you must follow through with this.

Present solutions to the issue. Corrective feedback is all about solutions. Chances are, you have what needs to happen in mind, but this may not always be the case. Additionally, using feedback as a way to collaboratively generate a solution builds accountability in the employee. When possible, ask the employee if they have a possible solution, but ensure you always have one yourself, too. Explore both solutions to determine the best path forward. To ensure the new solution sticks, role play it with your employee, and provide positive feedback when they demonstrate the solution.

Phew, we have just thrown a lot of rules at you. To help you remember them all, let's look at the following example that puts it all together.

Priya is a supervisor working in a clinic that services clients with who receive in home healthcare services. Her supervisee, Chris, is a therapist, who is tasked with delivering one-on-one services to his clients.

Priya read this feedback book (we know, we have a lot of readers!), and as a leader in her company, she would like to implement the strategies with her current employee, Chris. Chris is an excellent therapist and consistently does well all around. However, Priya has become frustrated with Chris's recent shortcomings. Priya's frustration with Chris lies with his inability to chart his client notes in a timely manner. Originally, she requested for notes to be completed on a weekly basis, but since it has been a struggle, she attempted to make it more consistent and asked for notes to be done daily. She has provided corrective feedback in the past, including verbal warnings, write-ups, and most recently, according to company policy, the threat of being put on probation. Chris always seems apologetic, but the behavior continues to occur.

Priya, frustrated that her feedback hasn't worked and fearing that she will have to let an otherwise excellent employee go, decides to try the steps listed above. She calls Chris in for a meeting the following day.

"Chris, I've called you in to this meeting to go over your recent performance," she begins. "You are consistently on time to your sessions, you are enthusiastic when interacting with your clients, you consistently follow the client's protocols, and you note the things that occurred during your visits in your log book. I appreciate your consistency in all these areas. In regard to your chart notes, I have noticed that neither the daily requirements nor weekly note requirements resulted in notes being completed on time. All notes must be entered into the client's chart each week to be considered on time. Without them, we cannot bill for our services, and if we cannot bill, we can't get paid. This has impacts for the company overall as we have weekly payroll. I know that entering notes may seem like a tedious activity, but it really does have large implications for the company and your colleagues. I want to determine a way that will help you successfully enter your notes on time."

"Honestly, I know how important the notes are," Chris responds, "but I am in school and constantly forget to complete them by the due date because I have so many other deadlines from school. I really try to remember, but I seem to forget more often than I am able to remember. It also takes such a long time for me to enter each note."

"Okay, Chris. Let me see if I understand. School takes up a lot of your time, and you're finding it difficult to coordinate all the deadlines? Is that correct?"

"Yes, that's correct. Entering the notes into the system also takes so long that sometimes I don't have the time to complete them. Also, sometimes I don't have Internet access, so I have to wait until I do to enter them."

"Understood, notes do take a long time, and the Internet is necessary to enter them."

At this point, Priya realizes that, among the verbal and written warnings, she has not contributed a possible solution for Chris. She follows up by focusing on potential solutions. "Chris, I know you understand that entering notes is important, and I want you to be successful. Let's brainstorm some solutions together. Have you tried setting an alarm?"

"I do understand, and I don't want to be the cause of people not getting paid. I have tried setting alarms. I tried to set them when I thought I would get home for the night, but found that it was so unpredictable with traffic. They kept going off while I was still driving, so I just started silencing them after a few weeks."

"Traffic is so unpredictable here, so it is hard to predict exactly when you will get home. I wonder if there is a different time that might work for you?"

"Once I get home, I try to get all of my work done and then turn everything off for a couple hours before bed to wind down," Chris replied. "I almost always finish my work around 10 p.m., though, and am always home by 9. Maybe I could set it for 9:30pm. That will give me time to get home and do some other work and then finish my night with entering my notes."

"That sounds like a great solution, Chris. Let's try that for a couple weeks to see how it works."

"Okay, I will try that."

"Okay, let's go over exactly what we'll be doing going forward and set up a meeting for 2 weeks from now to check back in and see how it's going. We reviewed the current issue of notes not being entered on time and discussed the reason this is so important. We also discussed some potential solutions and decided you would set an alarm for 9:30 p.m., giving you 30 minutes to enter notes before shutting down for the night. Do you agree?"

In the example above, Priya followed all the steps of providing effective feedback and had a productive meeting with Chris.

Before we end this chapter of dos and don'ts, there is one more don't we want to cover. It gets a section of its own because it is so commonly practiced and so very wrong.

And Finally...That Awful Feedback Sandwich and Why You Should Skip It

Ice cream sandwiches are the best. Every bite begins with a warm helping of dark chocolate that coats the inside of your mouth with a protective barrier of cocoa goodness right before an intense blast of ice cream shocks your taste buds into a freezing frenzy. Luckily, the experience concludes with a warm reminder of how much we all appreciate chocolate as it soothes the cold blast with a sweet, balmy aftertaste.

Unfortunately, though, the idea of comfort that comes from the chocolate at the beginning and end of every bite of an ice cream sandwich does not translate well to the delivery of feedback. The "feedback sandwich" happens when a leader begins the interaction with a positive statement followed thereafter by criticism of the individual's performance, which is then followed by another positive statement. Hence, the sandwich. The following is an example of a feedback sandwich:

- **Positive Statement:** Karen, great work decorating the office. It really brings out the color on the walls.
- **Criticism:** But I need you to do a better job with your customer service during phone calls.
- **Positive Statement:** Oh, and by the way, you did a great job planning the company event last week.

The above interaction usually takes place as a result of the employee, Karen, doing something that the supervisor finds unsatisfactory (presumably below-average customer service during phone calls). Rather than address this concern directly, the supervisor "sandwiched" the criticism between two positive statements.

Behavior of concern ----> *Positive Statement* ----> **Criticism** ----> *Positive Statement*

Supervisors often use the feedback sandwich to "soften the blow" of the critique, but there are plenty of reasons that this method of feedback should be avoided altogether and why it ultimately leaves a bad taste in everyone's mouth (except the supervisor—but that's who is consuming the sandwich). The feedback sandwich does not produce the desired results (reduction of ineffective behavior) and only ends up confusing the employee. Here are some reasons the feedback sandwich does more harm than good:

1. **It gives the wrong impression.** The employee may leave the interaction with the impression that they have mostly done well. In fact, they believe they have done two good things and only one bad thing, and the behavior needing improvement was minimized during the conversation. In reality, the "bad thing" might actually be something that needs to be addressed as soon as possible.

2. **The positivity is trivial.** The positive statements used in the sandwich may be seen as weak attempts at quickly finding something nice to say rather than an authentic statement delivered to praise a job well done.

3. **The employee doesn't know how to improve.** The criticism is usually presented without explaining how the performer can improve their behavior. Criticism is much more effective when presented with corrective actions. Remember, it isn't *performance* feedback unless you provide information to help them improve their *performance.*

4. **Learning happens the wrong way.** Every time you engage in a behavior, the odds indicate some form of learning will occur. Your behavior will either be reinforced, punished, or placed on extinction (in other words, in will stop happening after a while). When the feedback sandwich is used, the performer engages in a behavior that is immediately followed by a positive statement, a statement of criticism, then another positive statement. Will that *increase* or *decrease* the problem behavior? Unfortunately, the former is more likely.

5. **It can decrease the effectiveness of positive statements in the long run.** If the behavioral contingency holds true over repeated interactions, employees will learn that each positive statement will be followed by a criticism. If this happens enough times, the employee will begin to learn that positive statements will be followed by a "…but" statement that quickly negates whatever statement that came before it. Imagine hearing something positive about your work ("you did a great job today!") only for it to always be followed by a negative ("…but I need you to do this thing better").

6. **It reduces trust.** Remember, trust is the correspondence between what a leader says and what they do. While good intentioned, using the feedback sandwich can damage employees' trust in leadership in a number of ways:

   a. The positive feedback becomes superficial and is only there as part of a pattern, not because it is really meant.

   b. People focus on the corrective or negative feedback more, stop attending to the positive, and think that it is only there as a blanket to cover the negative.

   c. All of the feedback becomes superficial—it becomes this pattern of "you're awesome, but really you are a screw up, but I like you anyway."

d. It provides no help—people trust those who not only correct them but also provide a way for them to get better. Feedback sandwiches usually do not provide the receiver with a way to improve; instead, it's like saying "stop screwing up and do better!"

e. Feedback sandwiches, especially after repeated presentation, are easily spotted by other employees. When identified by other employees, feedback sandwiches can diminish trust in leadership, weakening the notion that managers will present an honest appraisal of staff performance.

Ultimately, people use the feedback sandwich to avoid blowback from an angry employee. Presenting a positive statement before and after the statement of criticism encloses the criticism in a protective sandwich of positivity that usually prevents people from getting upset with the interaction. So many companies nowadays are more concerned with avoiding the trouble that comes with a disgruntled employee than they are with improving performance. Unfortunately, however, feedback sandwiches usually end up making disgruntled employees even more disgruntled, exacerbating the problem rather than resolving it.

As we've stated before, if you need to give constructive feedback, don't be afraid, and follow the Nike™ slogan: "Just Do It"™. In the end, the employee will respect you more for your direct approach and transparency than if you tried to conceal the original intention of your meeting between two loaves of contrived positivity. Remember, meat without the sandwich can be just as appetizing.

The Worst Times to Give Feedback

When we discussed when to provide feedback, we stressed the importance of providing it as early and often as possible. However, some situations do not allow leaders to effectively deliver performance feedback that will drive performance improvement. Depending on the situation, waiting until another time may be the best suggestion. Here are some situations where you may want to wait to give feedback or possibly not give feedback at all:

1. You do not have all of the information about the situation or the individuals involved. In other words, you don't know what happened and/or you don't know what types of feedback to which the employee responds best. Identifying exactly what happened and how to respond best to your employee in a particular situation is absolutely mandatory for providing effective feedback. Preparation is important.

2. The performer cannot control the behavior you are proposing they change. A range of reasons they cannot change the behavior could exist, from a lack of resources to a lack of training. If it's not possible for the employee to change the behavior, don't ask them to do so.

3. The person receiving the feedback is highly emotional or especially vulnerable. Delivering feedback right after someone just showed up late to work or accidentally deleted an entire report on their computer may not be the best time to deliver feedback; both situations are emotional for most people.

4. The person receiving feedback has made an error; however, there is a large group around observing what happened. In this event, not only is the receiver likely emotional, but there are also several people to observe the interaction you will have. In this event, it is better to allow for a time when you can provide the feedback in a private location. Rather than immediately provide feedback in this situation, you may softly tell the employee to meet you in your office later in the day.

5. An employee is interacting with a customer. It can undermine the employee and send the wrong message to the customer for a supervisor to provide corrective feedback to an employee in front of the customer. If it is not a safety issue, it is better to wait until the interaction with the customer is complete before you provide feedback.

Another important aspect of knowing when to provide feedback is to consider the contingency: pairing vulnerability and high negative emotion (aversives) with feedback (neutral). If this pairing process is engaged in frequently, it will turn the feedback into a conditioned aversive. In other words, people will actively try to avoid feedback, specifically your feedback.

Here are some scenarios where you may be faced with high negative emotion. In these cases, it's okay to wait to provide the feedback.

1. You do not have the time or patience to deliver feedback appropriately. Managers have bad days, too. Delivering corrective feedback at 4:55 p.m. after a long, hard day probably won't go well for you or the employee, and you both will probably spend the rest of the night worrying about it. Go ahead and wait until the morning when you're refreshed, not rushed, and have a better outlook on the day.

2. The feedback is based on subjective opinions, not objective observation. Effective leaders can judge circumstances dispassionately and observe employee behavior objectively. Providing subjective feedback may set back employee performance instead of improve it; as with most subjective situations, there are three sides to the story. If you don't have objective data, it's better to remain silent until you do.

3. A more effective form of behavior is unknown. One of the worst things a leader can say is this: "You should not have done that. I'm not sure what you should have done, but you should not have done *that*." Such a statement erodes trust in the leader's competency and does nothing to improve the employee's performance. Remember, performance feedback is information about performance that creates an opportunity for the individual to improve. This can't be done without a replacement behavior.

4. You need to ask the performer to do something. Delivering feedback and then immediately asking the individual to complete a task can feel transactional and manipulative. Consider the contingency: Performer asks for feedback (behavior). You deliver feedback and immediately ask them to complete another task (consequence). Will this reinforce or punish their requests for feedback in the future? We assume the latter.

The Myth of Annual Performance Reviews—Revisited

We've touched upon this subject before, but it bares revisiting, especially when it comes to the issue of timing. Have you ever seen a performance review form? Of course you have. If you've seen one, you've seen them all. Annual performance reviews are problematic for many reasons, but we will only name a few for our purposes. First, they are filled with subjective rating criteria that use words like *meets* or *exceeds* expectations without any discernible measure to back up what that means. This not only leaves the supervisor to decide if someone has *met* or *exceeded* standards, but also leaves it for the supervisee to determine what that means. Second, as the label indicates, annual performance reviews only happen once each year and are based on an arbitrary timeline. We know now that timing is everything. Considering this, we know that the arbitrary timelines determined by the organization are likely not set at the most effective time.

All of this can lead to the delivery of feedback being considered uncomfortable. As a result, both the employee and employer avoid it, waiting until the last minute to deliver the performance review. All in all, annual or even semi-annual performance reviews turn feedback into something uncomfortable or an event that feels like punishment, which eventually results in leaders who don't want to conduct evaluation meetings and employees who don't want to attend them. The result of this? Stagnant performance.

One way of making the antiquated annual performance reviews obsolete once and for all is by making feedback a frequent and regular part of the employee's job. When feedback is given consistently, the employee has clear expectations, and miscommunications are kept to a minimum. Immediate feedback not only provides the employee an opportunity to immediately change the behavior but also prevents the employee from asking "Where did that come from?" when getting a less-positive-than-expected performance evaluation.

Consider the following ill-fated example:

Derek has a performance evaluation scheduled with his boss. He is excited for the opportunity to hear feedback about his first year with the company and possibly negotiate a raise. He has not received any corrective feedback throughout the year, so he expects a performance evaluation full of praise. However, during the evaluation, Derek's manager lists 10 different points of improvement he'd like to see, without providing much in the way of positive feedback. After Derek leaves the meeting, his productivity suffers. He begins engaging in disgruntled behavior, such as looking away when supervisors are speaking to him and talking back during meetings.

Why? Here's what Derek likely thought after the evaluation: *Why didn't someone tell him these things sooner? How could he have been so off?*

The example above is far too common. According to *Harvard Business Review* authors Peter Cappelli and Anna Tavis (2016), feedback is less effective when given months or weeks after the behavior occurs and can cause confusion and resentment in the employee. Giving feedback immediately removes confusion, ensures the behavior will be corrected quickly, and leaves the employee feeling more confident and knowledgeable about where they stand.

So why do people still use scheduled performance reviews if they're not effective? Here are some reasons scheduled performance reviews still happen and the common (and unfortunate) interactions that follow:

1. Scheduled performance reviews are often used to motivate employees, despite scientific evidence indicating they do anything but that.

    o Let's look at the following example to illustrate a common occurrence in many businesses. The unit employee is overheard talking with a peer saying, "I just don't feel like my job has a lot of meaning. I show up every day and work hard, but no one notices or cares." The unit manager takes the employee aside and asks why he is feeling this way, stating, "I did your performance review 6 months ago, and it showed that your performance is about average with your peers." The unit employee rolls his eyes and says, "Exactly. It's been 6 months, and I was told that I don't do anything that stands out. Why even try?"

    o Working hard only to be told that performance is "average" with no information about how to improve it, how to stand out, or how to know when you're performing better is demotivating. No one really wants to be told they are just average...especially if that's the only feedback they receive for an entire year.

2. Scheduled performance reviews are often (unfortunately) used to terminate employees. Companies complete performance reviews of employees they fire to avoid legal backlash.

o Have you ever had the following happen or heard of something similar? Kelly just got fired from the marketing department. The unit manager informed the HR manager of the event and was asked, "Did you make sure that you have her performance reviews showing her underperformance for the past year?" The unit manager states, "Well, her last performance review shows that she is making average progress, but she did several things that resulted in the firing. I will make sure I have them written down by the end of the day to show a more recent evaluation of underperformance."

o In addition to some ethical, if not legal, concerns in this scenario, the performance evaluation is being used to show a reason to fire an individual. If employees learn that this is what performance evaluations are being used for, they will begin to avoid them at even higher rates. Performance reviews should be helpful and provide feedback about how to improve when it is necessary and be used to celebrate when things are going right. They should not be used to build a case to fire an employee.

3. Conversely, scheduled performance reviews can be used inappropriately to promote employees who underperform.

o Jim just received his annual performance review, which has higher-than-average ratings. Because of growth in the company this prior year, a second unit manager was hired 2 months ago. The annual performance reviews were divided between the unit managers, despite the new unit manager only knowing employees for the past 2 months. Upon receiving Jim's performance review, the HR manager goes to the original unit manager and states, "This evaluation shows we should promote Jim." The unit manager responds with, "How could that be? He has been underperforming for the past 3 years in a row." The HR manager replies that she is not sure, but that the review better get changed before it is processed, or Jim will be promoted.

o There are several concerns with this scenario as well. In

addition to now having to go back and tell Jim that his performance review was actually incorrect, the evaluation clearly does not provide an objective measure of Jim's performance. This scenario also suggests that the annual review has had no effect on Jim's behavior, proving it to be an ineffective tool.

Despite the above all-too-common scenarios, scheduled performance reviews, whether quarterly or annually, are the accepted norm to deliver feedback. However, performance reviews and feedback are actually different things. Feedback is given to reinforce or change a behavior, and performance reviews (also known as *performance appraisals*) are used to evaluate past performance (Cappeli & Tavis, 2016). It's a small, but important distinction to make. If a behavior needs to be changed, it makes sense to make the change immediately and save the annual reviews for evaluations of overall performance. Ultimately, employers typically use scheduled performance reviews for two reasons: (a) they have to, and (b) that's the way it has been done for so long, regardless of their lack of success. Don't be that company or manager; even if you cannot change when performance reviews occur, you can deliver feedback in the moment when it really counts.

Consider this: If you wait until the end of the day to provide feedback, you will only have five opportunities to provide feedback per week. If you wait until the end of the week, you will only have four opportunities to provide feedback per month. And if you wait until the end of the month to provide performance feedback, you will only have 12 opportunities to provide feedback per year. So we ask you this: Is that enough feedback to improve performance to the given standards? Probably not.

CONGRATULATIONS

Wow! You made it. You completed your feedback journey and now know everything there is to know about providing effective performance feedback to your staff. JOB. WELL. DONE. We commend you on your perseverance and your dedication to this journey. For us, it was quite a long journey to reach this point, so we can imagine that it was for you as well.

Before we go, let's very briefly summarize all that we have learned.

Feedback is the information transfer from a mediator to a performer about the performer's behavior or action. *Performance feedback* is a specific type of feedback focused on the behaviors, actions, and outcomes related to the person's role and responsibilities.

We covered the many different steps and variables included in the Feedback Formula. In case you already forgot the formula, here it is again:

EFFECTIVE PERFORMANCE FEEDBACK =
[[Frequency] * [(The Behavior/Action/Outcome) + (The Person) + (The Number of People) + (The Type of Feedback) + (The Temporal Location) + (The Medium) + (Privacy) + (Formality) + (Physical Environment)]] / (Content + Delivery)

Remember that each variable in the formula can increase or decrease the effectiveness of your performance feedback.

Finally, we discussed some additional considerations, including how to determine if your feedback is effective, how feedback is affected by generational differences, how to teach your employees to accept feedback, and some final dos and don'ts when providing feedback.

We hope you enjoyed this journey as much as we did, and we thank you for coming along!

REFERENCES

Adkins, A., & Rigoni, B. (2016, June 2). Managers: Millennials want feedback, but won't ask for it. Gallup. http://news.gallup.com/businessjournal/192038/managers-millennials-feedback-won-ask.aspx

Binder, C. (1996). Behavioral fluency: Evolution of a new paradigm. The Behavior Analyst, 19(2), 163–197. https://doi.org/10.1007/BF03393163

Cappelli, P., & Tavis, A. (2016). The performance management revolution. Harvard Business Review.

Daniels, A. (2009). Oops! 13 management practices that waste time and money (and what to do instead). Performance Management.

Fredrickson, B. (2009). Positivity: Top-Notch Research Reveals the 3-to-1 Ratio That Will Change Your Life. Harmony.

Gallup. (n.d.). State of the American workplace. Retrieved January 23, 2020, from https://www.gallup.com/workplace/238085/state-american-workplace-report-2017.aspx

Geller, S. (2003). Should Organizational Behavior Management expand its content? Journal of Organizational Behavior Management, 22(2), 13–30.

Heath, C. & Heath, D. (2010). Switch: How to Change Things When Change is Hard. New York,

NY: Random House, Inc.

Klofstad, C. A., Nowicki, S., & Anderson, R. C. (2016). How voice pitch influences our choice of leaders. *American Scientist*, 104(5). https://doi.org/10.1511/2016.122.282

Ludwig, T. D., & Frazier, C. B. (2012). Employee engagement and organizational behavior management. *Journal of Organizational Behavior Management*, 32(1), 75–82. https://doi.org/10.1080/01608061.2011.619439

Vargas, J. (2013). *Behavior analysis for effective teaching* (2nd ed.). Routledge.

SUGGESTED READING SECTION

Books

Braksick, L. W. (2000). Unlock Behavior, Unleash Profits. McGraw-Hill.

Daniels, A. C. (2014). Performance Management: Changing Behavior that Drives Organizational Effectiveness. Atlanta, GA: Performance Management Publications.

Daniels, A. C., & Daniels, J. E. (2007). Measure of a Leader: The Legendary Leadership Formula for Producing Exceptional Performers and Outstanding Results. New York, NY: McGraw-Hill.

Daniels, A. C. (2016). Bringing Out the Best in People: How to Apply the Astonishing Power of Positive Reinforcement. New York, NY: McGraw-Hill Education.

Daniels, A. C. (2009). Oops!: 13 Management Practices that Waste Time and Money (and what to do instead). Performance Management Publications.

Lattal, A. D., & Clark, R. W. (2007). A Good Day's Work: Sustaining Ethical Behavior and Business Success. McGraw-Hill.

Mawhinney, T. C. (1996). Organizational Culture, Rule-Governed Behavior and Organizational Behavior Management: Theoretical Foundations and Implications for Research and Practice. Haworth Press.

Redmon, W. K., Mawhinney, T. C., & Johnson, C. M. (2013). Handbook of Organizational Performance Behavior Analysis and Management.

Taylor and Francis.

Reid, D. H. (2012). Supervisor's Guidebook: Evidence-Based Strategies for Promoting Work Quality and Enjoyment among Human Service Staff. Habilitative Management Consultants.

Rodriguez, M., Sundberg, D., & Biagi, S. (2017). OBM Applied! Volume 1: A Practical Guide to Implementing Organizational Behavior Management. Melbourne, FL. ABA Technologies, Inc.

Rodriguez, M., Sundberg, D., & Biagi, S. (2017). OBM Applied! Volume 2: Choosing the Right Solution. Melbourne, FL. ABA Technologies, Inc.

Rodriguez, M., Sundberg, D., & Biagi, S. (2017). OBM Applied! Volume 3: A Practical Guide to Implementing Organizational Behavior Management. Melbourne, FL. ABA Technologies, Inc.

Rodriguez, M., Sundberg, D., & Biagi, S. (2017). OBM Applied! Volume 4: Creating Lasting Change. Melbourne, FL. ABA Technologies, Inc.

Articles

Aljadeff-Abergel, E., Peterson, S. M., Wiskirchen, R. R., Hagen, K. K., & Cole, M. L. (2017). Evaluating the Temporal Location of Feedback: Providing Feedback Following Performance vs. Prior to Performance. Journal of Organizational Behavior Management, 37(2), 171–195. https://doi.org/10.1080/01608061.2017.1309332

Alvero, A. M., Bucklin, B. R., & Austin, J. (2001). An Objective Review of the Effectiveness and Essential Characteristics of Performance Feedback in Organizational Settings (1985-1998). Journal of Organizational Behavior Management, 21(1), 3–29. https://doi.org/10.1300/j075v21n01_02

Balcazar, F., Hopkins, B. L., & Suarez, Y. (1985). A Critical, Objective Review of Performance Feedback. Journal of Organizational Behavior Management, 7(3-4), 65–89.https://doi.org/10.1300/j075v07n03_05

Brown, K. M., Willis, B. S., & Reid, D. H. (1981). Differential Effects

Of Supervisor Verbal Feedback And Feedback Plus Approval On Institutional Staff Performance. Journal of Organizational Behavior Management, 3(1), 57–68. https://doi.org/10.1300/j075v03n01_05

Bucklin, B. R., Mcgee, H. M., & Dickinson, A. M. (2004). The Effects of Individual Monetary Incentives With and Without Feedback. Journal of Organizational Behavior Management, 23(2-3), 65–94. https://doi.org/10.1300/j075v23n02_05

Ehrlich, R. J., Nosik, M. R., Carr, J. E., & Wine, B. (2020). Teaching Employees How to Receive Feedback: A Preliminary Investigation. Journal of Organizational Behavior Management, 1–11. https://doi.org/10.1080/01608061.2020.1746470

Ford, J. E. (1980). A Classification System for Feedback Procedures. Journal of Organizational Behavior Management, 2(3), 183–191. https://doi.org/10.1300/j075v02n03_04

Ford, J. E. (1984). A Comparison of Three Feedback Procedures for Improving Teaching Skills. Journal of Organizational Behavior Management, 6(1), 65–77. https://doi.org/10.1300/j075v06n01_05

Frederiksen, L. W., Richter, W. T., Johnson, R. P., & Solomon, L. J. (1982). Specificity of Performance Feedback in a Professional Service Delivery Setting. Journal of Organizational Behavior Management, 3(4), 41–53. https://doi.org/10.1300/j075v03n04_05

Goltz, S. M., Citera, M., Jensen, M., Favero, J., & Komaki, J. L. (1990). Individual Feedback: Journal of Organizational Behavior Management, 10(2), 77–92. https://doi.org/10.1300/j075v10n02_06

Haas, J. R., & Hayes, S. C. (2006). When Knowing You Are Doing Well Hinders Performance. Journal of Organizational Behavior Management, 26(1-2), 91–111. https://doi.org/10.1300/j075v26n01_04

Henley, A. J., & Reed, F. D. D. (2015). Should You Order the Feedback Sandwich? Efficacy of Feedback Sequence and Timing. Journal of Organizational Behavior Management, 35(3-4), 321–335. https://doi.org/10.1080/01608061.2015.1093057

Johnson, R. P., & Frederiksen, L. W. (1984). Process vs Outcome Feedback and Goal Setting in a Human Service Organization. Journal of Organizational Behavior Management, 5(3-4), 37–56. https://doi.org/10.1300/j075v05n03_03

Johnson, D. A. (2013). A Component Analysis of the Impact of Evaluative and Objective Feedback on Performance. Journal of Organizational Behavior Management, 33(2), 89–103. https://doi.org/10.1080/01608061.2013.785879

Johnson, D. A., Rocheleau, J. M., & Tilka, R. E. (2015). Considerations in Feedback Delivery: The Role of Accuracy and Type of Evaluation. Journal of Organizational Behavior Management, 35(3-4), 240–258. https://doi.org/10.1080/01608061.2015.1093055

Kang, K., Oah, S., & Dickinson, A. M. (2005). The Relative Effects of Different Frequencies of Feedback on Work Performance. Journal of Organizational Behavior Management, 23(4), 21–53. https://doi.org/10.1300/j075v23n04_02

Lee, K., Shon, D., & Oah, S. (2014). The Relative Effects of Global and Specific Feedback on Safety Behaviors. Journal of Organizational Behavior Management, 34(1), 16–28. https://doi.org/10.1080/01608061.2013.878264

Ludwig, T. D., Biggs, J., Wagner, S., & Geller, E. S. (2002). Using Public Feedback and Competitive Rewards to Increase the Safe Driving of Pizza Deliverers. Journal of Organizational Behavior Management, 21(4), 75–104. https://doi.org/10.1300/j075v21n04_06

Mangiapanello, K. A., & Hemmes, N. S. (2015). An Analysis of Feedback from a Behavior Analytic Perspective. The Behavior Analyst, 38(1), 51–75. https://doi.org/10.1007/s40614-014-0026-x

Mihalic, M. T., & Ludwig, T. D. (2009). Behavioral System Feedback Measurement Failure: Sweeping Quality Under the Rug. Journal of Organizational Behavior Management, 29(2), 155–174. https://doi.org/10.1080/01608060902874559

Palmer, M. G., Johnson, C. M., & Johnson, D. A. (2015). Objective Performance Feedback: Is Numerical Accuracy Necessary? Journal of Organizational Behavior Management, 35(3-4), 206–239.

https://doi.org/10.1080/01608061.2015.1093059

Prue, D. M., & Fairbank, J. A. (1981). Performance Feedback In Organizational Behavior Management. Journal of Organizational Behavior Management, 3(1), 1–16. https://doi.org/10.1300/j075v03n01_01

Schwarcz, D., & Farganis, D. (2016). The Impact of Individualized Feedback on Law Student Performance. SSRN Electronic Journal. https://doi.org/10.2139/ssrn.2772393

Schwarcz, D., & Farganis, D. (2016). The Impact of Individualized Feedback on Law Student Performance. SSRN Electronic Journal. https://doi.org/10.2139/ssrn.2772393

Sigurdsson, S. O., & Ring, B. M. (2013). Evaluating Preference for Graphic Feedback on Correct Versus Incorrect Performance. Journal of Organizational Behavior Management, 33(2), 128–136. https://doi.org/10.1080/01608061.2013.785889

Tedick, D. and Gortari, B. (1998) "Research on Error Correction and Implications for Classroom Teaching" The Bridge, ACIE Newsletter. Center for Advanced Research on Language Acquisition, University of Minnesota, v1. [Online] /immersion/acie/vol1/May1998.pdf

Tittelbach, D., Fields, L., & Alvero, A. M. (2008). Effects of Performance Feedback on Typing Speed and Accuracy. Journal of Organizational Behavior Management, 27(4), 29–52. https://doi.org/10.1300/j075v27n04_02

ABOUT THE AUTHORS

Adam Ventura

Adam is a Board-Certified Behavior Analyst (BCBA) with over 15 years-experience working in behavior analysis. He is a graduate of Florida International University (FIU) and holds a bachelor's and master's degrees in psychology. Adam currently teaches as an adjunct professor within the behavior analysis department at FIU and is also currently serving as the Organizational Behavior Management (OBM) Network President. Adam has also worked in several different leadership positions at various companies holding positions in mid-level management as well as c-suite and executive tier positions. Adam has been a successful entrepreneur and has been involved with the founding and operation of over 10 separate businesses in various industries including behavior therapy, software, education, organizational behavior management (OBM), self-improvement, publishing, and business administration. Adam's last company, a behavior therapy organization stretched across three states and employed over 250 people. Adam has authored three books on topics including leadership (Leadership in Behavior Analysis), performance feedback (Feedback F!@#ups And How to Avoid Them), and professionalism (The RBT Professional) For more information, please visit his website at www.adamventura.com.

Natalie Parks

Natalie Parks, Ph.D., BCBA-D is a certified and licensed behavior analyst and licensed psychologist. She has worked in the field of behavior analysis for over 20 years. Her experiences draw from a complex set of experiences ranging from work within organizations, schools, clinics, hospitals, and homes. Dr. Parks currently owns and leads an organizational behavior management (OBM) company, Behavior Leader, Inc. and focuses on leadership development, diversity and inclusion, and systems and process development. She has co-authored two other books on topics of leadership (Leadership in Behavior Analysis) and OBM (OBM Entrepreneur) in addition to the publication of chapters and several research articles focused on early intervention and treatment for severe problem behavior. Dr. Parks' spends the majority of her time working with organizational leaders in companies that provide services to others, schools, and fire and police departments focused on leadership development, diversity and inclusion, and performance management. For more information about Dr. Parks and the services provided by Behavior Leader, Inc. visit www.BehaviorLeader.com.

Erica Crowley

Erica is a Board Certified Behavior Analyst with more than 7 years of experience in the field of applied behavior analysis. She graduated from the University of Florida and has a bachelor's degree in Psychology and a Master's degree in Special Education. She has presented workshops at conferences for both FABA and ABAI on how to effectively deliver feedback in the workplace. She currently works as the Center Director for a multidisciplinary clinic in Jacksonville, FL.

Dennis Uriarte

Dennis is a Board-Certified Behavior Analyst and has worked in the field of Applied Behavior Analysis for 10 years in supervisory, training, and instructor positions. During his time as a supervisor and a training coordinator, Dennis discovered his passion for the field of Organizational Behavior Management (OBM), specifically in the mentoring, guidance, and development of other professionals using the science of ABA. He graduated with his Bachelor's degree in Psychology from Florida International University and his Master's degree in Professional Behavior Analysis from the Florida Institute of Technology. His current research and work is centered around ways to improve the delivery of feedback, training and coaching employees and organizational leaders, and the incorporation of technology to improve these practices. Dennis also serves on the Board of Directors of the OBM Network as Director of Outreach, disseminating OBM through webinars, writing, and public speaking.

Made in the USA
Coppell, TX
13 November 2020

41329091R00183